VANDERBILT

Also by Anderson Cooper

Dispatches from the Edge
The Rainbow Comes and Goes

Also by Katherine Howe

The Physick Book of Deliverance Dane
The Daughters of Temperance Hobbs
The House of Velvet and Glass
The Appearance of Annie Van Sinderen
Conversion
The Penguin Book of Witches

VANDERBILT

The Rise and Fall of an American Dynasty

ANDERSON COOPER

AND KATHERINE HOWE

HARPER

An Imprint of HarperCollins*Publishers*

FIRST EDITION

Insert art credits: Page 1, top, Felix Lipov/Alamy Stock Photo; page 3, left, Courtesy of Charles Marlor; page 3, right, National Portrait Gallery, Smithsonian Institution; page 4, top left, 1894 by Louis Alman/From the collection of Michael Henry Adams; page 4, top right, Library of Congress, Prints & Photographs Division, LC-DIG-ggbain-05942; page 4, bottom, Gavin Ashworth/The Preservation Society of Newport County; page 6, top left, National Portrait Gallery, Smithsonian Institution; page 6, top right, Photo by Prince, New York; page 6, bottom, Mora, Museum of the City of New York. F2012.58.1460; page 7, bottom, Byron Company, Museum of the City of New York. 93.1.1.16376; page 8, bottom, Library of Congress, Prints & Photographs Division, LC-USZ62-10528; page 9, bottom left, Bettmann/Getty images; page 10, top right, Bettmann/Getty images; page 10, bottom, Collection of Anderson Cooper; page 11, top, Keystone-France/Getty images; page 11, bottom, *New York Daily News* Archive/Getty images; page 12, Horst P. Horst, *Vogue*, © Condé Nast; page 13, top, Bettmann/Getty images; page 13, bottom, AP Images; page 14, top, Collection of Anderson Cooper; page 14, bottom, Photofest; page 15, Tony Palmieri / Courtesy of Fairchild Archive; page 16, Bettmann/Getty images.

Endpaper credits: Inside front cover, right-hand page, clockwise from top left: © Archive Farms Inc/Alamy Stock Photo; © Painters/Alamy Stock Photo; © Pictorial Press Ltd/Alamy Stock Photo; José María Mora.

Inside back cover, left-hand page, clockwise from left: Courtesy of the author; Herbert Gehr; Toni Frissell Collection/Library of Congress; © IKE EDEANI/ the *New York Times*/Redux.

Frame art by Monory/Shutterstock, Inc.

Designed by Leah Carlson-Stanisic

Endpapers designed by Chip Kidd

Library of Congress Cataloging-in-Publication Data has been applied for.

ISBN 978-0-06-296461-8

23 24 25 26 27 LBC 13 12 11 10 9

To Wyatt.
—A. C.

To my mother, Katherine S. Howe, and to Charles.
—K. H.

Poor Vanderbilt! How I pity you; and this is honest. You are an old man, and ought to have some rest, and yet you have to struggle, and deny yourself, and rob yourself of restful sleep and peace of mind, because you need money so badly. I always feel for a man who is so poverty ridden as you. Don't misunderstand me, Vanderbilt. I know you own seventy millions; but then you know and I know, that it isn't what a man has, that constitutes wealth. No—it is to be satisfied with what one has; that is wealth.

—MARK TWAIN, PACKARD'S MONTHLY, MARCH 1869

Contents

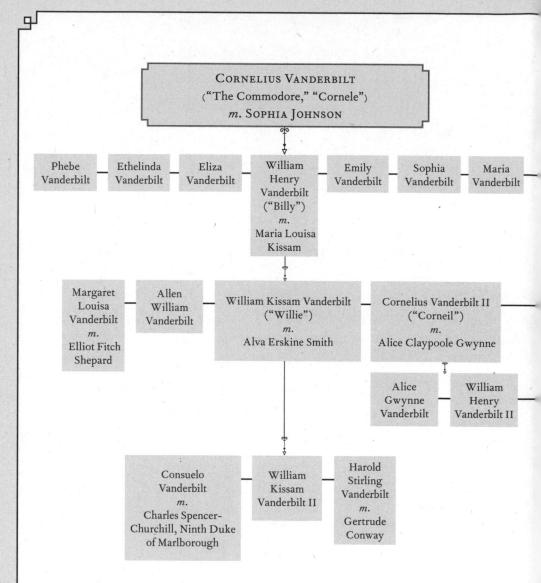

CORNELIUS VANDERBILT
("The Commodore," "Cornele")
m. SOPHIA JOHNSON

Phebe Vanderbilt

Ethelinda Vanderbilt

Eliza Vanderbilt

William Henry Vanderbilt ("Billy")
m.
Maria Louisa Kissam

Emily Vanderbilt

Sophia Vanderbilt

Maria Vanderbilt

Margaret Louisa Vanderbilt
m.
Elliot Fitch Shepard

Allen William Vanderbilt

William Kissam Vanderbilt ("Willie")
m.
Alva Erskine Smith

Cornelius Vanderbilt II ("Corneil")
m.
Alice Claypoole Gwynne

Alice Gwynne Vanderbilt

William Henry Vanderbilt II

Consuelo Vanderbilt
m.
Charles Spencer-Churchill, Ninth Duke of Marlborough

William Kissam Vanderbilt II

Harold Stirling Vanderbilt
m.
Gertrude Conway

Note: As this does not include all children, spouses, or branches, it is not a comprehensive family tree, but its aim is to situate the family members featured in the book.

❧ A PARTIAL GENEALOGY OF THE VANDERBILT FAMILY ❧

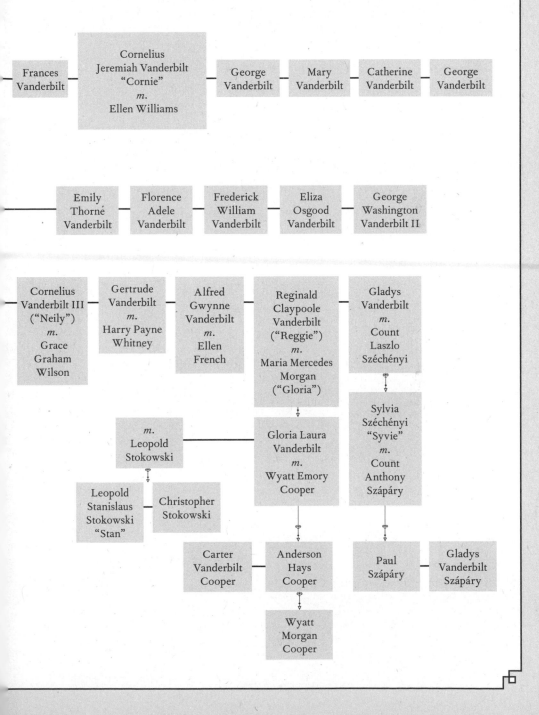

Introduction

For, as William Dean Howells once noted, "Inequality is as dear to the American heart as liberty itself," and it is only a step from this to arrive at something which passes muster for a Society definition of America: that all men may be born equal but most of us spend the better part of our born days in trying to be as unequal as we can.

—Cleveland Amory, *Who Killed Society?*

When I was six, my father took me to Grand Central Terminal in New York to see the imposing bronze statue of my great-great-great-grandfather "Commodore" Cornelius Vanderbilt. It stands high on a pedestal on the south side of the train terminal he founded, within sight of Vanderbilt Avenue and a hotel that, back then, was also named after him.

I knew little about the Vanderbilt dynasty. My mom, Gloria Vanderbilt, rarely talked about her tumultuous childhood or the fractious family she was born into in 1924. My father, Wyatt Cooper, grew up on a small farm in Mississippi during the Depression, about as far from the palatial homes of the Vanderbilts as you can imagine. But he wanted me to understand my mom's extraordinary history and her complicated feelings about it.

When we went to see the statue, my dad told me that the Commodore was a tough businessman and an unforgiving father and that, when he died, he was the richest person in America. I'm sure he said more, but I can't remember. I was, after all, only six. I do recall, however, that for weeks after our visit, I was convinced that all grandparents turned into statues when they died.

For much of my life, I wanted nothing to do with the Vanderbilts. I very much like the few Vanderbilt cousins I've met, but I never wanted to look too closely at the history of the family. I felt it had no bearing on my life. The Vanderbilt dynasty disappeared long ago, and my parents had made sure I understood early on that there was no "Vanderbilt money" or trust fund I'd be inheriting when I became an adult. They wanted me to be my own person, and I am grateful to them for that. I don't think I would have been as driven as I have been if I had grown up believing there was a pot of gold somewhere waiting for me.

I've always gone out of my way to avoid mentioning my relation to the Vanderbilts. When someone would find out and ask me, "What was it like to grow up a Vanderbilt?" my response was always the same. "I don't know," I'd say. "I'm a Cooper." That is how I viewed myself, and still do. I look to my father's large family, with its deep roots in the Mississippi earth, and I've taken their American story as my own.

But my mom's death in 2019 and the birth of my son, Wyatt, in 2020 began to change my perspective. In the weeks after she died, I began going through dozens of boxes stored away in her apartment and her art studio. They were filled with journals, and documents, and letters. She saved everything. Handwritten notes from her aunt Gertrude Vanderbilt Whitney and schoolbooks my grandfather Reginald Vanderbilt doodled in as a child. I found old wills and financial records, and as I read the contents of these files stained by time and mold, I began to hear the voices of those people I never knew. They were more than just characters in a history book, more than just one-dimensional members of an American dynasty. They were complex, flush with desire, their inner lives far more compelling than their public personae would have us believe.

When my son was born, I began to wonder, what will I tell him about them? What do I hope he learns from the lives they led, and the choices they made? In order to answer those questions, I began researching these people I had avoided for so long. This family. My family.

The Vanderbilt story somehow manages to be both unique and also, deeply, universally American. It is a saga of wealth and success and individualism, but as it turns out, those aren't necessarily the universal goods our culture likes to believe they are. A few central myths appear again and again in Americans' popular imagination: that success is available to anyone who is willing to work hard, for example, and that success is worthier of celebration if it is achieved without help. (As if any success were truly achieved alone: even the "self-made" Commodore got a crucial early loan from his mother when he was sixteen.) We still catch ourselves subscribing to this Horatio Algeresque celebration of entrepreneurship, of individualism, and, by extension, of wealth. We somehow, simultaneously, believe that we are all the same, all created equal, and yet we secretly suspect that the rich are somehow more special, that they have something figured out that the rest of us don't know. We see this embedded assumption play out every day in our modern celebrity culture and in our politics.

In writing this book, my coauthor, Katherine Howe, and I wanted to explore how some of the Vanderbilts—people with personalities and weaknesses and foibles, who found themselves living the ultimate American myth—actually felt as their lives were unfolding. The personal stories we recount focus on a few individuals rather than on the grand sweep of the Vanderbilts' business empire or the expansion of railroads into the wilderness.

Commodore Cornelius Vanderbilt founded a dynasty that would rule the Gilded Age, and his rise was dizzying. He possessed a genius and a mania for making money, but his obsession with material wealth would border on the pathological, and the pathology born of that wealth would go on to infect each successive generation in different ways. A family story about wealth and triumph becomes, in some respects, a story about sadness and isolation. But it's also a story of unexpected poignancy and truth that shifts our understanding and expectations about this name "Vanderbilt" that we imagine we already know.

The Vanderbilts were the original new-money arrivistes who burst on the scene, used their wealth to buy prestige and respectability, and churned through their fortune not in the cause of making lasting change, but on massive outlets for conspicuous consumption. Vanderbilt millions bought palatial houses, astonishing yachts, cars in the hundreds, and jewels both magnificent and rare.

But under the buckets of ink spilled on their exploits by newspapers and behind the magnificent, and temporary, marble walls constructed of the Commodore's money, unfolded private lives both messy and insecure, nuanced and complicated, sometimes irredeemable, but always fascinating. This is the story of the extraordinary rise and epic fall of the Vanderbilt dynasty. This is the story of the greatest American fortune ever squandered.

VANDERBILT

PROLOGUE

The Breakers

March 30, 2018

Whether a servant or the host or some other member of the family sees a guest to the door, the door is never closed until the guest is actually underway, by foot or by car.

—Amy Vanderbilt's Complete Book of Etiquette: A Guide to
Gracious Living, Part III, "Home Entertaining" [1952]

Gladys had to be out of The Breakers by four o'clock. That was the deadline they'd given her. Four p.m., Good Friday. She wasn't being evicted exactly. There had been no court proceedings, no sheriff serving her notice, nothing embarrassing like that. But she was being kicked out.

Her great-grandparents, Cornelius Vanderbilt II and his wife, Alice, built the seventy-room mansion in 1895, and a Vanderbilt had lived there ever since. Gladys would be the last. She worked as a nurse, but she had always dedicated herself to preserving the house and its history, just as her mother had, and, before that, her grandmother. Gladys served on advisory committees for the Preservation Society of Newport County and, over the years, kept an eye out for whatever needed repairs and maintenance.

No one's identity was as closely entwined with The Breakers as

Gladys's. After all, the grand palace with the velvet ropes and the precious artwork and the polished floors wasn't just a museum to her, an abstract symbol of a vanished age, one that now tolerated the prying eyes of a half million visitors each year. The Breakers was a home. Her home. Her history. Gladys knew every crack in the ceilings. She knew every creaking floorboard. As children, she and her brother, Paul, had clattered down the sweeping marble staircase on trays borrowed from the kitchen, something her mother had learned as a child from her own father. Every corner of their spacious third-floor apartment was full of such memories.

There weren't many visitors at the house that March day. Summer is the high season, and the crowds thin out in wintertime, as though the Newport mansions remembered that winter was for slumbering, their grand furnishings shrouded under white sheets. Those who do come to get a glimpse of a gilded past have to brave the cold winds whipping off the Atlantic Ocean as they walk toward the mansion's grand entrance. Anyone waiting for a tour of the house or walking the grounds that Good Friday probably wouldn't have noticed anything unusual. Gladys's apartment was off-limits to visitors, so no one would have seen her, Paul, and the few friends who'd been helping box things up for months, loading the old Otis elevator with heavy-duty black garbage bags and descending to the basement level. Before they made their final trip down, they went out on the terrace overlooking the ocean and toasted The Breakers with a bottle of champagne, remembering family and friends and a life now ending.

The Breakers is the grandest and most opulent of Newport's Gilded Age mansions, and it remains the most popular tourist attraction in the state of Rhode Island. During the summer, buses roll up Ochre Point Avenue, one after the other, disgorging visitors who crunch over the pea gravel drive that winds across grounds perched on cliffs facing the Atlantic. Hidden behind thirty-foot-tall wrought-iron gates set in limestone, like the bulwarks in European capitals designed to guard against civil unrest, The Breakers pretends to be an Italianate palace, though, unlike the real palaces of the aristocrats of Europe on which it was modeled, The Breakers is new. Ish.

When Cornelius Vanderbilt II built the house, he was president and chairman of the New York Central Railroad, the company his grandfather, Commodore Cornelius Vanderbilt, had founded after making his first fortune in shipping. Cornelius II and Alice hired architect Richard Morris Hunt to build them a summer retreat in Newport after the original house on the same site burned to the ground in 1892. Stonecutters from England labored with beelike urgency over marble imported from Italy. In two short years, The Breakers, named after the waves that crash ashore at the base of the cliffs behind the property, rose from the ashes of its former self, a temple to Vanderbilt money and ambition.

The house was small compared to Cornelius II and Alice's mansion in New York City, and in letters and calendars they referred to it simply as "home," but of course, they knew full well the grandness of what they had built.

The sheer size of The Breakers is hard to contemplate: Seventy rooms comprising square footage better measured in acreage than in feet—nearly three times as big as the White House. The morning room walls are paneled in platinum. The first floor alone sprawls with room upon room built on a scale more suited to grand city hotel lobbies than to a house meant solely to escape the heat in the drowsy days of summer. There are separate reception rooms for gentlemen and ladies, as befitting Victorian notions of propriety; a great hall ringed by a gallery with sculptured personifications of Art, Science, and Industry like those one might find in a university library, its ceiling painted with a trompe l'oeil sky; a music room with a gilded ceiling; a billiards room modeled in the style of ancient Rome, a civilization that never heard of billiards; and a dining room with a table designed to seat thirty-four. A library features a bust of William Henry Vanderbilt II, the owner's son, who died while a student at Yale, in bronze; one of his father, Cornelius Vanderbilt II, in marble; and a fireplace pried from a sixteenth-century French château to lend its historical cachet to the New World and its new wealth, with the inscription, "I laugh at great wealth, and never miss it; nothing but wisdom matters in the end."

Until recent years, tourists eager for a look inside this secret gilded world bought tickets in a tent situated near a row of Porta Potties; now most visitors reserve their tickets in advance online. They tour The Breakers in shifts. The summer sun is bright in Newport, but the sea air is soft, which makes the wait easier. Visitors to the great Gilded Age houses are no longer announced, as they would have been only a generation or two ago. They observe the rooms—with their ornate furnishings, walls studded with semiprecious stones, and bathtubs filled by hot and cold fresh or salt water piped directly from the sea—from behind velvet ropes. They are allowed to take pictures inside, but tour guides admonish those caught using a flash. A single ticket to tour The Breakers now costs twenty-six dollars, or about one dollar in 1913 money—just about what a scullery maid employed in the Vanderbilts' kitchen could have expected to be paid for a month of work. The Breakers has never been shy about its relationship with money.

Cornelius Vanderbilt II had been closely involved with every detail of its construction, but he didn't get to enjoy The Breakers for very long. He died of a stroke in 1899, just four years after the house was completed. He was fifty-five years old. Alice continued to use the house every summer until she died in 1934, bequeathing it to one of her daughters, Gladys Vanderbilt, who had married a Hungarian count, Laszlo Széchényi, in 1908, thereby becoming Countess Gladys Széchényi.

As is often the case with many things designed to impress, The Breakers proved to be an enormous financial burden. The house alone was challenging enough to maintain, but there was also a large stable and thirteen acres of meticulously landscaped grounds, as well as two capacious greenhouses for the palm trees and flowers needed for décor in The Breakers as well as in their mansion in New York. The house and grounds required a rotating staff of servants and workers—housekeepers, gardeners, maids, stable hands, and, if every seat at the dining table was filled, one footman to serve every three guests—who labored behind the scenes to keep it all going, and they all had to be paid. When The Breakers was first built, there was no federal income tax. After the Sixteenth Amendment was ratified in 1913, the great fortunes of the Gilded Age were exposed for the first time to taxation from the government, and Alice Vanderbilt was no exception. Then there were the property taxes and estate taxes, all of which ate away at the Countess's inheritance, as did the cost of the constant repairs and maintenance. The Countess loved The Breakers and had inherited an estimated $12.5 million, about $340 million today. But even that fortune wasn't enough. During World War II she had assets and property seized in Hungary and Czechoslovakia, and in 1948, running low on funds and desperate to find a solution that would keep The Breakers in the family, she arranged to lease the house for one dollar a year to the Preservation Society of Newport County, which began offering tours to the public. She moved out of the grand rooms on the first and second floors and decamped with her family into third-floor rooms that her brothers had occupied as children. They installed a small gate on the grand staircase, to stop any curious visitors from sneaking onto the floor, and converted a servant's room into a kitchen.

The deal with the Preservation Society helped the Countess by lowering taxes on the property, but she was still responsible for paying them and for covering the cost of most major repairs. She managed to hold on to the house until she died in 1965, but her children couldn't afford to keep it for long, and two generations after it was built, it passed out of family hands for good. In 1972 they gave much of the furniture to the Preservation Society as a gift, and sold them the house for $365,000, or about $2.3 million today. By contrast, Cornelius Vanderbilt II spent $7 million building the house in 1895, the equivalent of more than $220 million today. In its 77 years of existence, The Breakers saw the equivalent of nearly $218 million evaporate into thin air.

The Preservation Society's board of directors promised that one of Countess Széchényi's daughters, Sylvia Szápáry, could live on the third floor of the house for the rest of her life. Sylvia, who was called Syvie by her intimates, spent every summer at The Breakers along with her children, Gladys, who was named after her grandmother, and Paul. Syvie watched over the house with an eagle eye, trying to ensure it was cared for with love. She personally gave or loaned the Preservation Society hundreds of family heirlooms and photographs so they could be put on display for visitors.

The "secret" Vanderbilts still living in The Breakers, on an unseen floor no less, set the house apart from the other Gilded Age mansions of Newport overlooking the Atlantic Ocean, which, like The Breakers, had largely passed out of private hands by the mid-twentieth century, when they proved far too expensive to maintain. Tour guides made a point of mentioning that there were Vanderbilts still living upstairs, preserved, like rare specimens under glass. Sometimes tourists would catch a glimpse of Gladys walking her dogs on the grounds, or see someone peering over the third-floor banister and get excited, believing they'd had a sighting of one of the mysterious Vanderbilts rattling around, ghostlike, in the house. When Syvie died in 1998, the Preservation Society sent Gladys and Paul a letter allowing them to remain on the third floor, mentioning that "it will be helpful to us to be able to tell our visitors that the original owners' great-grandchildren continue to live in the house."

Gladys Szápáry wanted to make sure tourists—or "guests," as her mother had insisted they be called—had a good experience. True, she wasn't shy about speaking up when she saw things that could be improved upon, and yes, she was at times critical of the way the Preservation Society was running things. She complained about the shrinking budgets for repairs and maintenance, since something always needed restoration or protection from the ravages of time: the front gates, the Belgian tapestry over the stairwell, leaking windows, and family photographs bleaching away unprotected from direct sunlight. Gladys was chatelaine of the infinite list of minutiae that go into the running of a grand house, the very same minutiae that led to the house's sale a generation before.

Tensions started to bubble in 2013, when the Society proposed building a new visitor center on The Breakers's grounds to replace the drafty ticket tent and Porta Potties. Gladys preferred that it be built across the street, so it wouldn't alter the original Bowditch landscape design or intrude on the fantasy that visiting The Breakers meant stepping into another era. Whenever possible, in Newport, unpleasant matters are dealt with behind closed doors, in hushed voices, but this disagreement turned into a very public battle, fought in newspaper pages, in boardrooms, and before judges. The *New York Times* remarked that Newport on the whole resists change: its residents didn't like the America's Cup leaving their waters, they didn't like Bob Dylan going electric at the 1965 Folk Festival, and they certainly didn't like the idea of prepared food for sale at The Breakers. But the Preservation Society pointed out that the visitor center would be wheelchair-accessible. Change was coming. Change must come. In 2015, in a written statement, the Preservation Society pointed out that Gladys and Paul's use of the third floor "can be ended at any time." The threat was clear.

"I'm waiting for them to throw my clothes out the window," Gladys dryly told a reporter.

Those in Newport who followed such matters knew all that Gladys had done for The Breakers. She was smart and kind and well liked locally. As a teenager she was all over The Breakers, Eloise-like, working in the Children's Cottage gift shop, hanging out with the guides, visiting with the security guards, polishing the brass hinges on the oak doors before they opened every morning. But now some Preservation Society board members viewed her as a nuisance, and they wanted her out. The battle over the visitor center was the final straw. Gladys's efforts to stop construction failed. The Preservation Society got what it wanted. The visitor center would be built on the grounds of The Breakers. It would even sell sandwiches.

Gladys was summoned to a meeting at the Preservation Society in October 2017. She was told it was no longer safe for her to live on the third floor. Knob-and-tube wiring posed a fire hazard. The plumbing was antiquated, and a leak could destroy the showpiece rooms on the second floor below. The fire codes would not permit year-round habitation in the rooms where she and her family had always lived. Gladys had offered years before to get things up to code, but her suggestions had fallen on deaf ears. There wasn't much she could do. She was a guest in what she thought of as her family home, living there at the pleasure of strangers.

The statement put out by the Preservation Society was matter-of-fact:

> A year-long study by a preservation architect and an engineer concluded that the ventilation, electrical, and plumbing systems, while completely safe for museum use, were dangerously outdated for residential use, putting the structure and collections at risk. In view thereof, elements of the historic building's 120-year-old plumbing and electrical systems are being decommissioned on the upper floors. . . . The residential occupancy of the Vanderbilt family apartment on the third floor by Paul and Gladys Szapary, the children of Countess Anthony Szapary, has been voluntarily discontinued.

It was the final act of a years-long opera about the struggle for control over what The Breakers should mean and whom it should be for. Gladys was told she could stay until the end of the year. After that, she would be allowed in only to remove family property, accounting carefully for any historical items to prove that they did not belong to the Preservation Society. Over the decades, the boundary between what the family owned and allowed the Society to display and use and what the Society itself owned had blurred, waxed, and waned. Somewhere along the line, The Breakers had gone from a private family enclave into which the public was allowed a privileged view to something effectively owned by the public.

Gladys moved out at the end of December of that year, as ordered, but she was allowed back during the next few months to pack up. Every weekend, early on chilly mornings, half a dozen friends and preservationists from out of town would turn up to help her pack and label and hoist and move and store. Staff members from the Preservation Society had placed blue tags on furniture and whatever else they believed had already been given to the Society. Gladys had been preparing for this. She had gone through old files and carefully gathered documents and receipts for the loans she and her mother had generously made to the Society—photographs and furniture, baby carriages and christening clothes. Gladys always planned to one day make the loans permanent, but now she was reconsidering. There were other museums and historical societies that would happily take them. She and Paul and their friends bought hundreds of boxes from U-Haul and spent months carefully packing four generations of family history. Their grandmother's Louis Vuitton trunks were taken from the attic, as well as some children's sleds from the early 1900s. They shivered while they worked, as the Preservation Society had already turned off the heat on the third floor. Sheets of ice formed on the windowpanes inside, and as the sun warmed them each day, pools of water trickled down the glass to the floor.

On her last day, Gladys spent her final hours in The Breakers mopping the floors, shutting off lights, closing doors, and then packing her car with the help of her friend, preservationist Jason Bouchard-Nawrocki. Before getting into the elevator that final time, she took one last look around the rooms where she had spent so much of her life, now empty enough that her footsteps echoed over bare wood floors.

Finally, as the thin afternoon sun faded from the windows of the third-floor apartment, she rode down to the basement. She strode past the gift shop, whose staffers had been instructed not to speak to her—some even averted their eyes—and left through the service door, the only door she had ever used, rather than the grand front entrance. The service door was how, at age two, she had first entered the house her great-grandfather built, and it's how she wanted to leave it. She was tired. Her face was stiffened from the cold and by her determination not to show the anger and sadness she felt.

The chief of staff of the Preservation Society, Terry Dickinson, a sturdy former navy man, was waiting by the back door. Gladys marched over to him and put out her hand.

"Terry, thank you and good-bye," she said as they shook.

Gladys climbed into her car, pulled out of the small rectangular parking area, inched down the winding driveway past the Children's Cottage, and left through a side gate.

She never looked back. The Breakers now belonged to the Preservation Society of Newport County and to the public—perhaps to history as well.

There is something uniquely American about this faux palace, with its décor and fixtures ripped out of the ancient homes of European royalty. At first blush, a tour of The Breakers might feel like roaming the halls of an American Versailles, if all we notice is the grandeur and expense. But roaming Versailles's Hall of Mirrors in sneakers, taking pictures with abandon, is a revolutionary act—after all, the French palace, once a center of government and divine-right power, was seized by the people and never given back. The Breakers was the center of attention, the center of fame, and the center of envy without being a center of power. The house stands as a temple to excess.

If our country's mythos is based on the belief that anyone can be rich if they have enough gumption, have enough grit—or, as we shall see, have enough ruthlessness—then The Breakers is everything our culture tells us to want and promises we can have if only we are willing to work hard enough. It is arguably the most extreme expression of the loaded promises of the American dream.

The United States, a country founded on antiroyalist princi-
ples, would, only twenty years after its revolutionary burst into
existence, produce the progenitor of a family that would come
to hold itself up as American royalty, with the titles and palaces to
prove it. But their empire would last for less than a hundred years
before collapsing under its own weight, destroying itself with its
own pathology.

Part I

RISE

The Tycoon

January 4, 1877

The people who first come to virgin country usually arrive as workers, for every hand is needed, living facilities are at a premium, and there is little if any of the leisure or money necessary for the immediate development of an aristocracy. That is why all old American families such as mine have strong and simple roots here.

—Amy Vanderbilt's *Complete Book of Etiquette*, Introduction

Heavy clouds lay low over the sleeping city. A wicked cold snap had gripped the entire country that week, and reporters camped outside the town house at 10 Washington Place, huddled over ash can fires, stamping their boots to keep the blood moving in their feet. They had been out there for months.

Inside, a great man—or, certainly, a formidable one—was dying.

He was an upstart from Staten Island. He had overseen construction of the town house in 1846, when he was fifty-two years old, rich with an extraordinary fortune made in shipping, but he was only getting started.

Since then, he had lived in the double-width town house for more than thirty years, and in that time had made another great fortune, his second, in railroads, but he never considered moving or building a grander home. The Knickerbockers and other old-money families of Washington Square shunned him, but he didn't care. Money was his sole concern: making it, spending it, and making more. New York society could ignore him, but in the end, they couldn't ignore his money. No one could.

The house itself was stolid and elegant, built of red brick with brownstone trim. In the back, a courtyard led to stables along Fourth Street. The parlors on the first floor were well appointed, but the only valuable work of art was the Hiram Powers marble bust of the great man, made at the peak of his powers, when he was long-cheeked, tall, with sharp, calculating eyes and a shock of wiry hair rising over his high forehead. This was the man all the reporters were eager to hear from, to quote, maybe even to catch a glimpse of: "The Commodore," Cornelius Vanderbilt.

Months earlier, reporters asking after his health at the door of 10 Washington Place heard the old man bellow down the stairs, "I am not dying!" But he was. For eight wretched, painful months, he'd been ill and installed in his bedchamber, which connected to an office and to the boudoir of his second wife, Frank Armstrong Crawford, so named for her father's best friend, when her parents thought she might be a son. These rooms faced south and, on a less bitter winter day, would have let in bright beams of sunlight through the fringed Victorian curtains that likely hung there. But on this morning in January, the curtains were almost certainly closed.

The Commodore was eighty-two, and while his death was expected, when the end actually came, the reality of it surprised both his family and the city he had helped build. The previous night, according to the *New York Times*, he felt well enough to move from his bedchamber to a wheeled chair in his sitting room, his favorite room in the house, which was dominated by an imposing oil painting of his mother, Phebe. There he stayed up until ten o'clock at night, chatting with his family and a couple of friends. His son William H. Vanderbilt, called Billy when he was in favor, passed some of the evening with him and was confident enough in his father's health that he returned to his own home without undue worry.

But night comes for everyone, and it crept in on Commodore Vanderbilt before dawn as he lay in bed. At around four in the morning, a pallor touched his cheek, and his attending physicians summoned the members of the household to his bedside soon after. The *Times* reported that the Commodore was weak, but gratified at having his loved ones gathered around, and that he asked them to sing some favorite hymns to keep his spirits up. The death watchers, led by one Reverend Doctor Charles Deems of the Church of the Strangers—a congregation of Southern transplants in which Frank was very active—then joined together in prayer, and the Commodore tried in vain to sing with them. Presently, the spark faded from his eyes, and he sighed away in peace, his last words "That was a good prayer."

That's the *Times'* version, and it is certainly a complimentary one, aligning with Victorian fantasies of what a good and appropriate home and spiritual life should look like for a man of the Commodore's stature. But is it true? The breathlessly watching newspapers had been constantly warring for scoops on this larger-than-life man and his final days. The New York *World* reported that the Commodore had bemoaned that the devil was after him. The *New York Sun* agreed, claiming Vanderbilt told his doctor that he and the Lord were fighting the devil together. As for the cause of his death? The *Times* attributed it to "exhaustion," the *New-York Daily Tribune* to something else entirely: "venereal excesses." Adding insult to injury, the *Tribune* had been run by Horace Greeley until his death five years before, and the Commodore had always considered Greeley a friend.

Frank had been watching over her husband steadily since he first took to his bed and, on occasion, writing her own version of events in a journal. She'd thought he was going to die the previous May, as he shuddered through waves of pain that no amount of medicine seemed able to relieve. "Thy will O God be done," she records the Commodore gasping in late May as she and retinues looked on, "but if the Lord has anything more for me to do, be pleased to postpone the pain and enable me to do it."

The next day, she said, the Commodore laid his hand on Frank's hair and told her that she was the last link binding him to life on earth—not his children, notably; nor his grandchildren; not even his work (building the railroad into the American wilderness, or building a shipping network to cross Nicaragua); nor his fortune (greater than any ever amassed in the history of American business). Though, as the darkness gathered around him that spring, Frank wrote that he said he was grateful to have helped found the university in Tennessee that bore his name. The Commodore had stopped going to school when he was eleven, so having a university named after him likely gave him deep satisfaction. Proof, yet again, that with money, anything was possible.

Of course, the Commodore had laid many monuments to himself over the years. There were the ships and trains that bore his name and the portraits of himself he had commissioned and given to his favored children. In 1866 he bought Saint John's Park, a lush and exclusive enclave bordered by Varick, Beach, Hudson, and Laight Streets in Lower Manhattan, planned in the same elegant manner as Gramercy Park. It had been surrounded by grand houses, with a dignified church at the center of intersecting pathways meant for promenading during the afternoon. Vanderbilt knocked down the sweeping trees and removed the grass and pathways to erect the Hudson River Railroad Depot, an interchange for freight trains coming into Manhattan from New Jersey and other points west. In October 1869 (the same year the Commodore and Frank were married), upon the completion of the depot building, he installed, high up on the western wall, a statue of himself, flanked on either side by a bas-relief sculpture full of references to his shipping empire and his railroads, celebrating his victories over those who had tried to compete with him in business. When the sculpture was unveiled, *The Nation* magazine described it as a monument to "audacity, push, unscrupulousness, and brazen disregard of others' rights or others' good opinion." By the 1890s, the area around the depot had become a slum. The fine houses that had once surrounded the park, with tile floors and parlors wide enough for dancing a quadrille, had been converted into crowded tenements with clotheslines, washtubs, and stovepipes snaking into fireplaces. Today, the site is a traffic exchange that funnels cars to the Williamsburg and Manhattan Bridges. The statue he had built of himself was eventually moved some two miles north to Grand Central Terminal, where it still stands today.

On June 1, 1876, his illness seemingly worsening, the Commodore reportedly announced that he had forgiven all his enemies. "I bear no ill feeling to anyone," Frank records him saying, no doubt aware that there were plenty of people who still bore her husband ill will. The following day, he begged to be given the strength not to complain. On the eleventh, a Sunday, Frank quotes him saying, "You have been a true and faithful wife and done me good. Twas Providence that had thrown us together and I hope we will be united above."

Frank had married the Commodore eight years earlier, on August 21, 1869, when he was seventy-five years old and she was thirty. Born in Mobile, Alabama, she had traveled north in penury with her mother following the defeat of the Confederacy, eventually landing in New York City. They looked up Cornelius Vanderbilt, their distant cousin, and managed to ingratiate themselves so thoroughly that Frank and the Commodore eloped to Canada, a year after his first wife, Sophia, died. The wedding was attended by only a few friends of Frank's and none of Vanderbilt's children.

Frank was an unashamed Confederate sympathizer, a self-described Rebel, and it was through her influence and introductions that the Commodore put up $1 million for the Methodist Episcopal Church, South, to found the Central University in Tennessee, which would eventually be renamed Vanderbilt University in his honor. In theory, he made the gift as a gesture of peace to the South, after having given a million-dollar ship, the U.S.S. *Vanderbilt*, to help the Union Navy. With his endowment of the university, the Commodore successfully split the difference on public accolades.

Despite the accounts of his concerns about the devil, Cornelius Vanderbilt had never been a churchgoing man. It was only because of Frank's involvement with the Church of the Strangers that Reverend Doctor Deems was a frequent visitor to the Commodore's sickbed, leading the ailing man in prayer and joining Frank in song to keep his spirits lifted. Deems's devotion to the Commodore might also have been helped by the older man's donation of fifty thousand dollars to buy the Strangers their church building.

The Commodore spent much of June fretting over his younger wife. He told anyone who'd listen how good she had been to him and wished loudly that his family could understand this. He wanted her to be buried with him, in the family tomb he had erected, at no small expense, in Staten Island—if that was her wish. On June 5, he expressed a desire to add further to the university endowment and then told Frank that she should place her trust in his eldest son, Billy.

According to Frank, the Commodore prayed for God's forgiveness for his sins and transgressions and asked that He "change the hearts of his offspring and bring them all around." To what exactly, it isn't made clear. Likely, his late-in-life marriage, of which his daughters disapproved, or his plans for the dispensation of his fortune. The great man's children had begun to trickle in to see him at his sickbed, as rumors spread that he might be facing the end. He didn't always admit them upstairs if he didn't feel like it. On June 11, his son Cornelius stopped by Washington Place expecting to see his father, but was sent away. Despite being the Commodore's namesake, the younger Cornelius had always been a source of shame. Not even impending death would change that.

Frank tried to bring "Com," as she called her husband, to God—on that point at least, there is little disagreement. Few men, arguably, were more in need of God's forgiveness on the morning of January 4, 1877, than Commodore Vanderbilt. A master manipulator, disseminator, and inventor of his own legend, Cornelius Vanderbilt reveled in attention, in being feared by men in business with him and, certainly, by men in business against him. He was feared also by his children, whose lives he dominated with judgment and control. More than anything else, however, the Commodore thrived on money. He had blasted it out of the wilderness building railroads and had sieved it from the water with poles and sails and, later, steamships. When his final breath escaped his body, this man would leave behind a veritable monument of money.

Cornelius Vanderbilt started his life with next to nothing. He barely had any formal education, and yet, lying there in his bed, on the point of death, with his doctors and his wife and her minister watching over him, he was about to leave behind more money than any American at the time had ever accumulated: $100 million, the equivalent of more than $2 billion today. It beggared the imagination.

This financial feat, together with his talent for legend making and publicity—a talent shared by several of his descendants, even if many of them excelled more at spending than making money—made him the center of untold hordes of attention. *Frank Leslie's Illustrated Newspaper* would publish an engraving of Washington Place just after the Commodore's death, showing the street thronged with gawkers, lining fences three deep, craning necks from atop hansom cabs, bundled tight against the winter wind. No one could believe that the man who controlled one out of every twenty American dollars in circulation at that time could actually, finally die.

Before the sumptuous palaces of Fifth Avenue then being erected by his children, before the Upper East Side and Billionaires' Row, where Commodore Vanderbilt's figurative descendants now roost and preen, Washington Square was the beating heart of New York City society. The Commodore died just off the square, in his fine house nestled cheek by jowl with the social elites who never accepted him. The sedate, leafy block of Washington Place is a far cry from where Commodore Vanderbilt's story began.

New York has always offered up the possibility of forging a new self, a new identity, making new wealth out of nothing. New York has done this since before it was New York. Cornelius Vanderbilt may not have been the first person to remake himself in New York City, but his rise from hardscrabble rural obscurity to a level of wealth never before seen in America, and rarely paralleled since, places him squarely within the persistent American mythology that holds that success is tantalizingly available to anyone with the cunning and discipline to seize it.

Cornelius Vanderbilt was born on May 27, 1794, on Staten Island, in a small, undistinguished Federal-style farmhouse of modest clapboards, polite shutters, and a deep porch, in the fledgling years of the new republic. Descended from a Dutchman who came to the New World as an indentured servant before staking a claim in Brooklyn, the "van der Bilts" had farmed on Staten Island for almost a century by the time Cornelius was born. He was by all accounts a restless boy. The family farmstead—which he still owned at his death, together with a small cottage on Union Street that his mother, Phebe, had occupied and that, out of sentiment, he refused to sell—ran right up to the water. As a child, Cornelius watched from the shore as salt-crusted boatmen navigated small ferries through the difficult currents around Staten Island, their vessels laden with farm goods and, once in a while, a passenger, earning a few pennies here and there. Cornelius's father, with whom he shared a name, was one of them.

His father was an unambitious man. He farmed, he fished, he supported his wife and nine children, and the seasons drifted into each other on Staten Island, one year after another. Young Cornelius, who was called Cornele by his family, took after his mother, at least as far as cunning went. Phebe was English, pragmatic, sharp with money, and had already saved their farm from foreclosure once, by producing the required sum in cash that she had secreted away in a grandfather clock.

Cornele never cared much for school, preferring to work on his father's two-masted boat, known as a periauger. Though only a child, Cornele transported vegetables and passengers between Staten Island and Manhattan, a distance of about five miles, maybe an hour's sail if the wind and tide cooperated. The periauger was wide and shallow, good for carrying cargo. With Bermuda rig sails on its masts, and no keel, it was easy to maneuver in shallow water, quick before the steady winds of the harbor, polable when the winds died. Still, sailing a periauger through the currents of the Narrows was no mean feat for a boy of eleven, which is how old the child who would become the Commodore was when he left school and started earning money on the water.

Fragmentary anecdotes about Cornele's childhood have persisted over the years, though the man didn't write them down himself, and so they are next to impossible to substantiate. In fact, the Commodore was just this side of illiterate, and surviving examples of his handwriting border on the illegible. The stories could be myths or lies that Vanderbilt told to bolster his own legend or that writers—like the sober reporters of the *New York Times* who gave the hard-cussing Commodore such an angelic death—invented to color a childhood for which there is little trustworthy evidence.

The day after his death, the newspapers reported that one of the signal experiences of his early life occurred when he was six and raced a horse at top speed through the surf against another horse ridden by a boy about two years older than he. Historian T. J. Stiles, in his biography of Commodore Vanderbilt, writes that the boy was a neighbor's child slave. While no records have been found that indicate the young Commodore's parents owned slaves, many Dutch families in New York did. Stiles points out that in 1790, one out of every three families in northern Staten Island relied upon enslaved people. The *Tribune* even had this child Cornele once raced against reappear at the Commodore's bedside eighteen months before his death, in the guise of an elderly Black Methodist preacher of "advanced age" fondly recalling their boyhood together. This anecdote, typical of the white perspective on Reconstruction, is almost certainly untrue.

Another oft-repeated story supposedly occurred when Cornele was twelve. A ship ran aground at Sandy Hook, the spit of sandbar jutting from New Jersey into New York Harbor, southeast of Staten Island, and his father obtained a contract to salvage the cargo. This massive operation required the labor of several men, three wagons, and some rowboats. The twelve-year-old boy was tasked with moving the laden wagons from the beached ship on one side of the peninsula to the waiting rowboats on the other. When the scows were loaded, Cornelius the father took off with them, leaving young Cornele in charge of taking the empty wagons and teamsters overland to Perth Amboy, a distance of nearly thirty miles. Upon arrival in Perth Amboy, Cornele had spent all his ready money on food for the workers and feed for the dray horses, leaving nothing to pay for the ferry crossing back to Staten Island. The ferryman wanted six dollars. Cornele went to a nearby tavern to borrow the money, leaving a horse for collateral and promising to repay the loan within twenty-four hours. He kept his word.

The message of these stories, whether they are true or not, is that Cornelius Vanderbilt was headstrong, stubborn, manipulative, and willing to risk almost anything to make money. The second story also, Stiles has argued, established early in the young man's mind the freedom of the ferryman to demand whatever price he wanted.

Young Cornelius Vanderbilt also was secretive in his heart. He seemed to have held his father in vague contempt, though this didn't stop him from joining the ferry business with him. He certainly revered his mother, but his relationships with his siblings are elusive. There is no record, for instance, of how he reacted to the death of his brother Jacob, nor of how he might have felt when the next son born to Phebe was named Jacob to replace him. In Cornelius's history, there is little evidence of, or room for, delicate feelings or emotions. It was money he wanted. Not, as one might imagine, from a desire to better his family's circumstances, but for its own sake. With money came power. With money came freedom. And that is what the young man who would be the Commodore was after.

By the time he was fifteen, Cornele was bored running a periauger for his father. In May 1810, at the height of the Napoleonic Wars between England and France, as the United States was struggling mightily to remain neutral and still profit from the maritime trade, he declared to his mother that he was going off to sea. Phebe, however, wasn't fooled. She saw this announcement for what it was: a tactic. An article in the *New York Herald* published at the time of the Commodore's death reports what happened next.

Suggesting he would stay in New York if only he had a boat of his own, Cornelius hit Phebe up for one hundred dollars (or about twenty-one hundred dollars today) to purchase one. His mother was skeptical. She had the money, but she also knew that her husband was counting on young Cornelius's labor to work the farm and continue running his ferry.

She pointed to an eight-acre tract of land that was rocky and hard to cultivate. It was, if the story is to be believed, the first of May. "On the 27th of this month is your birthday," she said. "If by that time you have ploughed, harrowed, and planted that field with corn, I'll give you the money."

Cornelius did it. Not by himself—he enlisted a bunch of other boys to help him. That is how the story is usually told, but "enlisted" might be the wrong word. Rather than ringleading a bunch of friends to help out, like a real-life Tom Sawyer, it's possible Cornele had enslaved boys' labor at his disposal. There is no way to know for sure.

With the money from his mother, at the age of sixteen, he bought his own periauger at Port Richmond, Staten Island, and sailed it home. Within six months, he had run his own father out of the ferry business, putting in at Manhattan, near the Battery, at the same spot where the Staten Island ferry docks today.

Cornelius was a large boy, muscular, with the powerful legs and the wide back of a rower. He was drawn to the water not only because of the physical demands of sailing, the punishments of wind and tide and current, but also for the promise of self-determination. Running his own periauger meant that young Cornelius assumed all the risk, but answered to no one and didn't have to share in the reward. Ferrying was the perfect avenue for a young man of developing appetites who was impatient to get what he wanted. This sense of freedom infused the culture of the wharves around Staten Island and Manhattan, and Cornelius took to it like a fish to water. He drank and whored and didn't stand down from a fight. The wharves were the crucible in which Cornelius Vanderbilt's acquisitive hunger was forged. The older boatmen nicknamed him "the Commodore" during these years as a joke, but it stuck, and they didn't laugh for long.

A year after his mother loaned him the money, he paid her back, and when the British blockaded the East Coast of the United States to stop Americans' trade with France in 1812, the young Commodore saw a real moneymaking opportunity. American ships, including those used for regional and coastal trade, were trapped in port, and goods that used to move up and down the Eastern Seaboard had to travel over land. Cornelius had no qualms about striking a deal with the British, who had shut down New York's harbor. He moved supplies for the British military and, when possible, brought produce from up the Hudson River to hungry New Yorkers. The money Cornelius made playing both sides of the blockade allowed him to invest in two other peri-augers. He also had enough money to get married, and in 1813 wed his first cousin Sophia Johnson. He was nineteen years old.

Cornelius and Sophia had thirteen children, of whom twelve survived to adulthood: Phebe Jane (named for his mother), Ethe-linda, Eliza Matilda, William Henry (Billy), Emily Almira, Sophia Johnson, Maria Louisa, Frances Lavinia, Cornelius Jere-miah, George Washington (who died at age four, in 1836), Mary Alicia, Catherine Juliette, and the second George Washington. But only three of the children actually mattered to the Commo-dore: his sons, who would carry the Vanderbilt name. His nine daughters? They would get married and change their names, and, as far as the Commodore was concerned, their children would not be Vanderbilts.

George, the youngest, who was named for the brother who predeceased him, attended West Point but graduated without any distinction and was shunted aside in the army during the Civil War. He died of lung disease on the French Riviera while the war was still raging. Like the Commodore, he was tall and handsome, with mournful eyes that sloped down at the corners. Some thought he was the Commodore's favorite, but it's possible he simply died too young to have disappointed his father.

Cornelius Jeremiah, the second son, proved an embarrassment almost from the beginning, a point the Commodore never let him forget. He suffered from epilepsy, which his father took to be a mental illness and a mark of weakness. A failure in several dif-ferent business ventures, Cornie, as he was known, repeatedly leaned on his famous last name to procure loans and lines of credit, which he then squandered by gambling. Twice the Commodore had him committed to what were then called "lunatic asylums," and when those institutions proved unable to prevent financial and moral laxity, the Commodore resorted to warning friends and business associates away from him. "There is a crazy fellow running all over the land calling himself my son," the Commodore was quoted as saying. "If you come into contact with him, don't trust him."

No small wonder Cornie was shooed away from his father's sickbed when he tried to call on him in his final days. Even weakened, the Commodore maintained rigid control over all the people in his orbit. On an afternoon in June 1876, a doctor came to examine him, but before he could touch him, the Commodore applied spectacles to his nose with care and then closely examined the doctor's fingernails, running his own hands over them to make sure they were trimmed and wouldn't scrape him.

As the summer wore on, the heat in New York City grew heavy, and the Commodore showed no improvement. In the thick warmth of July, he liked to have one attendant stationed near his head, waving a handkerchief soaked in rum over his forehead. He had another person doing the same lower down, a third bathing his feet, and a steady supply of cracked ice brought to his bedside to suck upon. Moving him into his large-wheeled chair required the coordinated efforts of his physician, Dr. Ellsworth Eliot—the "long legged Yankee," as the Commodore called him—his nurse, Lizzie; and several attendants, all inching him from bed to chair. No one dared overlook any part of his comfort, but nothing his team of experts did could alleviate his illness.

On August 3, he underwent an operation of some kind at home, which put him in agony. Frank recalled that it seemed almost "too much for even his strong constitution," but when they tried to give him brandy to numb the pain, he reportedly refused it, on the grounds that he didn't want to meet his maker while under the influence of liquor. He had also reflected to Reverend Doctor Deems that he hoped he might get to heaven and see his mother again, so perhaps he didn't want to show up drunk for Phebe. During that dark night, the Commodore grew clammy, and Frank and the others lingered anxiously by his bedside, watching for what Dr. Eliot warned them was likely imminent. They slipped stimulants between his lips, and as dawn drew near, he brightened a little.

"Oh! That night of anxiety and terror!" Frank wrote later. "But he grew better and we were thankful."

What do pitiless and avaricious men dream about when they are at death's doorstep? In the Commodore's case, Frank notes that he dreamt he was walking with a group of people along a path in the shape of a horseshoe, along the edge of a cliff with water below. As each person walking with him neared the edge, they toppled and fell. When he drew close to the appointed spot, he felt himself slipping, slipping, nearly falling, but he caught himself and managed to carry on walking until the end. The end of what? Perhaps, despite all the claims of his newly Christian protestations about acceptance and readiness and God's will and being saved by Jesus, the Commodore didn't believe he would ever die.

The next day, his second-youngest daughter, Mary Alicia La Bau, paid a call on him. "Now don't be stubborn and give trouble," the Commodore told her, possibly forestalling what he assumed Mary wanted to discuss with him. "I have left you enough to live like ladies." Mary argued that she wasn't being stubborn, but her father dismissed her with a wave of his hand, unwilling to listen anymore.

That night, his fever and chills returned. Word was spreading among his children that the old man might finally be reaching his end. On the eighth, his long-suffering second son, Cornelius Jeremiah, appeared again and was finally received at his father's bedside. "Poor unfortunate boy," the Commodore said to him. "You make good resolutions but are not able to keep them from here to Broadway."

"It was pitiful to hear Com talk to CJ," Frank wrote later. She also noted that her husband had said for years that he would give $1 million or more to make young Cornelius right.

Attention wasn't coming only from his children. Visitors called at the house in a steady stream: business associates, friends stopping by for well wishes, but also reporters sniffing around for a story. Food deliveries arrived by the hamperful. The Commodore basked in the attention, by all accounts, but as the weeks wore on, he was still unable to get out of bed.

His iron control over his family remained unchanged, however. The Commodore forced his daughter Sophia to apologize to Frank for unspecified unkind remarks and urged his wife to meet her halfway. The apology was begrudgingly given, and it's worth noting that the recalcitrant daughter in this instance was fifty-one years old and the stepmother all of thirty-seven. Through it all, Vanderbilt's sharpness went undiminished, as he possessed a memory unwilling to give up the slightest detail or affair. When Frank marveled about this fact to the Commodore, he laughed and said, "I don't forget what I remember."

Periodically, they were visited by a Mrs. Danforth, a so-called "magnetic healer" who would minister to both the Commodore and his wife. Late in his life, the Commodore had grown intrigued by Spiritualism and clairvoyance. Evidence suggests that he began attending séances as early as 1864, but given the mainstreaming of Spiritualist practices in the 1860s and '70s, this was not as unusual as it may sound. The period immediately after the Civil War had seen a dramatic rise in the Spiritualism movement and other alternative modes of healing and perception, driven largely by the staggering loss of life experienced during the war. Significantly, this also would have been around the time that his youngest son, George, died. One example even survives of the Commodore asking in passing if a medium had been able to speak with George.

Perhaps most notoriously, in 1868, in the brief lull between his two marriages, Cornelius Vanderbilt encountered the Spiritualist sisters Victoria Woodhull and Tennessee Claflin. The pair had installed themselves at 17 Great Jones Street, about a five-minute walk from the Commodore's home. They advertised themselves as "magnetic physicians and clairvoyants," charging the queenly sum of twenty-five dollars per visit. "Magnetic healing" was a sort of laying on of hands, suggesting that magnetism could pass through the hands of the practitioner and into the body of the suffering person, to beneficial effect. The Commodore wasn't alone in discovering that being touched in a caring way by a beautiful woman was more pleasant, as treatments go, than being bled or given a powerful emetic by a man, beautiful or not. And the sisters were famous for both their "magnetic" powers and their beauty. He came to rely primarily on the ministrations of Tennessee Claflin, the more sumptuous of the sharp and wily sisters, but despite her tender touch, the Commodore's heart was already spoken for. In August 1869, he and Frank had eloped. She signed a prenuptial agreement first, relinquishing any claim to Vanderbilt's estate in exchange for half a million dollars in first mortgage bonds in the New York and Harlem Railroad. A Methodist minister presided over the quick ceremony, with the Commodore in a simple black suit, only diamond shirt studs suggesting the vastness of his personal fortune, and an overjoyed Frank in unfashionable traveling clothes. They took a private train car home, dodging the press, stopping over in Syracuse and then in Saratoga Springs, where the Commodore often headed to enjoy the horse racing. His social circle in Saratoga doted upon Frank, celebrating her with so much attention that she later expressed embarrassment about it to her mother. Some of the Vanderbilt children, most notably Billy, welcomed Frank with open arms, too, but most of the Commodore's daughters were aloof.

The Commodore's doting on his new wife didn't stop his other entanglements, however. In January 1870, the newspapers announced that Victoria Woodhull and Tennessee Claflin had gone into business for themselves, opening a brokerage house. Stranger still, the sisters suggested that their investment strategies were informed in part by spiritual visions. The two enjoyed the breathless interest of reporters, who couldn't believe that women could undertake such an enterprise. Their new offices on Broad Street prominently featured a portrait of Commodore Vanderbilt on the wall, but when pressed on whether the Commodore was backing them, Tennie was coy: "I know the Commodore and frequently call to see him on business, but I am not prepared to state anything as to whether he is working with us," she told the *New York Herald*.

As the days passed, though, the sisters dropped his name more and more into the papers, and the Commodore did nothing to disabuse the press of the suggestion that he was involved. Was he really their backer? Probably not. What seems most likely is that he continued to see them for "magnetic healing"—or, rather, massage—and found them entertaining and diverting. He may have been sexually involved with Tennessee Claflin or he may not have. What is clear is that Cornelius Vanderbilt always had a soft spot for iconoclasts with gumption, as they reminded him perhaps of the characteristics he most appreciated in himself.

The afternoon of September 3, 1876, the Commodore's daughter Sophia Torrance approached Frank and extended her hand. "I'm sorry anything unpleasant occurred," she said by way of apologizing for certain things said against Frank's character. "Father wishes us to become friends."

"I have nothing to do with it," Frank replied. "I said nothing. But I will do anything to please your father." She took Sophia's hand and shook it.

Frank later recounted the fragile reconciliation to the Commodore, who was gratified to hear it. Then Frank noted in her journal that she "rubbed him with electricity." Her ministrations, unfortunately, had little effect. That night, the Commodore was in the kind of agony that only opiates could relieve. After being dosed by his doctor, the great man slept fitfully, sometimes so nervous and afraid that Frank had to lie down beside him and hold him. She tried a flaxseed poultice, she tried singing—anything she could think of to keep the Commodore calm and relieve his pain. At its worst, he even spoke hard words to her, and later, when eased, he would warn her to stay away from him when he was in the worst throes of it, because he was afraid he would say things he didn't mean.

The Commodore was suffering from dysentery, which was treated with codeine and paregoric (a tincture of opium) as well as flaxseed poultices and enemas. His autopsy would later reveal a constellation of painful internal conditions, including an enlarged prostate, cystitis, anal stenosis, and diverticulitis, the last of which was exacerbated by his taking opiates, which were the only truly effective modes of pain relief available to him. Frank wrote that she was "miserable about him," crazed with worry. By October, the Commodore was in so much pain that he loudly wished he could die, if only he could take Frank with him.

Frank's journal of her husband's final illness ends on October 19, 1876, with some notes of levity. On the sixteenth, the Commodore had an easy night and was feeling more himself, so they were surprised when a telegram from a Mr. Barton, who had just left the house, arrived asking if the Commodore was dead, as he had seen in the papers. The telegram's arrival just beat a crush of reporters, according to Frank, all asking "comical queer questions" that "amused Com greatly." So great was his amusement that he even forgot his pain for a short time, spending the afternoon in his wheeled chair in the sitting room chortling over the wildfire rumors. He had the evening newspapers read aloud to him, many of which included details of his death, so eager were the reporters to scoop one another.

On the eighteenth he was visited by his son Billy, together with some other gentlemen from the railroad. By late October, the newspaper reporters had taken up the death watch themselves. Daily they filed reports of his health, its ups and downs, their predictions and their anticipations.

As late as December, the Commodore still weighed in on business matters with Billy from his deathbed. But the problems in his colon only worsened, and peritonitis set in. His long, gradual decline meant that the stock market was prepared when the end finally came, even if his family wasn't. It was, as Stiles has noted, his last gift to Billy, into whose hands would pass the Vanderbilt railroad empire.

On January 4, 1877, the Commodore lay surrounded by Billy, Frank, and several of his daughters, listening as the Reverend Doctor Deems offered up prayers. In a telegram that Billy sent that night, he noted that the Commodore perfectly understood everything that was said around him, keeping control and consciousness to the last. At nine minutes before eleven in the morning, Cornelius Vanderbilt expired.

"A great loss," Billy wrote, "which we hardly realize."

His last words have been a matter of some debate, with every newspaper reporting them differently. The *Times* has him saying "That was a good prayer." To that sentiment the *Tribune* adds that he breathed a single word: "Home." But one account has him giving Billy the most urgent instruction possible, an instruction designed to protect the legacy that Cornelius Vanderbilt was leaving to the children hovering by his bedside and to generations of grandchildren to come: "Keep the money together."

Van der Bilt

c. 1660

Every generation has its immigrants. Many of us are descendants of the Irish who emigrated here during the potato famine in the nineteenth century, of Italians who came to supply our labor pool or bolster our artisan class in the nineteenth and twentieth centuries, of early Dutch settlers dissatisfied with opportunities at home and who came to trade and colonize in New Amsterdam.

—Amy Vanderbilt's Complete Book of Etiquette,
Part II, "Dress and Manners"

In this nation of immigrants, the idea that people seen as nouveau riche, or "new money," first arrived on North American shores in the 1600s might seem counterintuitive. The Vanderbilt money was made in the nineteenth century, but the family itself had been around since New York City was New Amsterdam.

The first family arrival that we know of was Jan Aertsen, a broke, undistinguished farmer from a village named Bilt, in the Utrecht region of Holland, an inland hamlet about thirty miles southeast of modern-day Amsterdam. He was born there around 1627, and his name was recorded as Jan Aertsen van der Bilt, or "from the Bilt."

Passage to the New World wasn't cheap, so Jan Aertsen signed up to be an indentured servant to afford it, a common practice at the time. Terms of indenture varied. Often would-be servants would contract their labor for several years in exchange for passage to the New World and "sufficient Meate drinke and App[arel] during his said time," according to one surviving example from the eighteenth century. "Redemptioners" were indentured servants who agreed to work off the cost of their passage within a stated period of time after arrival; if they failed to do so, the ship's captain who had arranged their passage could then sell their labor to the highest bidder.

Jan Aertsen sailed on a ship owned by the Dutch West India Company, the corporation granted an exclusive charter by the Netherlands to run the Dutch Atlantic slave trade between the Caribbean, West Africa, and the Americas and the lucrative fur trade along the Hudson River as far north as present-day Albany. When he arrived in New Netherland, as New York State was then called, Jan was indentured to Peter Wolpherson, a landholder who'd brought fifty colonists to work the company-owned land he had been granted. The Wolphersons traded on the side with the Native peoples who lived in what would become the city of New York, and when Jan Aertsen's time as an indentured servant expired, he obtained a small holding of land in the area we now know as Flatbush, in Brooklyn.

Jan Aertsen married a woman named Annetje Hendricks, and they had at least one son, Aris Janse van der Bilt, around 1653. It is not known exactly when Jan Aertsen arrived in New Netherland, but records show that in 1687, he swore an oath of allegiance to the English Crown and indicated he had lived "off Breucklijin" (modern-day Brooklyn) for the past "26 Jeare." So he was certainly there by 1661, and died in 1705. These dates draw boundary lines around Jan Aertsen's life, but what of his world emerges from beneath the silt?

Dutch New Amsterdam, much less Dutch Breucklijn, is hard to see in today's New York. We may remember that Wall Street is so named because it used to have a wall running along it, south of which lived most of the colony; the wall was designed to protect against unknown forces in the wilderness, be they Native or English or French. Maybe we've wandered the narrow streets of the Financial District in Manhattan, dimly aware that they follow an early modern labyrinthine path, so unlike the clear grid plan that begins at Fourteenth Street. But successive fires that tore through New York City in 1776 and 1835 consumed any remnants of Dutch-period architecture that would have been left standing. Unlike Boston, which nearly sanctified its seventeenth-century buildings and wears its eighteenth-century identity on its sleeve, New York City keeps its Dutch past largely hidden. Historian John Van Dyke, writing in 1909, bemoaned:

What seventeenth-century Dutchman, could he wake up, would recognize in the ponderous new Custom House the site of the old Dutch fort in New Amsterdam; of in Beaver Street the beaver trail leading over into the marsh now called Broad Street; or in Wall Street the place where the wall to keep out invading foes was erected; or in Broadway the Heere Straat, which in 1665 was remarkable for containing twenty-one buildings? The burghers in pot hats and bag breeches that wandered along Perel-Straat (Pearl Street) when it was the water-line of the East River, and the faithful huis-vrouws in balloon skirts that chattered along the cow path (Beekman Street) leading through the Beekman farm up to the (City Hall) park would never be able to orient themselves in the new New York.

But remnants of Dutch life sometimes peek through the rocky soil of Manhattan, buried under twelve generations of silt, offering a window into what Jan Aertsen's world might have felt like. Archaeological evidence suggests that life for Dutch inhabitants of seventeenth-century New Netherland wasn't as much of a crude struggle for survival as one might imagine. The 1600s were something of a golden age in Dutch culture, and some of that relatively high life traveled with Dutch settlers when they came to the New World. Jan Aertsen's lifespan overlaps with that of Johannes Vermeer, a painter in Delft with an unusual eye for individual faces, domestic moments in time, and light. The material world of Vermeer's paintings—the tile floors, gathered breeches, ripples of linen and wool and taffeta, paper maps pinned to the wall, poured milk, that one pearl earring—gives us a sense of the tactile experience of middle- and upper-middle-class Dutch life. An indentured servant would not have had access to pearls, of course, but the scent and sound and sight of milk pouring from an earthenware pitcher would not have been strange to someone like Jan Aertsen or his wife, Annetje.

This picture of everyday Dutch life stands in contrast to archaeological evidence of English settlements in New England, which suggest a plainer existence. New Englanders, while no strangers to the profit motive in their settlements, were self-abnegating religious extremists, carving out a foothold in wilderness that Puritan minister Cotton Mather memorably termed "once the Devil's territories." The Dutch, for their part, didn't initially envision establishing permanent settlements in the New World, and New Netherland was designed as a temporary outpost, a means for access and export of beaver fur. Many people came expecting to return to the Old World after their fortunes were made.

A daily pleasure in this vanished life was also a common New Netherland item used for trade with both Native populations and with the English: clay tobacco pipes, which appear frequently in archaeological digs up and down the Atlantic coast. One source says that pipe smoking was especially common among women in the seventeenth century. The colonists enjoyed some everyday comforts here and there: A will and testament names a taffeta underskirt with gold braid, not unlike the rustling fabrics of Vermeer. Crushed bits of glass and pottery appear at the bottom of privies where early modern people relieved themselves and often tossed their garbage, one reason privies are a rich archaeological resource today. Street plans list copious breweries, suggesting that New Yorkers, then as now, liked a good tipple. But some differences from home show that New Netherland would have been an alien landscape to Jan Aertsen when he first arrived.

New Netherland was always more than just Dutch; it was cosmopolitan from the start. Consider that Dutch houses were rarely built from wood, yet houses in seventeenth-century New Netherland were often constructed with a wooden plank cellar—essentially, a finished basement, kept dry and more practical for storage. This same construction method extended to New England, with even brick houses often overlying wooden frames. The Dutch and English colonies didn't function in isolation from each other. The remnants of Dutch ceramics appear both in New England to the north and Virginia to the south, illustrating the interconnectedness of trade among all the colonies regardless of origin.

An inset elevation view from a map dating from around 1684 and drawn by Dutch cartographer Nicolaes Visscher gives us a picture of "Nieuw Amsterdam" on Manhattan Island as seen from the harbor. To anyone familiar with the glass-and-steel cliff faces that wall off Lower Manhattan today, the landscape is simply unrecognizable. On the left, a square-rigged ship rests at anchor, pennants hanging loose from atop the two visible masts. In the foreground, two hazy figures propel a canoe through the water, and a few more schematic, hatted men ferry small sailboats to

Brooklyn and points south. In the foreground, at the lip of the water, stands a wooden scaffold for unloading cargo, and behind it sit tidy rows of Dutch houses of the same A-shape seen in antique Amsterdam houses today. Rolling green hills press up from the water to the right, with further neat rows of houses situated along a ridgeline. A map key illustrates "Het Fort" (the fort), "de Kerck" (the church), "de Wintmolen" (the windmill). The tallest structure in this vision of early not-yet-New-York-City is a flagpole, which the legend tells us is for running flags up whenever ships enter the harbor. Taken as a whole, the inset paints a picture of an orderly, staid little colony, a company town run by the Dutch West India Company for company purposes.

Of course, the tidiness of a map obscures some of the harsher truths of what it meant to live in the seventeenth century. Jan Aertsen would have stepped into a town in which enslaved Africans did backbreaking work. The Dutch West India Company first brought captured African men to New Amsterdam in 1626, to build infrastructure, and in the ensuing years, reliance on slave labor only grew. Enslaved Africans slept in attics and cellars in houses all over the settlement, and their forced labor went into building Fort Amsterdam, the wall on Wall Street, docks, and churches.

The New-York Historical Society estimates that as many as 20 percent of residents in colonial New York were enslaved, and 41 percent of pre-Revolutionary New York City households used enslaved labor as servants and for domestic businesses—numbers more in line with what was seen in Charleston, South Carolina, than in Boston. By the 1738 census, of Flatbush's 539 inhabitants, 129 of those counted were enslaved.

Thirty years ago workers constructing a federal office tower at 290 Broadway in Lower Manhattan uncovered intact human skeletal remains dozens of feet below the surface of the city streets.

They had happened upon the "Negroes Buriel Ground," six acres containing the remains of more than fifteen thousand people of African heritage, both enslaved and free, who had lived in colonial New Amsterdam and New York between the 1630s and 1795. Archaeological research revealed that some of the people interred there had died with broken bones not yet healed, or with injuries wrought by extreme violence. Those sweetly reflective Vermeer interiors don't reflect the truth of life in New Amsterdam for most people, it turns out.

Calling the settlement that Jan Aertsen joined "Dutch" was itself something of a misnomer or, at least, a new and shifting concept. The settlers of New Netherland would likely have identified more with the particular region from which they came—Utrecht, in Aertsen's case—than with the Dutch Republic. They would have spoken different languages, followed different religions and customs, and in some cases even used different systems of weights and measures. Though many of them were broadly Protestant, and from Northern Europe, in truth, the most dominant cultural affiliation for these early immigrants would have been to the Dutch West India Company itself. Perhaps it's fitting that the Vanderbilt family origin story would be inextricably tied with the history of a corporation.

Jan Aertsen would have been accustomed to a homeland that was diverse relative to other European countries, but still dominated by Europeans. When he arrived in New Netherland, he stepped into a realm peopled by other Northern Europeans as well as Native populations speaking distinct variations of Algonquian and Iroquoian languages and people of African descent, both enslaved and free, from different regions within Africa, South America, and the Caribbean. New Netherland was from the beginning a unique community, something related to its European antecedent, but wholly distinct from it. Who were some of the people living out their lives in this new and separate place? Some clues derive from the most famous map of the settlement below Wall Street. Its original translated title is "Picture of the City of Amsterdam in New Netherland," but it is now referred to as the Castello Plan, because it was rediscovered in the library of the Villa di Castello in Florence in 1900.

The map was drawn up around 1660 and is remarkable for its detail as to ownership of each individual plot of land in the colony at that time. Though Jan Aertsen, who had already settled in Flatbush, does not appear, the key nevertheless gives us a sense of what kind of community he would have moved within as he carved out a living from the land.

On one block, a Dutch Reformed Church minister, Dom Johannes Megapolensis, lived next door to a skipper named Lucas Andries, while tavernkeeper Lucas Dircksen installed himself up the street. One block over, Peter Stuyvesant kept an orchard, selling part of it to Captain Jan Jacobsen de Vries in September 1660. Evert Pels, listed in 1656 as a "rich merchant," lived in the same block as the orchard. New Yorkers have always loved their nightlife, and so, on the same block, Pieter Wolfertsen van Couwenhoven erected a house and brew house, not concerned that he was next door to the Latin school.

The next block over was busy with renters and widows and the buying and selling of houses, both for home and profit, among people who worked as smiths, barrel makers, soldiers, glaziers, and tailors. Also on the block, you could find a tanner, a shoemaker, and the overseer of the weigh house. Hendrick Willems, overseer of bakers, lived next door to Frederick Gijsbertsen van den Bergh, a merchant of wine and tobacco. This block even held the Deacon's House for the Poor, which the map notes contained eight people.

In a block on the other side of the island, Paulus Heymans in

1653 worked as an "overseer of co[mpany] of Negroes." Another overseer lived on the same block as Peter Stuyvesant's Great House, along with a panoply of tapsters and carpenters and sailors. The Dutch West India Company's house for enslaved laborers was built before 1643, near the house and garden of shoemaker Jochem Beeckman.

Most of the early settlers in New Amsterdam were men. (The Castello Plan lists a trumpeter, for example, but no housemaids.) The colony that would become New York City was a well-ordered machine for the creation of profit, and profit was maximized by the maintenance of the monopoly of the Dutch West India Company. The ideology of New York City was, is, and probably always will be profit.

The English took over New Netherland in 1664, to the consternation of the Dutch people living along the Hudson, up to Albany, and into Long Island—like Jan Aertsen. The latter half of the seventeenth century was an uneasy time everywhere, but for Dutch settlers living along the edge of the waterways of North America, the years after the English takeover were especially so. English began to be spoken in the streets more than Dutch, and the sets of laws governing everyday life derived from a different authority. Though the settlements all around what would one day be New York City were also dependent on the goodwill and trading relationships with the Native peoples, those relationships could be unpredictable. Tidy square plots of land, tidy square meadows dotted with tidy cows and tidy houses, and tidy braid-trimmed clothing created a semblance of order, but outside the wall that would become Wall Street, away from the fort with its defiant little flagpole, they were surrounded by the unknown.

In the 1660s, Dutch colonists like Jan Aertsen had to worry not only about hostilities between themselves and the new English bubbling constantly under the surface of everyday trading and business, but also the growing economic influence and pressure of the French to the north, in what would become Canada, and occasional hostilities exploding among differing groups of Native people, whom the Dutch called *de luiden*, "the people," or, more often than not, *de wilden*, "the wild ones" or "the savages." The Mohawk, allied with the French, spent half of the 1660s thrashing it out with the Mohican in the wilderness around Albany. The Dutch around Albany kept their heads down, but they couldn't avoid the conflict entirely. Through the Native lands was the path to valuable beaver fur—the promise of wealth that had brought the Dutch West India Company to the Hudson River in the first place.

Then, in 1673, when Jan Aertsen was around forty-six years old, England and the Dutch Republic went to war. A Dutch fleet sailed up New York Harbor in triumph to reclaim New Netherland, but the restoration of Dutch rule lasted only one confusing year, a year full of uncertainty over names and places and who was in charge. The colony of New Netherland was gifted back to Charles II of England, traded away like so much lustrous beaver fur.

After 1675, more English people streamed into the colony, bringing with them their language and customs and religions and hostilities with other Native peoples. The governor-general on Manhattan Island let it be known that burghers must report on anyone (neighbor, family, or friend) who might take mutinous action against the English king. New York City was, as the English say, well and truly New York City now. There was no turning back.

The region of Brooklyn where Jan Aertsen van der Bilt settled then became known as Flatlands (and would remain so up until the nineteenth century). Jan's son Aris married a woman named Hillitje Hillegonde Vanderbeeck in 1677. They had several children, including Jacobus (Jacob) Aertse van der Bilt, who was born in 1692—the year of the witch trials in Salem, Massachusetts, though not as dramatic a year in the rolling farmlands, on the wagon-rutted king's highways, or on the busy waterfronts of Long Island. Jacob married and had a son, also named Jacob, and by 1731, he'd ventured with his family across the choppy Narrows of New York Harbor to settle and farm Staten Island.

It was from this Staten Island branch of van der Bilts, a mere two generations later, that the Commodore would spring. Hard to imagine that the man who made the Gilded Age according to his whims and who died on the cusp of the twentieth century had a great-grandfather born the same year as the Salem witch trials, but such are the long spans of generations. The changing of New Amsterdam for New York, the Anglicization of the Dutch colonies, inscribed itself in the Vanderbilt family, too; the second Jacob Vanderbilt married an Englishwoman, Mary Sprague, on Staten Island in 1746. This meant that the Commodore's father, the first Cornelius Vanderbilt on Staten Island, was half-English, and his mother, Phebe Hand, was fully so. Despite his name, Commodore Cornelius Vanderbilt was only one quarter Dutch.

That iconic name, too, took some time to cohere from "van der Bilt" before the family decamped for Staten Island. In the militia roster for Flatlands in the eighteenth century—a militia headed by a Captain Schenck—there is a long list detailing whether the men have three important possessions: wagons, horses, and weapons (muskets, bayonets, cartridges, powder, and balls). Possessions in this instance could be seen as a proxy for social rank. Captain Schenck, for instance, had a wagon, four horses, and a driver named Sam.

"Jeremiah V. D. Bilt," in contrast, is in possession of one musket, one cartouche, nine cartridges, but no wagon or horse. The overall impression from these fragmentary records is that in

Flatlands around the time of the Revolution, the Schencks were the family to deal with. They had the resources, and the leadership among the company of Flatlands men. The van der Bilts were there, but they had less to offer than families with names like Lott, Voorhees, or Van Sinderen.

At one point, Jeremiah seems to have obtained the rank of major, and by 1777, is in charge of the transport and identification of some prisoners of war held at the home of his neighbor and fellow Guardsman Dr. Van Buren. Jeremiah signs his name "Jeh Vander Bilt," and his handwriting is clear and legible, albeit lacking in flourish, so he was literate.

By 1792, two years before the Commodore's birth, there are fewer Vanderbilts in Flatlands. Jeremiah's name does not appear in an accounting of Flatlands townsfolk's respective responsibilities with regard to a fence around the town's meadow taken that year, and by the time a subscription is gotten up for the building of a new Dutch Reformed Church meetinghouse for Flatlands, no Vanderbilts appear among the pew subscribers.

The shades of the English and Dutch past that haunt the Vanderbilt origin story matter insofar as they tell us about the Commodore, and New York, and the specific set of circumstances that combined to create the opportunities that the Commodore was able to exploit. The Dutch West India Company ran New Amsterdam as a monopoly, and the English, in many ways, continued this tradition, granting exclusive rights to essential services like mills, bridges, and—crucially, for our story—ferries. In a very real way, the Commodore was part of the first generation that truly made the United States into America as we know it now, with its disorderly market culture and its thirst for competition.

In 1817, when Cornelius Vanderbilt was a strapping twenty-three-year-old ferry captain with a young wife and two baby daughters, a businessman named Thomas Gibbons hired him to run a Hudson River steamboat between New Jersey and New York. Cornelius kept his own ferry boats running on the side, but he assumed control of Gibbons's ferry concerns as well. But while Vanderbilt's ferries all ran within New York State, Gibbons's ferries were interstate, and technically illegal. He was breaking a long-standing monopoly on that essential service (echoed by the battle between medallioned yellow taxis and ride-hailing apps in New York City today). None of this rule breaking bothered the Commodore.

In 1807, the New York State Legislature had granted a steamboat monopoly to Robert Livingston, a descendant of the Livingstons who had been influential in and around New York City since it was New Amsterdam, and to Robert Fulton, a steamboat designer. Both men were long dead before Cornelius Vanderbilt came on the scene, but their monopoly lived on, controlled by their heirs, like latter-day patroons, the title granted by the Dutch West India Company to those seventeenth-century colonists granted tracts of land in New Netherland. These heirs leased the monopoly—the way a taxi medallion is leased today—to a man named Aaron Ogden.

Gibbons hated Ogden with the fire of a thousand suns; he wanted to bankrupt him. But he needed a ruthless business manager who was willing to smash the monopoly alongside him—first, by slashing prices, a competition-beating technique that Vanderbilt would gladly use to destroy business rivals in the decades to come; and second, by bringing a case before the U.S. Supreme Court challenging the legal basis of the monopoly.

Cornelius moved his young family from what is now called Staten Island to New Brunswick, New Jersey, which was a stop on the steamship ferry line that he was now managing. His wife, Sophia, opened an inn and used the rich profits she was able to generate to feed and clothe their growing brood of children. Vanderbilt, meanwhile, went to Washington, DC, and hired attorney Daniel Webster to argue for the overturn of the monopoly.

On March 2, 1824, the Supreme Court ruled in Gibbons's favor in *Gibbons v. Ogden*, a case still cited frequently today, which marked the turn in America from monopolies to markets. The case doesn't bear Vanderbilt's name, and he didn't appear in the news around it, but it is covered in his fingerprints in its declaring that individual states had no standing to interfere with interstate commerce. The last of the protected Dutch-era monopolies were washed away in the unfettered competitive churn of steamboats plying between New York and New Jersey. That seawater churn would froth higher and higher, heaping up great clouds of profit around the descendants of Jan Aertsen van der Bilt, to a level that a seventeenth-century indentured servant or an eighteenth-century farmer who owed one horse to his militia could never have possibly imagined.

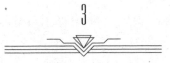

3

The Blatherskite and the Namesake

April 2, 1882

*We all mourn the deaths of those we love, but the healthful thing
is to accept the loss as well as we can and gradually make our
adjustment to the life we must live without this beloved person.*

—Amy Vanderbilt's Complete Book of Etiquette,
Part I, "The Ceremonies of Life"

Cornelius Jeremiah Vanderbilt sat on the edge of his bed in room
80 of the Glenham Hotel, a nickel-plated Smith and Wesson revolver in his hand. It was five minutes before two on the afternoon
of April 2, 1882. The fifth-floor room faced Fifth Avenue, just
high enough to escape the worst of the street noise, the rattles and
creaks of passing landaus, the stamping of horse hooves, and the
constant thrum of human activity on one of the busiest avenues
in the city. There was always the stink of horse manure in Manhattan, an odor thickened with the drum of rain every spring, but
with the windows closed, it wasn't too oppressive this high up.

Cornie had spent much of his adult life in Hartford, Connecticut, away from the stresses and excitement of the big city where
he was born. But he was never very far from the expensive temp-
tations New York offered, or the yearning urge to satisfy them,
even when finances or common sense would suggest otherwise.

He found himself back in New York this time after a trip to Hot Springs, Arkansas, to take the cure. In the adjoining room, George Terry moved softly about, conducting business of his own. George was his constant companion. They said it was because of Cornie's epilepsy. He never knew when a fit might fall upon him, rendering him insensible. He could collapse in a restaurant, at the theater, in the street. George was there to help him, but they were far more than just traveling companions. They ate together, read together, slept together. George tried to safeguard not only Cornie's body, but his mind, too—he had been institutionalized before, for weakness of character. That was Cornie's father's judgment, anyway: that his son was weak, an embarrassment, a drain on the old man's resources, a drain on his name. It was hard being the son of the Commodore, harder still to be named after him and judged only on the differences between them. Always being found wanting.

The gun was small enough to fit in his pocket, and Cornie had carried it for years, another attempt to make himself feel safe that had never seemed to work. He was never safe. Not from the constant comment and observation, not from his creditors, and certainly not from his father's cool, gray-eyed judgment. The Commodore had been dead a little more than five years, but even from beyond the grave he hounded Cornie. The lawyer Cornie had hired to try to break the Commodore's will was suing him for payment. The selfsame will that had left nearly everything, $100 million, to Cornie's brother Billy—William H. Vanderbilt.

The Blatherskite. That's what their father had always called Billy. The blockhead. Well, he may have been a blatherskite and a blockhead, but Cornie and his sisters were convinced Billy had swayed their father in his interest, consolidating his control over the Vanderbilt fortune through undue influence in the waning days of the Commodore's final illness. Cornie was desperate: he was in debt up to his ears. Imagine! A man in his fifties, from one of the greatest fortunes in the world, with a family that controlled all the railways into and out of the greatest city in America, and Cornie didn't have anything of his own, not really. Even the few hundred thousand dollars the Commodore had left for him in a trust was administered by Billy, like an allowance doled out to a petulant child.

For his whole life, Cornie had been seen as less than the Commodore. While his father was universally praised as sturdy, rugged, and physical, with his early exploits on the Staten Island waterfront becoming the stuff of legend, the younger Cornelius was to some extent imprisoned by his body. Cornie was over six feet tall, like his father, both of them a head above most other men of their day, but Cornie had the build of a man whose pleasures were indoors. He was slim, a bit stooping, un-muscled, his skin paled to a nearly consumptive pallor. Some observers called his features delicate, and by the time he was thirty, his hair was already streaked with gray. In his forties, Cornie had started to effect a closely trimmed beard to give his face some strength and definition. In further contrast to his father, Cornie considered his greatest quality his geniality. He was likable, dry-humored, a bit ironic. Easily swindled, maybe, but he thought, hardly to blame for the financial straits in which he continually found himself.

In December 1877, Mr. Scott Lord, the attorney who was now after him for unpaid fees, had attempted to persuade the Surrogate Court of New York that Cornie's financial problems weren't his fault. His elder brother, Billy, had clearly manipulated their father into leaving Cornie with the meager competence. What kind of father cuts off his namesake and all his daughters? How could Billy have fooled him?

"A long time anterior to the months of October and November 1874, a period about a month before the execution of the will,

Cornelius J. Vanderbilt was a man of good habits," Mr. Lord said to the court. "This was known to Commodore Vanderbilt, who promised to aid him and said what naturally gave him high hopes of the future. Harmony and good will existed during the months mentioned between the Commodore and Cornelius J."

What Mr. Lord said next shocked everyone in the courtroom. Was it the truth? Well, if Cornie's lawyer said it was, who could argue? "William H. Vanderbilt began a conspiracy to have Cornelius J. personated by a man of bad habits, and through his agent, employed detectives to follow that person to houses of infamy. That person was followed by the detectives, who reported to the agent, and then to William H. at his house, and then to Commodore Vanderbilt, that Cornelius J.'s conduct was dissipated in regard to liquor, women, and gambling. The Commodore became greatly excited in consequence, made the deepest expressions of sorrow, and said at the same time that he had been led to think differently. Afterward . . . the Commodore absolutely refused to do anything or to hold out any hopes for the future whatever."

That afternoon, Mr. Lord summoned Cornie to the stand in support of this argument. Before a packed gallery stuffed full of onlookers and newspapermen hungry for sordid details of life behind the curtains at 10 Washington Place, Cornelius J. Vanderbilt was asked to account for himself—for his frailties, for his failings.

"In October and November 1874, I did not visit any gambling houses," Cornie swore. "I never entered a house of ill-fame; I never was in the habit of drinking liquor; I never in my life purchased a lottery ticket in Wall-street or elsewhere; when my father was in his last illness I was in the City; I saw him but once during that period; I was at his house every day for three or four months, and often two or three times a day, and I made efforts to see him, but was refused; it was Mrs. Vanderbilt chiefly who kept me from him; I asked William two or three times for some position in the office of the New-York Central; he told me, 'I can't interfere with father for you; if I should he would damn me up hill and down, and I dassent do anything myself without asking him'; this was after William was made Vice-President of the road; during the Winters of 1870 and 1871 my wife and myself were in this City; William never called upon us but once; on that occasion he told my wife that father sent him around to give her a little New Year's present; he gave her a $50 bill."

That fifty-dollar bill was a symbol, and a particularly cruel one. It was the weekly rent that Cornie and his wife, Ellen, were paying a landlady in the city who had dared ask the Commodore to serve as guarantor. The very idea that Cornie couldn't be trusted to pay his own fifty-dollar rent was galling enough. Worse still was that his father had initially refused to guarantee it. And then, in 1872, Ellen had died. She had been the only thing in Cornie's life that the Commodore approved of.

Mr. Lord tried to get testimony of what Billy had told Cornie after their father's funeral: "Don't make any fuss about the will," his brother had assured him. "I'm the best friend you've got in the world, and I'll see you're all right." But then, when the will was read, leaving everything, absolutely everything, to his brother and cutting off Cornie and his sisters with a mere pittance, Billy feigned amazement. Of course he did! Any fool could see that Billy knew the contents of the will ahead of time, because he'd bent the Commodore's ear in his own interest. But the Surrogate Court excluded the testimony, and Mr. Lord had nothing further to ask. The Surrogate asked Billy's lawyers if they cared to cross-examine.

They certainly did.

"Yes, Sir," answered Mr. Henry Clinton, attorney for the defense, with some feeling. He first endeavored to establish that

Cornie was in the habit of referring to himself as "Cornelius Junior" when transacting business, ostensibly to pass himself off as Billy's son, Cornelius Vanderbilt II, who had good credit, a sterling reputation, and was considered the Commodore's favorite grandson. The old man had even left him $5 million in his will. Cornie said he used that name sometimes, but after all, he had a prior right to it, didn't he? Wasn't he named Cornelius Vanderbilt, after his father, who was also named Cornelius Vanderbilt? Hadn't Cornie been named Cornelius longer than his nephew?

Then the attorney zeroed in on Cornie's time in lunatic asylums. He had been sent to the Bloomingdale Insane Asylum when he was nineteen or twenty, and again at twenty-four, the first time because his father had insisted he go, but Cornie didn't remember how long he was there—longer than two weeks, but less than six months. The second time was the result of his activities in Washington.

"While in Washington, was any criminal charge brought against you?" asked Mr. Clinton.

"I drew some money on Father and he did not pay it," Cornie replied truthfully. The Commodore was always churlish about settling his wayward son's debts.

"Were you not arrested on a charge of forging your father's name?" the lawyer pressed.

"No," said Cornie.

"Were you in [the] charge of the criminal authorities?" Mr. Clinton clarified.

"I think I was in jail," Cornie said, and the entire gallery erupted in laughter.

"Don't you know what is meant by criminal authorities?" the lawyer said, clearly annoyed.

"It is hard to tell what is criminal nowadays," Cornie responded ruefully.

Mr. Clinton struggled to keep his irritation in check. "Were you arrested on a criminal warrant and lodged in jail?"

"I don't know whether it was a civil or criminal action," Cornie said drily.

Then Mr. Clinton went in for the kill: "Was not your release obtained upon the ground that you were insane and not responsible for your actions?"

"No."

"Didn't you consent to go to the asylum to escape the criminal consequences of your arrest?" Mr. Clinton insisted.

"No, Sir," Cornie said, refusing to be rattled. The lawyer then went on about Cornie's epilepsy, and Cornie assured him that if he had a fit on the stand, it wouldn't interfere meaningfully with the cross-examination.

"Did you think yourself insane at the time?" Mr. Clinton wanted to know.

"No; nor anybody else," Cornie said, to the general laughter of the audience at court, causing his remark to be stricken from the record.

Cornie continued, unperturbed about publicly disclosing his time in the asylum. It was, after all, common knowledge—New York never felt more like a small town than when it came to gossip. "Father came to the asylum to see me," he said, "and I told him that I had stayed long enough; I then came away; I don't know whether anybody came with me; I don't recollect where I lived after that, but I think in New-York City."

Bloomingdale lay nestled in the verdant hills of Morningside Heights, to the north end of Manhattan, where the air was thought to be more healthful and restful for someone suffering from what the Commodore had described to doctors as "dementia," a term then used to refer to bizarre mental states or behavior. It was, notably, the same asylum where the Commodore had committed his wife, Cornie's mother, Sophia, in 1846, against the wishes of all the children except Billy, who seemed willing to do almost anything to stay in his father's good graces. The Commodore had sent her there ostensibly for her instability during what he referred to as her "change of life," but in truth, he wanted her out of the way so he could spend time with his children's governess unfettered by the constraints of marriage.

For a while after his time in Bloomingdale ended in 1850, Cornie tried his hand at this and that profession: reading the law, dealing in dry goods. None of his efforts ever amounted to much. He did develop his taste for gambling during those years, but when he met Ellen Williams, a minister's daughter, she took him in hand. For a time, it seemed as though Ellen was all Cornie needed to set himself to rights. They married in 1856.

"After I was married I worked a small farm my father gave my wife in West Hartford," he told the court. "It consisted of ten acres laid out mostly in fruit; I did not perform any manual labor; I attended to its cultivation; I lived there fifteen years; during that period I came to New-York and took a position in the revenue under Joshua F. Bailey, and stayed until he left himself."

Billy's attorney interrupted: "He left between two nights. He was a defaulter."

"How often have you been an inmate of the debtor's jail?" the court asked.

"I was twice in Ludlow Street Jail," Cornie said. Ludlow Street was nothing to be ashamed of, not really. Even Boss Tweed had passed some pleasant evenings there, not to mention the fact that one of Cornie's father's magnetic healers, Victoria Woodhull, had been an inmate at Ludlow Street. It was almost gentlemanly of Cornie to have stopped by.

"Were you not arrested four times by Deputy Sheriff Mac-Gonigal in civil suits on charges of fraud?" pressed the defense.

"I don't know the gentleman," Cornie said truthfully. It was, to be fair, hard to keep track of the people who came to him to collect on debts.

"Would you know him if you should see him?"

"I don't think I would; he belongs to a class of people I never took a particular fancy to," Cornie said, and great laughter rocked the halls of the Surrogate Court. But Mr. Clinton wasn't finished talking about Cornie's relentless need to spend money that didn't belong to him.

"During the time you lived in Connecticut, did you run in debt to a considerable extent?"

"I believe I owed some money," Vanderbilt allowed.

"At the time of his death did you owe Horace Greeley for borrowed money, and how much?"

Nothing drove the Commodore to ranting as much as Cornie's habit of borrowing money from Greeley. He felt that his layabout son was abusing his friendship with the famous newspaperman, but Cornie didn't see why it should matter, especially after Greeley died before the Commodore did.

"I borrowed $40,000 from him during his lifetime," Cornie admitted. "At the time of my bankruptcy he sent me my notes and made me a present of them, but when I was discharged, I gave him new notes."

"Do you owe his estate now $70,000 borrowed money and interest?" Clinton continued.

"No; I arranged it with the Executor, I think, for $40,000." The estate had let him off the hook for the interest. A lucky thing.

"Did you ever make any payments?" Clinton asked.

"My father gave the children $10,000. Individually I did not," Vanderbilt said. How did they expect him to make any payments with no profession and no money from the family? It was laughable.

"At the time of your father's death how much did you owe altogether?" Mr. Clinton asked.

"Leaving Greeley out," Cornie mused, "about $50,000."

"Do you keep a list of your creditors?"

"I do, and that is what I go by."

"Do you owe Mr. Zachariah E. Simmons, the lottery-policy man, any money?" Clinton said in an accusatory tone.

A dark shadow crossed Cornie's eyes. "That's my private business," he said.

Mr. Lord objected, but Mr. Clinton shouted: "It will appear that there was a conspiracy—not such a conspiracy as has frequently been spoke of in this trial, but one of the rankest ever known in the history of jurisprudence!"

Presently the truth came out: Cornie owed to an infamous numbers runner an amount of money he hadn't bothered to keep track of, and the two men saw each other every couple of days. Illegal gambling and loan sharking went hand in hand, and without Simmons taking his wagers and floating him cash, there was no way for Cornie to meet his considerable expenses. For the first time, the true depths of Cornelius Jeremiah's financial straits were laid bare for the public to see and feast upon. He told the Surrogate Court of his suit pending in the Supreme Court for $1 million against Billy, "on the ground that he promised me that sum if I would withdraw my opposition to the probate of the will."

The trial had nearly broken him. No matter how many trips he took to take the waters, no matter how many cures or visits to Florida or afternoons with George Terry, always the anxiety of the trial stalked him. It pressed in on him now, as he sat in his hotel room. Cornie weighed the revolver in his hand. Outside, a Sunday afternoon in April in Manhattan carried on just as sunny afternoons in April always had. He could hear George in the next room, moving quietly about.

Dear George. What would he have done without him?

Of course, Cornie hadn't had the wherewithal to try to break the Commodore's will by himself. In that enterprise, he had joined with his sisters Ethelinda and Mary. They would have been mad not to. One hundred million dollars, all to Billy, with only a few hundred thousand dollars for everyone else? They filed a formal objection to the probating of the will in Surrogate Court in March 1877, two months after the Commodore's death, serving Henry Clinton, Billy's attorney, as Billy was both chief beneficiary and executor. Ethelinda, whose married name was Allen, and Mary, now Mrs. La Bau, made nine different allegations, and Cornie himself made seventeen. They claimed, among other things, that the "instrument proposed to probate is not Cornelius Vanderbilt's last will and testament; that it was not properly executed; that if it was made and executed by Cornelius Vanderbilt, it was obtained by fraud, circumvention, and undue influence exercised by William H. Vanderbilt and other persons; that by reason of age, delusion, mental disorder, and loss of natural affection the testator was disqualified from making a will, and that he had a mania on the subject of concentrating his wealth in William H. Vanderbilt and the children of William H. Vanderbilt, and an unwarrantable aversion to his other children." The internal contradictions in this statement didn't dim the siblings' confidence that they would prevail.

Cornie knew that these charges might mean a public airing of the family's dirty laundry, but it would be worth it if the will were broken. By early 1878, as the trial wore on, Mr. Lord was arguing that, in effect, the Commodore's avarice should itself count as a mental illness, which should mean he was not in his right mind when making his will.

"I wish to show," Mr. Lord said, "that the Commodore was in the habit of taking property which had no good title; that he held many 'floating' deeds, which he settled on property belonging to widows and infants; this was well known and he was no more responsible for his acts in certain moods than is the kleptomaniac who filches goods. . . . He told the truth to Mr. Simmons," with whom the Commodore had been called upon to deal in the course of settling some of Cornie's outstanding debts, "when he said, 'I have been insane on the subject of money-making all my life.'"

Mr. Clinton objected on the grounds that this assertion defamed the dead. But Cornie didn't see how that was true. Everyone knew the Commodore had a mania for making money.

Billy's lawyer was having none of this argument. "The counsel takes the broad ground that every act of the Commodore, from the time he was eighteen years old, bears out the assertion of mental mania—because, forsooth, these acts do not happen to agree with the habits and opinions of morality possessed by his client who sits behind him—Cornelius J. Vanderbilt—who, by evidence is the moving spirit in these proceedings."

It was true Cornie didn't share his father's hunger for money-making. Or at least, he didn't share his talent for it. He certainly lived a life that was perpetually in need of funds.

But was the Commodore's avarice really a mental disease, as Cornie's lawyer was trying to insist? A mental disease pronounced enough to render the Commodore incompetent to make his own will? That same day in court, that March, Dr. Ellsworth Eliot testified that he attended the Commodore in his final illness. When asked if Cornie's father was of sound mind, Dr. Eliot answered, "I should say he was of sound mind; he showed no sign of old age, mentally. I never knew an instance of a man so old who had so strong a mind."

Mr. Clinton asked the doctor, "Did you read to him the obituary notices of himself, when he hadn't died?"

"Yes, frequently," the doctor answered. "They seemed very

gratifying to him, so I read them. Sometimes he called me blatherskite, blockhead, or old fool."

To be sure, Cornie's attorney, Mr. Lord, did his level best to paint the Commodore as old, and not in his right mind. On April 10, 1878, the *New York Herald* reported that Mr. Lord was determined to prove that Commodore Vanderbilt had a "morbid impulse" for making money. To speak to this point, the attorney summoned Mrs. Helen S. Clark, a "magnetizer," who claimed to have spent many hours in confidential conference with the late railroad scion when treating him. She asserted before a packed courtroom that the Commodore dismissed his namesake Cornie as "generous, but wasteful," while praising his son William as "avaricious, like me." She went on to add that the Commodore claimed to her that he knew there would be trouble over his will, but that it was unbreakable, following the model of the Astors. She said that the Commodore believed the undivided mass of money he was leaving behind would be a monument to his name.

A good story, Mrs. Clark provided, and a plausible one, given the Commodore's interest in magnetic healing. However, upon cross-examination, Mr. Clinton dismantled the magnetist's supposed insights by proving that, in fact, she'd never even set foot inside the Washington Place house. When Billy's attorney pressed her, she couldn't name a single person she had met at the Vanderbilt home. She claimed that on her first visit, she was let in by a male house servant who ushered her up to the Commodore's room. After that, Mrs. Clark said, she saw and spoke to no one on her visits, instead hurrying straight up to his room at his express request. And yet it was well established that Mrs. Vanderbilt, Cornie's youthful stepmother, was always at the Commodore's side in his final days, as Cornie himself had testified. It was she who often barred him from seeing his father.

The magnetic healer still insisted she was telling the truth, but she proved unable to describe the interior of the house she claimed to have visited so often. The nurses who attended the Commodore on his deathbed were unfamiliar to her as well. She seemed to have drifted in and out of the town house like a vapor, or like the invisible "magnetic" fields in the human body she purported to manipulate in the name of restored health. Her insights into the Commodore's thinking were presumably just as substantial.

The court case dragged on and on. Even the press grew restless and tired as Mr. Clinton and Mr. Lord jousted back and forth on the most arcane, picayune details of legal procedure. At one point, the *Tribune* noted that "in the afternoon the testimony of the two witnesses taken on Friday was read. It proved to be about as entertaining as a patent office report, and was a soporific powerful enough to cast into a deep sleep an old gentleman with a beard like Rip Van Winkle's and a head like a billiard ball."

By June, Cornie had to admit that their challenge to the will was on the ropes. Billy appeared in court, as he did most days, to watch the proceedings unfold, resting his head on his great, heavy hand, looking particularly jovial. He was on the point of winning, and the newspapers noted his "sly little eyes glisten[ing]" as the Surrogate Court slowly dismantled the challenges to the will.

Cornie's elder brother was modest in his comportment, typically wearing all black and daily driving his carriage to the courthouse himself. His figure inclined to be stout, his head balding on top but offset by a lush mustache, muttonchop sideburns, and sharp blue eyes. Compared to Cornie, Billy was controlled in his appetites, be they for tobacco, food, liquor, or women. He had married Maria Louisa Kissam, the daughter of a Presbyterian minister in New York City, in 1841, and eight of their children had survived to adulthood, including Cornelius II, whom Cornie had been accused of impersonating when he needed lines of clean credit.

But the Commodore had not always evinced a preference for Billy. Far from it. Not only was Billy's family nickname "the Blatherskite," but he had been browbeaten and shunted aside by his domineering father for most of his life. Ethelinda, and especially Mary, dated the beginning of Billy's special influence over the Commodore to the moment when he was the only one of the children to take their father's side when he sent their mother, Sophia, to the asylum in 1846. Billy was twenty-five at the time, and may not have liked seeing his mother locked away, but he was also a pragmatist. If the Commodore wanted other women, he would have them. At least if it was the governess who was involved, Billy could exert a modicum of control.

His alliance with his father grew firm in the 1850s. While Cornie was wending his way in and out of institutions, Billy demonstrated enough nascent business acumen that the Commodore brought him in from exile on a farm in Staten Island to run the affairs of the New York Central Railroad. Billy proved to be as adept a businessman as their father, with the added benefit of also being well liked. The Commodore named Billy president of the New York and Harlem Railroad in 1864, and within a few years he became vice president of the entire Vanderbilt railroad empire, expanding along the Great Lakes and establishing a monopoly on all rail travel from the East Coast to as far as Chicago. By the time of the trial over the will, Billy served in his father's place as president of the Lake Shore and Michigan Southern Railway, the Canada Southern Railway, and the Michigan Central Railroad, with further holdings in the Chicago, Burlington and Quincy Railroad; the Chicago and Canada Southern Railway; the Detroit and Bay City Railroad; the Hudson River Railroad; the Hudson River Bridge; the Joliet and Northern Indiana Railroad; the Michigan Midland and Canada Railroad; the New York Central and Hudson River Railroad; the New York Central

Sleeping Car Company; the New York and Harlem Railroad; the Spuyten Duyvil and Port Morris Railroad; and the Staten Island Rail-Road. In 1883, the newspapers caricatured him as a colossus standing astride all rails into the rapidly growing American Midwest.

For all his capability as a manager, for all his cunning in getting along with Tammany Hall, Billy didn't share the Commodore's relentless drive to innovate, and he didn't have the mania for money the Commodore had. If anything, Billy was afflicted with anxieties not unlike those that haunted Cornie, his only surviving brother. He had always wished for their imperious father's approval and never truly felt he'd gotten it. Despite all this, Billy would go on to more than double the Commodore's fortune in just eight years—the only one of the Vanderbilt descendants to add to the wealth they'd been handed. By 1885, when he died, Billy had amassed a staggering fortune of some $200 million, the equivalent of about $5.4 billion today.

Cornie was never afforded an opportunity to ingratiate himself with the Commodore, a point illustrated when his sister Mary La Bau took it upon herself to testify before the Surrogate Court about their father's feelings toward his wayward son. When she took the stand in March 1878, the papers reported that she had "the family features, and an expression of much firmness. She showed perfect self-possession and her answers were given with much clearness, though in a low voice. Her testimony was mainly in regard to the Commodore's violent temper, his opinions, and his treatment of his two sons."

One of their attorneys suggested that because of Cornie's ill health, the Commodore conceived a violent dislike for him, and thus Cornie received no moral training, except the bad example of his own father. "It was needless to say," Mr. Lord claimed of Cornie, "that he became addicted to certain vices."

"A man's peculiar views and prejudices do not unfit him for making a will—so declares the law," countered the defense. "The objection is levelled against the law of the land, not against this will."

The Surrogate broke in: "All the benefits to be derived from the prejudice of the Commodore against Cornelius seem now to be in the case. From what has thus far been given of the domestic relations of this family, I think that neither the court, the counsel, nor the public are to be edified by a closer view of the family circle."

Mr. Lord wasn't ready to cede the point, however. Referring to Mary, he said, "I offer to show that this witness in 1848, being in her room, heard screaming from the room of Cornelius. Going into the room, she found the Commodore beating his son with a riding whip; that she interfered and grasped her father's hands." Cornie was eighteen at the time. Mary was fourteen.

The public demonstration and proof that the Commodore never really loved him came to nothing. It didn't matter. None of it mattered. Cornie and his sisters couldn't break the will. Billy would get everything. The unfairness of it all didn't matter one whit.

The challenge to the Commodore's will ended abruptly on March 4, 1879, when one of his former lawyers produced a chain of successive wills, all of which were completely consistent in leaving Cornie small segments of interest in his father's possessions and proving, as one newspaper reported, that the Commodore "clearly intended always to treat him as a wayward child requiring trustees' guardianship and restrictive provisions."

Billy offered to give Cornie a million dollars if he made the suits go away. They settled, and the public's hunger for a dramatic denouement for the sordid family battle thrashing out in the newspapers was left to devour itself. Cornie took the money, accepting that some of it would remain in trust, and fled with George Terry to Europe. But the money didn't last, of course. How could it in Cornie's hands?

He was finally able to pay his debts to Horace Greeley's daughters—with interest—and built a thirty-room house in Hartford, but after that there was nothing left. And he had no hope of ever getting anything more. When, in January 1882, Mr. Lord sued him to recover thirty thousand dollars in unpaid legal fees, it was all too much.

On that Sunday afternoon in Manhattan, tucked away in his hotel room, Cornie was exhausted. He was fifty-one years old, he had never become what his father wanted him to be, and he would never be able to escape the long shadow of his father's disapproval and disappointment. As Frank had noted in her journal, the Commodore used to tell anyone who would listen that he would gladly pay a million dollars if someone could make Cornie get his act together. (He would pay someone *else*, that is.) But for Cornie, he would leave nothing more than a few hundred thousand dollars held in trust.

The suit against him from Mr. Lord was scheduled for a hearing the next day. Cornie had summoned his friend and attorney Judge E. O. Perrin to come that morning and advise him, but when Perrin arrived, Cornie was too tired to see him. His epileptic fits always left him feeling wrung out and despondent, and he had suffered one that very day. He just wanted to rest.

Around two in the afternoon, alone in his room at the Glenham Hotel, Cornelius Jeremiah Vanderbilt placed his Smith and Wesson revolver to his temple and pulled the trigger.

The moment the report of the pistol rang out, George Terry dropped what he was doing and rushed through the folding doors separating the adjoining rooms. He found Cornie sprawled across the bed on his back, a neat hole in his right temple streaming blood down the right side of his face, and the left side of his face blackened with powder. George fell to Cornie's side and found his dearest friend still breathing, albeit heavily. He spoke to him, but Cornie couldn't answer.

A blur of activity took immediate hold in the room. The hotel owner was called, and Dr. Robert Weir was sent for and came at once. He tried to stanch the bleeding, but it was no use. Everyone present saw immediately that Cornie's wound was a fatal one. There was nothing more to do but send for Billy.

The eldest Vanderbilt son got to his brother's hotel room as quickly as he could, with his own sons in tow. They found Cornie on the bed, with a doctor and George and a few hotel employees crowding around. Hours passed while Cornie breathed heavily, unconscious, quiet, and seemingly not in pain. Everyone clustered around him, watching and waiting.

Billy stayed with him until 4:30, then stepped out, believing he had a few more hours before the inevitable. But without uttering another word, Cornie breathed his last around forty-five minutes later. The papers didn't report what, if anything, Billy may have said to his dying brother that afternoon, but they did say he was "deeply moved." Billy took charge, as he had been accustomed to doing in family matters for years now. He gave instructions for what to do with the body. Arrangements for a funeral at the Church of the Strangers were hastily made. Some friends arrived and a couple of his sisters' husbands, but the person who mattered was Billy. Billy, and George Terry. George never imagined Cornie would do such a thing, or he would never have left him alone, he said later. Cornelius must have risen and retrieved the revolver from its carrying case. It certainly wasn't under the pillow, or George would have known about it.

The hotel released a statement saying that Cornie had been struck with apoplexy at 2:00 p.m. and died at 5:00, but after initially suggesting that he had died of an epileptic fit, Cornie's friend E. O. Perrin finally informed the press that Cornie had killed himself. He had been under great mental excitement, the judge said, refusing to believe that Cornie was responsible for his actions. Cornie, as everyone knew, had suffered with epilepsy for more than twenty years, which caused physical and mental collapse. After suffering one of his fits, he was taken with "nervous prostration." He had never given any indication that he might take his own life.

He left no note.

He left no monument.

In his will, he left the newly built Hartford house to George Terry.

The *Baltimore Sun* theorized that Cornie's wayward attitudes could be traced to his coming of age after the Commodore's fortune was made, rather than during its making, as Billy had. Because of his lack of understanding of what the Commodore's fortune meant, or how it had come about, Cornie "began early a course of reckless dissipation whose good nature was its only redeeming trait." It was almost as though the Vanderbilt fortune itself was Cornie's affliction—the access to it, the lack of access to it, the assumption of it, the theft of it, his father's affection for it. Epilepsy is a disease. But the money was like a parasite, or contagion, preying upon Cornie's body and on his mind.

"Corneil was always a singular sort of an individual," a friend of his who elected to remain anonymous remarked that night to a reporter at the Hoffman House, the glamorous Flatiron hotel most famous for the rye whiskey in its barroom and the Tammany politicians haunting its gilded hallways. "From the time he began to crawl he was always at outs with everybody. The only thing he ever did which pleased the old Commodore was in his marriage with a Connecticut lady . . . While his wife lived[,]

Corneel for a time led a comparatively correct life, but the reins were not always strong enough to hold him. He had no children, and when his wife died[,] there was left not a single influence in all the world to influence him for good."

When the coroner was done with him, late that night, the sexton of the Church of the Strangers arrived at the Glenham Hotel with an icebox. He was the same sexton who had overseen the funeral of the Commodore five years before. A service was scheduled for the next morning, with a discourse preached by the same Reverend Doctor Deems who had called upon the Commodore in his final illness, and it took place in the same church the Commodore had paid to build. Then Cornie's body was to be carried on a train to Hartford, leaving from Grand Central—out of the station built by the Commodore, traveling on railroad tracks the Commodore had owned. Cornie died as he had lived, an echo, following along on a path laid out for him, paved for him, made only for him, by his father.

Society as I Have Found It

October 22, 1883

> *Once the effort to break in socially is made, the newcomer finds most big cities culturally stimulating and financially reward-ing, as small towns can rarely be.*
>
> —Amy Vanderbilt's Complete Book of Etiquette,
> Chapter 2, "Dress and Manners"

It is a truth readily acknowledged that a Vanderbilt heir in pos-session of a great fortune must be in want of ways to spend it. Fortunately, for Billy Vanderbilt, New York was a city unlike any other for opportunities to spend a great deal of money. And while Billy undoubtedly facilitated the rise of the Vanderbilt fortune, as the only one of the descendants actually to build upon the great monument of wealth left by the Commodore, he also initiated its fall, by inaugurating the Vanderbilt siege on the gilded gates of New York society that ushered in the truly astonishing excess for which the Vanderbilts would become famous.

In the Gilded Age—the name given by Mark Twain to the glit-tering years from the 1870s until around 1900—New York soci-ety was personified by two inscrutable consuls, leaders elected by their own guile and consenting to reign together, ruling over the patricians who cowered at their feet: Caroline Astor and Ward

McAllister. They were the keepers of the gates, the makers of the taste, and the arbiters of who could be said to belong and who would be excluded. But like many seemingly time-honored institutions in New York City, society in the Gilded Age was itself something of a myth—or, perhaps more accurately, a recent invention. Embedded in the idea of society lay not just social prominence and influence, but also a degree of power and a representation of an American ideal that would communicate to the rest of the world what the young nation might mean, might be capable of, and ultimately, what it valued. Of course, the Commodore's descendants would want to have a say.

Caroline Astor was born Caroline Schermerhorn in 1830 to an old Dutch family of famously staid respectability and decent money. In 1853, she married William Backhouse Astor Jr., descendant of a family that had originally made its fortune in fur trading. (The Astor Place subway station mosaics today feature silhouettes of beavers in homage to the family's roots.) William was a younger son who—not unlike Cornie Vanderbilt—resented his elder brother John Jacob Astor III for having been the favorite of their father and for having a snobbish demeanor.

A famous portrait of Mrs. Astor painted in 1890, at the peak of her power, which presently hangs in the Metropolitan Museum of Art, shows a brunette woman with arched dark brows and flawless cream skin, her mouth set in an imperious and judgmental line. She is dressed in the height of fashion for the moment, with finely wrought lace netting over a black satin bodice and ballooning sleeves, one hand hidden by a dove-gray opera glove. Throughout the 1890s, the flesh-and-bone Mrs. Astor, who was nicknamed Lina by her friends, hung this portrait in her palatial home, and she would stand under it to receive her guests, creating the impression of a doubling of her power to anyone privileged enough to approach her.

The combination of Caroline Schermerhorn's Dutch lineage and the Astor fur fortune was a powerful nexus, but one crucial ingredient was still needed to vault Mrs. Astor into the stratosphere of American social influence: a war that would call into question what American culture really was.

In 1862, Mrs. Astor and her husband built a brownstone town house at 350 Fifth Avenue, hastening the movement of fashionable New Yorkers northward from their former strongholds around Washington Square. From there, and from her summer cottage in Newport, Mrs. Astor watched as New York City grew and changed at a whiplash-inducing pace in the years after the Civil War. With each new wave of arrivals of immigrants from Europe, new money from the Midwest, and expatriate former Confederates (like Frank Vanderbilt), Mrs. Astor felt more keenly the imperative to define and codify who should qualify as polite society, preferably in terms that would also consolidate her own power and influence.

Whereas the Old World enjoyed clear arbiters of class and distinction in the form of art, music, culture, and aristocratic titles and heritage, the United States of the immediate postbellum period was suffering an identity crisis. Mrs. Astor's signal insight turned on the necessity of laying claim to a heritage, even if it was an invented one. In her schema, social ambition could be seen as a nationalist project, an investment in Americanism at a moment during which the concept of "American" was far from fixed. She also recognized early on the importance of money in a country without landed aristocracy. In New York, society and money would never be divorced again.

Another piece of the shifting social terrain onto which the Vanderbilts were about to step was the invention of celebrity, a concept made possible by new technologies for the cheap dissemination of images. Not many years before, Cornie Vanderbilt could have been accused of impersonating his own nephew when he was in need of good credit because his appearance would have been familiar only to individuals with whom he was personally acquainted. With the growth of lithography and the rise of illustrated weekly magazines such as *Harper's* and *Frank Leslie's*, fame unlike anything seen in the years before the war was suddenly possible, and it became its own currency. Lavish balls and parties could be seen as an extension of a nationalist project, for even though the guest list was restricted, rampant coverage in the press meant that anyone with a penny to spare could read what Mrs. Astor had served her rich and glamorous guests for dinner.

Mrs. Astor, however, couldn't quite consolidate her hold over New York society alone. She needed a gadfly, someone elegant, who had traveled in Europe and knew all the Old World mannerisms; someone well versed in the rules of etiquette, who knew the fashionable chefs, the fashionable artwork, the dances, and the modes of entertaining most apt to surprise and delight guests. She needed someone who had just the right touch, an instinct for publicity and exclusion that would attract the right attention and envy, from the quarters of the social world over which she wished to dominate. But also—someone whom she could control.

She needed Ward McAllister.

Samuel Ward McAllister was born in 1827 in Savannah, Georgia. He studied for a time at Yale and then went west with the Gold Rush in 1852, where he reportedly saw, as one newspaper put it, "some pretty wild life." Upon his return to New York, he married a fellow Southerner, Sarah Gibbons, but then refused to read law as his family expected and instead traveled to Europe to give himself the requisite amount of polish. On his Grand Tour, McAllister made a careful study of all aspects of social life: court manners, architecture, fashion, food, drink, watering spots, dances. He returned to the United States as what one contemporary called "the most complete dandy in America," and established himself in New York as essentially a professional snob. Wiry brows over lidded eyes and a high, receding hairline gave him an avuncular air, and he commonly sported a wide handlebar mustache and bristly little beard. He was perfect for Caroline Astor.

Under McAllister's guidance, Mrs. Astor began to Old Worldify herself completely: she instituted livery for her servants, began collecting French art, hired a French chef, served dinner on French and German china. American society would make up for its youthful inexperience by taking the class signifiers of Europe for their own.

"It is our fancy for things ancient, more than for things beautiful, that induces us to lift marble mantels from Venetian palaces and to place them in Fifth Avenue houses," writer John Van Dyke grumbled in 1909, reflecting on the Astor-led impulse of aping European taste. "To hang our walls with tapestries from France and pictures from Italy and Holland, to cover our floors with Dagestan rugs, and to put in our drawing-rooms wormeaten chairs from Paris and Nuremberg. Their inappropriateness in their new western setting is glazed over by the statement that they are 'very old'—a statement which might, with equal pertinence if less interest, be made about any pudding-stone from the neighboring hills."

But taste was only part of what the twin consuls of New York City wanted to codify. They sought to rate people according to a hierarchy as much as they wished to rank food or clothing or interior décor. To that end, Ward McAllister divided the social world along two axes: "nobs" on the one hand and "swells" on the other.

"It is well to be in with the nobs who are born to their position," theorized McAllister in writing. "But the support of the swells is more advantageous, for society is sustained and carried on by the swells, the nobs looking quietly on and accepting the position, feeling they are there by divine right; but they do not make fashionable society, or carry it on."

Caroline Astor was a "nob," someone with a long pedigree and old money. The Vanderbilts, in contrast, were "swells," nouveau riche arrivistes who were ready to lavish their fortunes on social climbing. Mrs. Astor and Ward McAllister together had the genius and distinctly American insight that society would result from the knitting together of these two worlds—carefully, of course, and under their expert tutelage and domination.

"A nob can be a swell if he chooses, i.e. if he will spend the money," McAllister elaborated. "But for his social existence this is unnecessary. A nob is like a poet—*nascitur non fit*; not so a swell—he creates himself."

But how should they determine who was acceptable and who wasn't? The Commodore, despite his wealth, had been a boor. Everyone knew this, and no one disputed it. His manners had been coarse. He chewed tobacco; he could barely read. He damned people up one side and down the other. He was, in fact, proud of his lack of refinement. For McAllister, unapologetic crassness would never do, but neither would poverty.

"If you see a fossil of a man, shabbily dressed, relying solely on his pedigree, dating back to time immemorial, who has the aspirations of a duke and the fortunes of a footman, do not cut him," McAllister wrote. "It is better to cross the street and avoid meeting him."

Mrs. Astor determined that for acceptance into society, one must be at least three generations removed from whoever's hands had been dirtied in the making of money. As her own husband was living off the fortune made by his grandfather, whose hands had been stained with beaver blood, Mrs. Astor herself was just in the clear. And then, of course, there was the amount of money under consideration. The consuls didn't settle on a specific number, unless that number was "more."

"A fortune of a million," McAllister remarked to the *New York Tribune*, "is only respectable poverty."

European taste, plus aristocratic pretension, plus vast postbellum wealth—this was the recipe Mrs. Astor and Ward McAllister drew up for social acceptance in New York City. But with so many rich new people pouring into the city with each passing year, it was hard to tell who was in and who was out. What they really needed was a list.

To that end, in 1872 McAllister founded an organization that he named the Society of Patriarchs. This group instituted a series of Patriarch Balls, designed for introducing young people to society and to one another. Each Patriarch was issued a finite number of invitations that he could disseminate to young men and women of his choosing for each ball. The name was rather transparently designed to create the impression of a long-standing tradition, completely belying the fact that the society was a new invention of his own. Under McAllister's system, there were only twenty-five Patriarchs, defined as "representative men of worth, respectability, and responsibility." They were essentially chosen by him and Mrs. Astor from the ranks of both the old Knickerbocker families of the city, like the Schermerhorns and Lorillards, and the new money, like the Goelets and Rockefellers. The Patriarchs gave balls through Dodsworth's Dancing Academy and, later, at the famous Gilded Age restaurant Delmonico's. They were, as McAllister said, a "stepping stone to the best New York society."

Ward McAllister's biggest triumph of branding, however, was not the institution of the Patriarchs, but the naming of a number: four hundred. Ostensibly referring to the number of people who could fit in Mrs. Astor's ballroom (a rumor that has since been put to rest), McAllister determined that New York society was led by "the Four Hundred," no more and no less. Any more than that, he asserted, and you were bound to encounter people who were not comfortable in a ballroom, or whose presence made others uncomfortable. Several years would pass before a list of the supposed Four Hundred was published, so, for a time, McAllister could grant or rescind membership almost at will. (Several more years would pass before the list was published in the form of a "blue book," which persists today as the Social Register.) The artificiality of this distinction, the sheer invention of it, marked New York society then as much as it does now. Even the oldest of old New York was brand spanking new.

So, where did this leave the Vanderbilts? The Commodore may have built his house near what was then New York's most fashionable neighborhood, Washington Square, but he never tried to soften his calloused edges to gain acceptance by the city's oldest and wealthiest families. It wasn't until after his death, as his eldest son, Billy, consolidated his position as the head of the family, that the Vanderbilt siege on New York society began in earnest. Under Billy's stewardship, the Vanderbilt fortune ballooned, and while Billy himself was only one generation away from his father's rough beginnings on the Staten Island waterfront, his own children—including Cornelius II (who would finish building The Breakers in 1895) and William Kissam—qualified for inclusion in society by Mrs. Astor's rules. They had the distance. They had clean hands, so to speak. And they certainly had the money. All they needed was the polish. By the 1870s, Billy stood ready to use his fortune to land himself and his children on New York's social map. But where to begin?

Cornelius II managed to score some Patriarchs invitations, only because Ward McAllister thought that the sheer size of the

Vanderbilt fortune meant their social triumph was inevitable, but most polite society hostesses kept the Vanderbilts at arm's length through the 1870s. No one was willing to "take them on," as it were, before Caroline Astor indicated that she was ready for them to be included. So, they waited.

An early skirmish in the social war between the houses of Vanderbilt and Astor took place at the Academy of Music, at Irving Place. The "sociable old Academy," as novelist Edith Wharton called it, was where old New York went to the opera and where important balls were held. In a society built on display and spectacle, the holding of a box at the Academy offered a very public means of demonstrating one's old New York bona fides. The eighteen boxes were closely controlled by Knickerbocker families and passed down from one generation to the next. Mrs. Astor had one, of course. As did the Schermerhorns, Livingstons, Beekmans, Schuylers, Roosevelts, and Lorillards. Notably absent were the holders of more recent industry fortunes, such as the Goelets, Goulds, Rockefellers, and Morgans. Also absent? The Vanderbilts. Billy tried to buy a box at the Academy for the princely sum of thirty thousand dollars, and was refused. The Academy considered adding boxes to meet the surging demand, but the multiplication of wealth in Gilded Age New York meant that there would never be enough.

The newly rich Academy rejects, led by Billy Vanderbilt, instead banded together and enlisted architect Josiah Cady to erect a new Metropolitan Opera House on Broadway between Thirty-Ninth and Fortieth Streets. In true nouveau riche form, the Met pulled out all the decorative stops, presenting a plush riot of gilding, gas-lit crystal, and warm red velvet, like the rich lining of a jewelry case, designed to maximize the sparkle of the gems presented within. (Even today, the carpeting of the Metropolitan Opera, which relocated to Lincoln Center in 1966, is lush red velvet.) Next to the newly built opera house, the Academy looked downright shabby. To meet the demand for settings in which to show off their wealth and influence, the Met offered social climbers three tiers of boxes to which to aspire, including the so-called Diamond Horseshoe, for the richest of the rich, which set their occupants on display as brilliantly as the singers performing on-stage. The new opera house opened to great fanfare on the fine and mild night of October 22, 1883, featuring soprano Christine Nilsson singing *Faust*.

The symbolism of this particular soprano singing this particular opera would be enshrined in literature when Edith Wharton began her Pulitzer Prize–winning novel of the Gilded Age, *The Age of Innocence*, with the line "On a January evening of the early seventies, Christine Nilsson was singing in *Faust* at the Academy of Music in New York." No more symbolic reference to the sweeping away of the old guard could Wharton imagine. The new-money people bounded in with a fat checkbook and bought the taste and distinction they had neither the time nor the inclination to cultivate.

The papers reporting on the Met didn't fail to notice the meaning of the choice of programming. "The opening of the splendid new opera house is an occasion of so much interest to the fashionable world that a performance of much less artistic merit than this one promises to possess would serve the purpose," mused the *Times*. "An enormous, richly dressed, and distinguished audience will surely be present."

And present they were. The night the new opera house first opened its doors, the social news of New York spoke of little else. Papers reported the lines of carriages were so long that at 8:23 p.m., as the maestro lifted his baton to begin the opening notes of *Faust*, scores of attendees were still streaming through the doors and crushing into the hallways, trying to find their seats. Almost immediately an unanticipated snag in the opera house design appeared: so much more attention had been paid to the display of patrons in the boxes that the architects had forgotten to consider the quality of the acoustics. Throughout the brand-new Met, the orchestra and operatic notes sounded muddy and difficult to make out. (Wharton alluded to this embarrassing error when she described the Academy as being cherished "for its excellent acoustics, always so problematic a quality in halls built for the hearing of music.") But of course, the hearing of music was only a small part of the purpose of the new opera house. Gas chandeliers provided enough warmth to illuminate the glitter of jewels and subtly highlighted cheekbones without being so glaring as to reveal every freckle and line. But the newspapers decried the warm, orangey red color of the hallways and their narrowness and insufficient ventilation, which, when crowded with eager bodies, made the spaces feel close, hot, and sweaty.

Even these relative drawbacks could do nothing to dampen the triumph of the new opera house or, by extension, of the new money that had funded it. "William H. Vanderbilt developed an unusual degree of sociability during the evening," the *New York Times* reported the following day. "He is the owner of three boxes, two of which he occupied at different times. He also paid two or three visits to the boxes of his friends, and while passing through the lobby stopped frequently and talked with various acquaintances. He was apparently in excellent spirits," though the paper then went on to add that "as he walked about it was plain to see that he is growing round-shouldered." Billy had succeeded in buying an opera box not only for himself, but one for each of his sons. His triumph was total. But heavy is the head that wears the crown.

"All the nouveaux riches were there," sniffed an anonymous critic with a more pointed perspective than the newspapers. "The

Goulds and Vanderbilts and people of that ilk perfumed the air with the odor of crisp greenbacks. The tiers of boxes looked like cages in a menagerie of monopolists. When somebody remarked that the house looked as bright as a new dollar, the appropriate character of the assemblage became apparent. To the refined eye, the decorations of the edifice seemed in particularly bad taste."

Caroline Astor, with her keen instinct for the nuances of social warfare, had arranged to be out of town the evening that the Metropolitan Opera House opened. She was biding her time, waiting to see which way the social winds would blow—or, rather, which way the calling cards would fall. Perhaps unsurprisingly, for New York, they fell toward money. Almost immediately, the old New York families caved and consented to rent boxes at the new opera house. By 1885, only two years after the Met's opening, the Academy of Music had closed its doors.

That same year, Billy "the Blatherskite" Vanderbilt died at the age of sixty-four. Each of his daughters inherited around $10 million, but the bulk of his fortune was split between his two eldest sons, each of whom got $65 million, about $1.7 billion today.

Cornelius II assumed control of the family's business interests. He was the obvious choice. He had the ambition of his grandfather, which probably explains why the Commodore had liked him above all his other grandchildren, and was more concerned with business than social pursuits: he didn't breed horses; he didn't have a yacht. Unlike his namesake, however, Cornelius II softened his ambition with an interest in religion. He had met his wife, Alice Claypoole Gwynne, when they were both teaching Sunday school at St. Bartholomew's Episcopal Church on Fifth Avenue, and by all accounts, he remained a religious man over the course of his life. But some critics called him imperious and autocratic, smug and intimidating. His wife, Alice, who came to be known as Alice of The Breakers, kept a tight control over her seven children and reveled in her husband's wealth, wasting no time throwing it into the creation of enormous palaces on Fifth Avenue and in Newport.

Alice and Cornelius II had the money, to be sure, and were enough generations removed from the Commodore to claim the respectability necessary for social success according to Caroline Astor and Ward McAllister. What they lacked, however, was "ease of manner," perhaps what in subsequent generations might be termed "cool." Though Billy had jimmied the door open for the Vanderbilt family's entrée to society, it was another Vanderbilt who would elbow her way through. On which, more in a moment.

As one set of social arbiters rose, so another had to fall, and Ward McAllister was not immune to this rule. A kingmaker like no other at the beginning of the 1880s, by the end of the decade he began to lose his grip on the orb and scepter of New York society. First, in 1889, he alienated the powerful society hostess Mamie Fish, also known as Mrs. Stuyvesant Fish, when he had the audacity to publicly criticize a dinner she gave, and he further humiliated her husband when he joked about an event the family was planning, by saying, "I am glad I had nothing to do with such a Fish ball." But the ball came off beautifully, regardless of McAllister's lack of involvement. Caroline Astor attended and even led a dance while President Benjamin Harrison and the First Lady looked on. Mamie Fish would later take up a new consul, Harry Lehr, and would enlist Mrs. Astor's approval in making him the next most-favored "extra man" at New York society balls. There could be no clearer indicator that McAllister was losing his favored status with the queen of New York.

Then he made a final, fatal error. McAllister let slip that he was writing a memoir about his society friends. He had for years had a reputation as a genial, unassuming, even somewhat sloppy, chit-chatty fellow, constantly peppering his discourse with speech fillers like "Don't you know" and "Don't you see" and "Don't you understand." Reporters enjoyed teasing him for his verbal tics, but always found him to be, as one newspaper put it, an "interesting and intelligent talker" who was never afraid to say exactly what was on his mind. Unfortunately, the same traits exercised in print would be his undoing.

His book, *Society as I Have Found It*, was published in 1890, a meandering mishmash of breathless gossip, reminiscences about parties and costumes and conversations, and opinionated remarks on entertaining and fashion, heavily padded with advice on letter writing and stationery. McAllister craved the attention the book would bring, but frankly, he also needed the money. Reaction was swift and total: Ward McAllister was out. Stuyvesant Fish dismissed him as "a discharged servant." Though his accounts of his famous friends were largely complimentary, he had broken their confidence, and his status among elite New York could never recover. Without naming her explicitly, McAllister described Caroline Astor thusly:

> A silent power that had always been recognized and felt in this community. . . . having all the qualities necessary,—good judgement and a great power of analysis of men and women, a thorough knowledge of all their surroundings, a just appreciation of the rights of others, and coming herself from an old Colonial family, a good appreciation of the value of ancestry; . . . But also understanding the importance and power of the new element; recognizing it, and fairly and generously awarding to it a prominent place.

He could at least give credit where credit was due. But Mrs. Astor would never forgive him. McAllister's situation worsened in

1892, when, in a flagrant bid for relevance, he gave a list of the Four Hundred to the *New York Times*. The release of the closely guarded list caused a furor, not least because it contained just over three hundred names instead of four hundred. McAllister basked in the press attention and the seeming confirmation of his status as social arbiter. But then word started to go around that he could be bribed by the nouveau riche to introduce them into society. This rumor wasn't entirely untrue; it was McAllister, after all, who paved the way for the ultimate Vanderbilt triumph, as we shall see. But even worse than his influence being available for a fee, McAllister had also violated a cardinal rule of society: he was freely spilling details about his fancy friends to reporters. While no New York society figure would disavow the importance of publicity, they felt it must be rigorously controlled, and the indiscreet McAllister was clearly speaking out of turn. Soon, a measurable distance began to yawn between him and Caroline Astor. At one point, while in Chicago for the 1893 World's Columbian Exposition, McAllister rubbed enough people the wrong way that he was called Mrs. Astor's "Head Butler" and a "New York flunky."

McAllister realized that the book had been a mistake, but it was too late. "Oh, I shall never write another book," he said to a reporter in an interview near the end of his life. "People don't read books nowadays, don't you know. They live too rapidly. They read newspapers. Newspapers have more that's interesting in them on Sundays than most of the new books, don't you see. I write for two reasons. I enjoy it and it pays me." No one could ever accuse Ward McAllister of an excess of sentiment, but his assertion that he would never write another book had more to do with the social death knell that his book had rung for him than with a lack of widespread interest in books.

In early February 1895, word shot through the throngs of revelers at the annual Charity Ball that Ward McAllister had died. The news of his death shook the ranks of New York society. He had taken suddenly ill with an attack of "the grippe," a Gilded Age term for influenza, after a dinner at the Union Club the previous week. His case wasn't thought to be that serious, and so his abrupt death stunned everyone. The *Times* called him "a man of foibles," but also acknowledged his indispensability in matters of etiquette of the parlor and the dining room and extolled his famous deference to women.

Ward McAllister was the first and greatest of what would later be called a "walker," a gentleman friend whose special skill lies in escorting society ladies whose husbands have other interests or limited time and yet whose comportment does not leave the ladies vulnerable to intimations of scandal. He was married and had produced three children, though his wife, Sarah Gibbons, was rumored to be an invalid and was never seen in society. She presided neither at his farm dinners in Newport nor his smart evenings in New York, but her invisible existence was enough to render McAllister socially safe for squiring Caroline Astor or the subsequent ladies who might have wished to enlist his help. The right walker, after all, can make or break a woman in society, and Ward McAllister was the original. His death meant that the Four Hundred—all three hundred of them—would never be the same.

When asked if the annual Patriarch Ball, long set for the end of February, would go forward as planned, an unnamed Patriarch suggested that it might be canceled in the wake of McAllister's death. In fact, the Patriarchs themselves as an institution would barely survive the loss of their figurehead. By 1897, the organization had disbanded, but society debuts, balls, and cotillions proceeded all the same. "Poor McAllister!" the anonymous Patriarch exclaimed, considering the impact of the loss on the social land-scape of New York. "What a pity it is that he wrote a book!"

And what of Mrs. Astor? Her seemingly infinite iron reign over New York society lasted only about twenty years, from around 1872 to around 1892, when any pretense to patriotic or cultural values would be wholly eclipsed by the gross orgy of excess that Thorstein Veblen would name "conspicuous consumption" in *The Theory of the Leisure Class*, published in 1899. Aping Old World taste and manners might establish compelling faux-aristocratic ideals, but over-the-top excess made for better newspaper copy.

As society shifted and changed around her, Caroline Astor's primacy waned. Around 1895, she decamped farther north, to a lavish, elegant palace at 841 Fifth Avenue, at the corner of Sixty-Fifth Street, facing "the Central Park," as it was then known. That same year, she gave a ball in her new home, hosting six hundred people, a newsworthy event in that she hadn't done it for some time. All went off in true Gilded Age, Old World, Astor style. The ball didn't begin until midnight, as all the guests were first attending a performance of *Carmen* at the Metropolitan Opera. The ball was held in the expansive art gallery of her splendid new home, all done up in ivory and gold, with a scarlet carpet and blue silk drapes. Banks of tropical foliage had been brought in for the occasion, as well as hampers full of American Beauty roses and bunches of violets. The cotillion began after one in the morning, led by Elisha Dyer Jr. (a subsequent society walker) and Caro-line's daughter-in-law Ava, draped in thick white silk trimmed in point lace, her hair heaped up and pinned in place with an aigrette of diamonds. The guest list included Lorillards and Winthrops, Drexels and Cuttings, and the August Belmonts (on whom more in a moment). The newspaper did not mention any Vanderbilts in attendance—though, by this time, their social triumph was so complete that they had no need for Mrs. Astor's invitations or seal of approval. The peace had always been an uneasy one anyway. The dinner menu for Mrs. Astor's ball was French, as the now-forever-banished Ward McAllister would have insisted.

In *Society as I Have Found It*, without naming her explicitly, McAllister calls Caroline Astor a "true and loyal friend in sunshine and shower."

Mrs. Astor did not attend his funeral.

Venetian Princesses

March 26, 1883

I dislike display and foolish expenditure in the sense of what Veblen called "conspicuous waste," that is, spending to impress those who have less, as well as to impress associates. I dislike chi-chi.

—*Amy Vanderbilt's Complete Book of Etiquette,*
Introduction

The crowds had begun to gather in the afternoon. They knew they would never get past the door, but New Yorkers have always insisted that they own the sidewalks of Manhattan, and on the afternoon of March 26, 1883, both sides of the street outside the grandiose mansion at 660 Fifth Avenue belonged to the people. Anyone—housemaid or newsboy, "tough girl" or Bowery "b'hoy"—was free to gawk on the sidewalks of New York, a fact as true then as it is today. The crowd was studded here and there with reporters, their pencils poised to jot down all the details of who would soon be arriving, what they were wearing, what the flowers were like—and what about the music? The hostess had been leaking them details for weeks, but now the public hungered for the story, and the reporters stood by ready to feed them and slake their newfound thirst for celebrity.

Around five that afternoon, a team of workmen set about erecting a great awning over the front door of 660 Fifth Avenue, whose windows blazed with light as the final preparations inside were under way. The number of loiterers on the street continued to grow, hordes of people streaming to the address to gawk with the same hunger and curiosity of a crowd outside the Oscars or a Met Museum gala today. They had been reading about the preparations for weeks and wanted to see the spectacle for themselves. The crowd crushed in so close together that the Metropolitan Police had to forcibly hold back the wall of onlookers to create a path from the street to the doorway.

At around seven, gentlemen in all the fashionable neighborhoods in town were seen in brown coupes hurrying home from their hairdressers' with unusually powdered hair. Meanwhile, at Fifty-Second Street, onlookers buzzed with interest as an express wagon rolled sedately up Fifth Avenue and stopped at 660 to off-load a cargo of wooden horses covered in real horse hair, which were rumored to be for one of the dances that night. Imagine killing and skinning a horse just to mount its hide on a fake horse, for a single dance. The onlookers could hardly believe it.

Finally, at half past eight, footmen dressed in white powdered wigs and eighteenth-century-style maroon livery, which the Vanderbilts had taken to using, stepped out of the grand front doors of the mansion and unrolled a thick, gold-edged maroon carpet under the awning and across the sidewalk. The greatest ball of the nineteenth century, the Vanderbilt ball, was about to begin.

The *New York Times* reported on the scene outside: "Carriages containing the more youthful and impatient of the maskers drove past the mansion before 10:30 o'clock, the occupant peering surreptitiously under the curtain to see if others were arriving as he rolled by." By eleven, maskers were streaming in. "Pretty and excited girls," the *Times* continued, "and young men who made desperate efforts to appear *blasé*, were seen to descend and run up the steps into the brilliantly lighted hall. Club men who looked bored arrived singly and in pairs and quartets, in hired cabs, and whole families drove up in elegant equipages with liveried coachmen and footmen."

Because of the incredible complexity and weight of the costumes planned for the evening, many of the society women in attendance had brought their maids along, but the maids were refused entry and told they had to spend the evening waiting outside in the carriages. Gentlemen's valets were given the same news. They were numerous enough that one wonders what kind of shadow party took place in the parked carriages on the side streets surrounding 660 Fifth Avenue that night.

As the revelers alit under the temporary canopies, helped out of carriages by ushers, light wraps clutched about the ladies' shoulders against the spring evening chill, the waiting crowd was treated to a spectacle unlike anything seen before on the streets of New York. "Out stepped what appeared to be the ghosts of all the great dead since the world began," the *Tribune* gossiped the following morning. "Joan of Arc, complete with solid silver mail; Christopher Columbus; Louis XVI; Queen Elizabeth I in a bright red wig; the goddess Diana; Daniel Boone. By 11:30 a bouillabaisse of kings, queens, fairies, toreadors, and gypsies blocked Fifth Avenue." Of all the guests stepping from carriages onto the plush maroon carpet on the sidewalk of Fifth Avenue, pretending indifference to the gawkers craning their necks to catch a glimpse of them, bejeweled and bedecked in silks and furs and ropes of diamonds, only two men appeared not in costume: William Henry "Billy" Vanderbilt and his friend Ulysses S. Grant. They both wore white tie.

But perhaps we are getting ahead of ourselves. Before we talk about the ball, and the flowers, and the food, and the quadrilles, and the money—good lord, the money! And the fact that the entire face and trajectory of New York society was changed in one evening, at a costume ball in which some of the attendees wore electric lights in their hair, in 1883, a time when virtually all homes and spaces were lit by gaslight and candles—before we get to all that, we have to talk about Alva.

Where to start with Alva Erskine Smith?

In 1883, on the night of her infamous ball, to which around thirteen hundred invitations were issued and which she deliberately scheduled after Lent, so there would be no competing balls or entertainments to distract public attention from her bid for social domination—traditionally, Lent brought the city's high social season to its end, but Alva had very little patience for tradition—Alva was known as Alva Vanderbilt. The wife of William Kissam Vanderbilt, one of the two surviving sons of Billy the Blatherskite and a grandson of the Commodore, she was mistress of a nine-hundred-acre estate on Long Island called Idle Hour and queen of the brand-new so-called Petit Chateau at 660 Fifth Avenue, a French Renaissance–style palace designed by Richard Morris Hunt under Alva's particular direction.

At that time, Alva was already years into a rivalry with Alice Vanderbilt, her sister-in-law, over which of them would mount the most serious challenge to Caroline Astor's iron rule over New York society. But anyone who knew Alva—and an awful lot of people knew Alva—would have had no doubt about who would reign supreme in that contest. Alice was so snobbish and removed that later in her life people would say she'd rather be driven around the city for hours than condescend to speak to her chauffeur to give him the exact address for where she was headed. Alva, by contrast, was brilliant, witty, cunning, and utterly ruthless. Her daughter, Consuelo, would later write that her mother was a "born dictator." There could be little doubt that Alva would triumph; the only question was: how and when?

William Kissam Vanderbilt, Alva's husband, was born in 1849. Together with his brother Cornelius II, he would be the main beneficiary of their father's astonishing $230 million fortune upon Billy's death in 1885. But even before their father died, "Willie," as he was called, received $3 million from the Commodore, which set him off on the first stage of what would be a lifelong spending spree. Whereas his brother, Cornelius II, whom he called Corneil, was more given to the business side of Vanderbilt life, and had the sternness and seriousness required to oversee the railroads, Willie was more given to refined pleasures. He was educated in Switzerland and felt at home in Europe, so he faced something of a rude awakening when he returned to New York and discovered that for all his wealth and distinction, New York society still found him unacceptable.

Willie was a party boy; he was stout, reddish-faced, with an athletic build that would soften to chubbiness with age. He admitted to having no professional aspirations at all. He loved the pleasures that his wealth afforded him, like Idle Hour, which Richard Morris Hunt built for him, where he could enjoy yachting and soft ocean air. He had a taste for horses, too. But Willie belonged to the first generation of Vanderbilts to feel that their primary purpose in life was to consume, which wasn't much of a purpose. In 1920, shortly before he died, he was quoted in the *New York Times* saying, "My life was never destined to be quite happy.. . . Inherited wealth is a real handicap to happiness. It is as certain a death to ambition as cocaine is to morality." What Willie himself may have lacked in ambition, however, was more than made up for by his wife, whom he met in 1874, when he was twenty-five years old.

Alva Erskine Smith was an expatriate Confederate, born in Mobile, Alabama (like Frank Crawford Vanderbilt before her), in 1853, to a family rich in Kentucky cotton money. She was raised with a taste for brutality, and she freely admitted that as a girl she enjoyed abusing the children who were enslaved by her family. Just before the Civil War, her parents moved her, with slaves in tow, to New York City, where they spoiled six-year-old Alva in a mansion on Fifth Avenue. When the long-simmering hostilities between North and South finally erupted, the Smiths decamped to Paris, finding even Southern-sympathetic New York City not aligned enough with their Confederate point of view.

Throughout the rest of her childhood, all of which she spent in Europe, Alva's taste was further influenced by the high style of the Second Empire under Napoléon III, Haussmannization, and rich French opulence. The family returned to New York in 1870, but then their fortunes collapsed: Alva's mother died, and her father's remaining money evaporated in the fluctuations of the postbellum stock market. Alva was seventeen, a homely, square-chinned young woman with nothing to recommend her but her exquisite taste, her wide-ranging connections, and her unrelenting ambition. Her task was clear: get married—and make sure he was rich.

Alva's shortcomings in the marriage market were clear: she wasn't pretty, and she was no longer rich. But she was sharp and cunning, with boundless social ambition and a sparkling, sarcastic wit. She possessed all the strength and self-assurance that good-time-guy Willie Vanderbilt was lacking. Alva would lay siege to the cloistered world that Mrs. Astor ruled and would use the Vanderbilt coffers to accomplish her goals. She and Willie were married in April 1875, and two years later, Alva had a daughter, Consuelo, named for her best friend, Consuelo Yznaga. A year later came Willie Junior, and then Harold in 1884.

At last, by the early 1880s, there was a Vanderbilt wife with the will and guile necessary to crack New York society. Alva was a close student of the Astor set and its mores and knew that the way to ensure attention, the way to really make a splash, was to give a party unlike anything New York had ever seen. She must plan and host an entertainment that would seize the imagination of the public, dominate talk of the social world, and most importantly, bring the queen of New York into her camp. She had to win over the impossible, impervious Caroline Astor.

For this, Alva would need more than money, more than the right flowers, the right food, the right music—though, she would of course need all those things. She would need someone on the inside. She would need Ward McAllister. Any society lady worth her salt cellars wanted McAllister's advice on décor, menu, and arrangements for music and dancing. He was the man who mattered. Alva knew that the first step to her social success would involve consulting with him.

One of Alva's greatest insights was to recognize the power of the press, and as she schemed with McAllister on the plans for the ball, she used her instinct for publicity carefully. She arranged for details to slip out—a whisper here, a hint there. Anonymously sourced tidbits of information bubbled up in the press. First, she let slip the rumor that the ball would take place after Easter, well past when the usual social season was over. Alva arranged for the rumors to be officially confirmed the week before Lent, which meant an entire month of not much happening during which anticipation could build, among not only potential attendees, but also the general public.

The whispers were tantalizing to a city newly hungry for celebrity gossip, and they could find it in newspapers like *Town Topics,* and for the first time see reproduced images of fashionable people in *Harper's* and *Frank Leslie's.* It was to be a costume ball, and so, potential invitees had not only to conceive of a creative, luxurious, and stunning persona in which to costume themselves, but also to track down dressmakers able to craft the necessary raiments—no easy feat, as the number of dressmakers in New York City equal to such a task was finite. Rumor had it that Alva and Willie would host more than a thousand people at the Petit Chateau. The ball would feature a midnight supper and two different orchestras. The palatial house at 660 Fifth Avenue would be full to overflowing with hothouse orchids out of season and American Beauty roses by the thousands—at a cost, it was rumored, of more than $11,000 (some $280,000 today).

When the appointed day for the party finally arrived, the *Times* reported breathlessly that "the Vanderbilt ball has agitated New York society more than any social event that has occurred here in many years. . . . It has been on every tongue and a fixed idea in every head. It has disturbed the sleep and occupied the waking hours of social butterflies, both male and female, for over six weeks."

Those six weeks were a crucial preparation time for young attendees, not only because of the necessary, pleasurable, but also stressful details of arranging one's sumptuous historical costume, but also because of the need to practice the steps for the various thematic dances, called quadrilles, whose performance was an integral part of the spectacle of balls during the Gilded Age. Broadly speaking, a quadrille is like a square dance, with rigidly choreographed steps. It traces its origins to French court dances of the seventeenth century. The participants were chosen ahead of time; the themes and costumes were elaborately planned. Being chosen as a dancer was, too, a marker of one's social rank. The best ones would also be rewarded with "favors," like ribbons or sometimes exquisite pieces of jewelry, to be worn at the party. One had to practice for weeks ahead of time to make certain one knew the steps and to maximize the possibility of showing oneself off well to a watching and judging audience. For young women of marriageable age, performing well in a quadrille at a ball as hotly anticipated as Alva Vanderbilt's would have acquired colossal significance. Knowing the quadrille and being able to perform it well was part of the all-important quality of being "at ease in a ballroom," which Ward McAllister had cited as a crucial trait for social success.

In the weeks leading up to the ball, one of the most excited young people was none other than Carrie Astor, who had started practicing her quadrille in anticipation. Carrie, the twenty-two-year-old daughter of "the" Mrs. Astor, had been out in society for a couple of years already. Carrie had all the refinement of features that Alva Vanderbilt lacked: a slender, oval face; wide-blinking pale eyes; and a delicate mouth. Her practicing steps echoed happily in the Astor brownstone at 350 Fifth Avenue, and given who her mother was, Carrie had every expectation of being invited.

But shortly before the ball was scheduled to take place, Alva let it be known that, unfortunately, because Mrs. Astor had never called on her, she would be unable to invite Carrie. In fact, Mrs. Astor had never called on any of the Vanderbilts, ever. Carrie was devastated. How could she not be invited? She, alone, of all girls who were out?

The practice of paying calls was one of the more arcane, time-consuming instances of social theater practiced by upper- and upper-middle-class women in the Gilded Age. Women maintained visiting lists of people on whom it was appropriate to pay calls—in effect, Ward McAllister's "Four Hundred" was a codified, publicized version of such a list—and passed set times in the afternoon creaking along in landaus from brownstone to brownstone, as often as not sending a footman to the door to leave cards on behalf of themselves, their husbands, and their children without bothering to try to step inside for an actual visit. Society hostesses were expected to maintain hours when they would be "at home," which meant they were prepared to receive visitors, not just physically in their houses. (An Eastman Johnson painting from this period entitled "Not at Home," which shows a fashionably dressed bourgeois woman in a dimly lit Gilded Age New York interior mounting a staircase, suggesting that she is avoiding receiving whoever is at the door, now hangs in the Brooklyn Museum.) Calling was as much about reaffirming networks of power and acquaintanceship as it was about actually passing pleasurable time in one another's company—perhaps more so.

The snub of Caroline Astor's daughter was a masterful maneuver. According to the rules by which their society functioned, Alva Vanderbilt was being scrupulously correct. That Mrs. Astor had never deigned to call on her suggested that she believed Alva Vanderbilt did not socially exist. How, Alva reasoned (and made sure society knew she reasoned), could she then invite the Astor children to her costume ball?

Mrs. Astor had a choice: stick to her guns and risk New York society's leaving her behind while bitterly disappointing her marriageable daughter, or give in.

One chilly spring afternoon, a thin-lipped Mrs. Astor rode in her carriage the one long mile from her mansion in Murray Hill to 660 Fifth Avenue. When the carriage arrived at the curb, she sent a footman, dressed in the rich blue livery the Astors used, to ring the bell at the Petit Chateau. The door was opened by another footman, this one dressed in the Vanderbilts' maroon livery. A few words were exchanged. An engraved calling card passed from one servant's gloved hand to the silver tray held by the other. The door shut, and the blue-clad footman returned to the carriage. Then the Astor carriage jounced slowly away from the curb, horse tail flicking. It's possible that someone was watching the carriage's departure from behind a curtain, but of course we cannot know for sure.

Mrs. Astor and Mrs. Vanderbilt did not meet face-to-face; no words were exchanged between them personally. But delivery of the calling card, according to the complex set of rules they lived by, meant that Alva Vanderbilt had won. She had forced Mrs. Astor to acknowledge her. Carrie Astor would be invited to the masquerade ball and would perform her quadrille. And New York society would never be the same again.

After weeks of Alva's planning, scheming, purchasing, ordering, dropping hints to the press, and countless hours of standing for costume fittings, her night, the night of the Vanderbilt ball, finally arrived. The *New York Herald* described the scene as "like an Oriental Dream . . . never rivaled in Republican America and never outdone by the gayest courts of Europe." The palatial rooms of 660 Fifth Avenue shimmered with orchid chains, palm fronds, and vases and silver baskets of Jacqueminot, Gloire de Paris, and American Beauty roses alternating with potted palms. The whole house was ablaze in flowers and lanterns, alive with music and revelers in costumes the likes of which had never before been seen.

Alva's triumph could not have been more complete: Mrs. Astor herself attended the ball. She was costumed as a Venetian princess, as befitted her position as queen of New York, dressed in dark blue velvet embroidered with real gold thread, pearls, and lace. She wore almost all her diamonds, including a tiara of diamond stars glinting in her pitch-black hair. (Mrs. Astor, like the New York society women who would succeed her in the twentieth and twenty-first centuries, arranged at great expense not to have any gray hair.) Her ears sparkled with diamond drop earrings, her chest glittered with a diamond bow and lovers' knot brooches, and her décolletage was weighted down with heaps of diamond necklaces. A diamond-and-pearl stomacher graced her waist, and every movement of her arms glimmered in the paper lantern light with diamond bracelets over the wrists of her long white gloves. As always, Ward McAllister accompanied her, costumed as Count de la Mole, the lover of Marguerite de Valois, his costume crafted of purple velvet and crimson silk.

Most of the ball attendees chose long-deceased royalty as the inspiration for their costumes. Though Alva's father-in-law, Billy Vanderbilt, at that time the richest man in the world, appeared in simple white tie, his wife, Louisa, came dressed as a lady-in-waiting to Marie Antoinette. Alva's brother-in-law Corneil outfitted himself as Louis XVI, dressed in cream-colored satin embroidered with gold and silver thread, silk stockings, slippers with diamond buckles, and a feathered tricorn hat on top of a voluminous powdered wig and carrying a low-slung sword with a diamond-crusted hilt around his hips.

Alva's rival for preeminent Vanderbilt hostess, Corneil's wife, Alice, went in a more abstract direction for her costume: she came dressed as an electric light. Her gown was made by the famous dressmaker Worth, of yellow and white satin (the same colors and textures as her husband Corneil's costume), with skirt panels of dark blue satin embroidered with pearls. Her bodice, made from cream satin, was trimmed in diamonds, silvered lace, and feathers. Most remarkably, Alice carried a gilded torch in her right hand, its light powered by a concealed battery. Wittingly or not, the Vanderbilts were giving an entertainment that paid homage to the past while single-mindedly lighting the path of the future of society—her torch and tiara preceded the Statue of Liberty by three years.

Other costumes were designed to be shot through with wit as much as opulence. Willie's sister Eliza Vanderbilt Webb, for instance, costumed herself as a hornet, rustling about in a brown velvet skirt with a bright yellow satin bodice, trembling brown gauze wings, and diamond antennae. Mrs. Henry Sloane went costumed as a witch, with thick satin embroidered pythons coiling around her gown and winding up her pointed black hat, as befits a "pythoness" (back then, another term for "witch").

Alva's husband, Willie, dressed as the Duc de Guise, sporting an eighteenth-century-vintage yellow silk waistcoat and jacket over matching stockings with a dramatic black velvet cape. The real Duc de Guise had been assassinated in 1588 at the Château de Blois, which was the architectural inspiration for the house at 660 Fifth Avenue where they all stood talking, laughing, and drinking champagne, their feet grinding the occasional fallen orchid into the floor. No clearer equivalence could possibly be drawn between the old aristocracy of Europe and the new, self-crowning industrial aristocracy of New York.

And then, of course, there was Alva herself. Taking a page from Mrs. Astor, Alva received her twelve hundred guests while standing magisterially in a François I–style salon beneath a full-length portrait of herself painted by Raimundo de Madrazo y Garreta. In a further challenge to the reign of New York's queen, Alva also had costumed herself as a Venetian princess. She appeared in a queenly yellow-and-white brocade gown, with an underskirt patterned in deep orange and pale butter. Her overskirt and bodice were hand-worked in blue satin and decorated with gold thread and beading. Her arms appeared almost naked in the long, transparent gold sleeves that gathered at her shoulders, and her costume was finished with a train of pale blue satin embroidered with gold and lined with rich crimson velvet. Alva crowned her long corkscrew curls with a velvet tiara featuring a jeweled peacock. Most notable, though, in her outfit was the rope of pearls that had belonged to Catherine the Great stretching to her waist. At this moment in time, before the advent of culturing, a string of perfectly matched pearls was rarer, and more expensive, than diamonds. Alva had out-Astored Mrs. Astor on every level.

The most shocking costume, however, was neither an abstract concept nor a famous aristocrat lending Old World cachet to New World wealth. Writing in his memoir, Ward McAllister recalled that the most remarkable costume at the famous Vanderbilt ball was that of a young woman, Miss Kate Fearing Strong, who came dressed as a cat. Her costume consisted of a gown made of white cat tails with a bodice of skinned cat heads and was topped with a hat made of a taxidermied white cat curled up and perched upon her heaps of blond curls. Around her throat, Miss Strong wore a black velvet ribbon with a bell and the word *puss* spelled out on the choker in large diamond letters.

The existing photographs from this ball completely fail to capture the riot of color bursting through the Petit Chateau—from the gleam of brightly hued satins and silks, to the glitter of diamonds at every earlobe and throat, to the heady scent of perfume and roses and wine wafting through the air. The images are all staged and static: Alva standing stock-still, taxidermied white doves alighting on her hands, creating the illusion that she is feeding them. But in life, the ball would have been cacophonous, with the echoing of conversation in marble hallways and footfalls on stairs, exclamations over who was there and what they were wearing, murmured gossip, squeals of laughter, the occasional shatter of a broken glass. As the clock inched toward eleven, the hundred participants in the evening's six quadrilles milled about upstairs, talking and laughing and maybe shuffling their steps as they waited for the other eleven hundred guests to crowd together in the galleries on the first floor, a veritable beehive of satin and silk and jewels. At the stroke of eleven, a battery of trumpeters burst into a fanfare at the top of the grand staircase, and everyone proceeded to the dining room for the dancing.

The first dance was set to be the Hobbyhorse Quadrille, in which dancers entered the room to fanciful circus music, carrying the wooden horses that the fascinated onlookers on Fifth Avenue had watched be unloaded that afternoon. The young men were all costumed in matching scarlet hunting coats with satin breeches, and the young ladies similarly clad, in hunting coats and white satin skirts, with their costumes finished by horse-shaped frames suspended from their shoulders and upholstered with real horsehide, including manes and tails, bobbing and bowing as the dancers moved in their complicated pattern. In a quadrille, a caller announces each dance move in French, so the Hobbyhorse Quadrille would have featured not only deafening music played by a live orchestra, but also shouted dance moves booming to be heard over peals of laughter at the bobbing horses, the clapping and chatter of onlookers, and the rhythmic pounding of satin-slippered feet.

Next up, the Mother Goose Quadrille starred dancers costumed as characters from fairy tales, followed by the Opera Quadrille, with outfits copying those of characters from famous operas. Carrie Astor made her long-anticipated appearance in the Star Quadrille. This dance, which a contemporary described as "containing the youth and beauty of the city, was the most brilliant. The ladies in it were arrayed as twin stars, in four different colors, yellow, blue, mauve, and white. Above the forehead of each lady, in her hair, was worn an electric light, giving a fairy and elf-like appearance to each of them." The effect of these tiny lights, in the soft glow of candles and Chinese lanterns strung between forests of lush tropical foliage, orchids, and roses, together with the cold glint of diamonds against youthful skin, would have been nothing short of magical to a nineteenth-century participant.

The next performance was the Dresden China Quadrille, in which the dancers wore white satin and white powdered wigs and pretended to be porcelain figurines, collectible trinkets that serve only a decorative purpose. The final formal dance was a Go-as-You-Please Quadrille, with a variety of costumes chosen at the whims of the dancers. It's worth noting that the themes of all the dances were variations on expensive diversions, like sports, the arts, collectible doodads—each of them a frippery of fripperies.

At two in the morning, an eight-course supper created by the chefs from Delmonico's was served in the gymnasium on the third floor, which had been festooned into a riotous imagination of a tropical forest. Every surface exploded with palm fronds, ferns, walls of roses, dangling orchids, tiny electric lights, and bougainvillea hung with paper lanterns. At either end of the grand apartment babbled two artificial fountains, filling the air with the plashing of freshwater under the clink of crystal and fine china and silver.

At one point during the course of the ball, Alva was observed to be in confidential discussion with Mrs. Astor, two Venetian princesses whispering together in the indoor tropical forest. Around them, the dancing continued even as the thin, gray light of morning began to creep its way through the sleeping city. The last dance of the night was a raucous Virginia reel, led by a laughing and delighted Alva herself. After the music finally stopped, everyone went home, yawning, sore-footed, driven by exhausted (and bored) coachmen just after dawn.

"We here reach a period when New York society turned over a new leaf," wrote Ward McAllister ten years later, reflecting on Alva's ball in the book that would be his undoing. "Up to this time, for one to be worth a million of dollars was to be rated a man of fortune, but now, bygones must be bygones. New York's ideas as to values, when fortune was named, leaped boldly up to ten millions, fifty millions, one hundred millions, and the necessities and luxuries followed suit." It was rumored that the Vanderbilt ball cost a quarter of a million dollars, about $6.4 million in today's money. Six-point-four million dollars for a party. For comparison, one of the maids who left Alva's ball to await her mistress in a carriage parked on Fifty-Third Street as the spring evening grew cold and sharp, maybe stealing a nip of gin from the coachman, maybe flirting with a valet to pass the time, would have been paid around $350, in a year.

The day after the Vanderbilt ball, the press tripped all over itself with superlatives in describing the evening, drawing comparisons to "the Orient," the courts of Europe, the ancient world—in all instances, using references that underscored the otherness, the inaccessibility of that degree of privilege and sumptuousness. Suggesting that one woman's costume party could be compared to the opulence of ancient Rome presented Gilded Age society as the natural successor to these great things and, intentionally or not, positioned Alva Vanderbilt's entertainment as part of a nationalist project, just as Caroline Astor had imagined society could be. Was a ball like this just frivolous entertainment, an excuse to burn through money at a rate never before attempted or imagined? Or was it evidence of superior taste, of a new elite establishing a truly American class and culture that would stand atop the world? What story about the newly united United States would the world read and believe?

The night of the Vanderbilt ball, in a small Illinois town named Braidwood, about sixty miles outside Chicago, a similarly sized crowd gathered in anticipation of another event that had been in the making for over a month. On February 16, around the time Alva announced that the ball would take place, after days of unseasonably warm rain and melting snow, frigid groundwater burst through the shaft walls of the Diamond coal mine, instantly filling its narrow, winding passageways—four feet high and six feet wide—with rushing, bubbling water. A whistle blew the alarm, and women and children sprinted to the mouth of the mine, screaming in terror and held forcibly back from rushing into the maelstrom below to save their fathers, husbands, brothers, sons.

Years later, George Atkins, the son and nephew of two of the men trapped inside, would write, "I stood with Mother at the mouth of the mine and watched the water boil up to the surface[,] sealing doom of all below." One terrified man, streaked with mud and coal, was climbing the airshaft holding the body of his lifeless son, with his wife reaching her arms down to help him, when he lost his grip and plunged to his death in the water at the bottom of the shaft.

Immediately, the pumps were set to work, but the mine wasn't dry enough to access again until March 26, thirty-eight days later, the day of Alva's ball. That night, hundreds of people, including the families of the seventy-two men trapped inside the mine, watched as workers eased into the shaft, slick with water and treacherous with rockfall, to retrieve the bodies of the miners, some of them boys as young as thirteen, many of the workers immigrants from Poland, Germany, Ireland, Scotland, and Wales.

The first victims discovered at the bottom of the mouth of the shaft were in miners' suits, and one was dressed only in an undershirt, pantaloons, and a belt. They had surprisingly undistorted faces, a reporter wrote, hard to believe given that they had been submerged in water for more than a month. Around midnight in Illinois, just as supper was about to be served in Alva Vanderbilt's improvised tropical bower one time zone away, the first load of bodies was hoisted out of the mine and conveyed to a makeshift morgue before hundreds of onlookers, the stricken faces of miners' widows and orphans lit orange and hot by a flaming bonfire, the night sky broken by prairie grass fires winking in the distance, like fairy lights from a living nightmare.

The state of Illinois appropriated $10,000 for the relief of the families who had lost men in the mine disaster—$1,000 less than Alva spent on flowers. Other states contributed as well, with New York putting up $2,197.70. From these funds, a family of six or more could expect to receive $1.50 each per week. Widows wanting to move away from Braidwood could get a one-time settlement of $300. As one newspaper wrote, "[T]his bountiful provision made for the relief of the physical wants of these unfortunate people, has done much to alleviate their sufferings, and as an expression of the universality of human sympathy, constitutes the only redeeming feature of the situation."

These two events—Alva's ball and the recovery of the bodies from the Diamond coal mine tragedy—shared equal space on the front page of the *New York Times* for March 27, 1883.

The following year, 1884, Alva Vanderbilt appeared at Caroline Astor's annual opera ball for the first time. The arrival of the Vanderbilts was complete.

American Royalty

November 6, 1895

Of all life's ceremonies that of marriage is the most touching and beautiful.

—Amy Vanderbilt's Complete Book of Etiquette,
Part I: "The Ceremonies of Life"

Consuelo Vanderbilt was sobbing. She had spent the morning alone in her suite of rooms in her mother Alva's new house. There were no giggling girlfriends, no doting dowager relatives—none of the usual fuss and hubbub that attends a young woman on her wedding day. Not even Alva was there with her. Consuelo mopped her eyes alone, with no sound but the steady breathing of the footman who'd been posted outside her bedroom door to prevent her escape.

The hour was drawing nearer, and it was time for her to start climbing into her wedding finery. Sniffling, her eyes red and puffy, Consuelo felt herself moving like an automaton, a sense of numb unreality seizing hold of her as she slowly pulled lingerie made of hand-worked lace over her shoulders and slowly unrolled white stockings made of real silk over her legs. One foot, then the other, went into stiff white satin shoes.

The press—God, the press! They wouldn't leave her alone.

It had started when her parents, Willie and Alva Vanderbilt, separated. The divorce was finalized in March. The stories had been horrid, of course, full of gossip and innuendo. But once the wedding was announced, the attention had shifted to Consuelo. No detail, it seemed, was too intimate. When they couldn't find something salacious to write about, they just made it up. Consuelo's cheeks burned at the thought that they'd dared suggest her wedding outfit included garters with gold clasps studded with diamonds. No less a news outlet than the *New York Times* ran an article about her trousseau, complete with an actual illustration of one of her supposed corsets. Her reason rebelled at being asked to forget such vulgarity, but she knew this was the kind of attention paid to the great-granddaughter of the Commodore. We have a window into how Consuelo felt on her wedding day because of a ghostwritten memoir she published in 1952 called *The Glitter and the Gold*.

A soft knock came at the door, and a maid appeared to help Consuelo into her voluminous wedding dress, a frothy confection of Brussels lace falling in tiers over heavy white satin. High-necked and long-sleeved, it was a dress that befitted a wedding at noontime. When it had first arrived, Consuelo realized with a sickening drop in her stomach that her mother had ordered the dress when they were still in Paris, before the Duke had officially proposed. That's how immutable Alva's plans for her were. Of course Consuelo would have a wedding dress from Paris her mother had picked out when she married the man her mother had chosen. She didn't even have a say in the final date. Consuelo and the Duke had originally chosen Guy Fawkes Day, which meant nothing to Consuelo, but apparently meant something to the Duke. But it was changed to the next day, November 6. Nobody even asked her.

The maid did up an infinity of buttons enclosing a high, tight lace collar around Consuelo's throat. Long, fitted sleeves encased her arms. The maid affixed the court train, heavy with seed pearls and silver embroidery and falling in billowing white folds from her shoulders. The weight was prodigious, and not only physically. The train hung on Consuelo with all the pressure of her mother's ambition; of the attention of the press and the salivating public; of the gossip about her parents; of the expectations of her name; of the triumph of American money marrying into actual honest-to-God British royalty—a massive mantle draping over her, smothering her.

The final, finishing piece of Consuelo's bridal costume floated over her head. A cloud of tulle and old lace descended over her blotchy face and fell all the way to her knees. A wreath of orange blossoms crowned her masses of dark hair. A bouquet of orchids from Blenheim, the palace owned by her fiancé, the Duke of Marlborough, was expected but had not yet arrived.

Moving as if in a dream, numb and filled with a kind of detached horror, Consuelo made her way downstairs to meet her father and her retinue of eight bridesmaids, all chosen by her mother, most quite a bit older than Consuelo. They wore matching gowns of heavy white satin with long blue sashes and gigantic blue velvet picture hats topped off with pale blue ostrich feathers that moved softly on the faintest breath of air. Each wore a delicate brooch set with turquoise, a gift from the Duke. The bridesmaids looked beautiful. And Consuelo—swan-necked, slender, with dark hair and eyes set in an oval face, like John Singer Sargent's imagination of a Spanish dancer—they all agreed, looked radiant.

It was the worst day of Consuelo's life.

She had first met Charles Richard John Spencer-Churchill, Ninth Duke of Marlborough, in 1894, just a year before. She was seventeen; he was twenty-three. They'd been seated next to each other at a dinner, by the design of one of her mother's friends. The

Duke was slimmer than average, pale, with a proud forehead, aquiline nose, a light fringe of mustache, and dark hair like her own. He shared Consuelo's enjoyment of bicycling, and he was rather keen for tennis. Though he was genial and unpretentious about granting interviews after their engagement was announced, the American press could never agree on the Duke's salient characteristics, which effectively implied he had none. He was neither a genius nor a snob, though he had been called both. He had also been called "an empty-headed sprig of decayed nobility" and, alternatively, "a magnificent specimen of old-time aristocracy"; "a money-seeking foreigner" and "a young man of noble impulses." "If he were what he is pictured as being," the *Washington Post* remarked, "he would be a composite of all the rascals and gentlemen, dunces and geniuses in the universe."

He went by "Sunny," the typical sort of jocular nickname one might expect for a young man who possessed a 150-room (or was it 300? The papers could never agree) palace but not the fortune necessary to maintain it. For her own part, Consuelo found him smart, if a bit serious, and he was certainly attractive. But he didn't turn her head. Alva would have to turn it for her.

Consuelo and her retinue rolled up in their carriages to the curb outside Saint Thomas Church twenty minutes late. The corner of Fifth Avenue and Fifty-Third Street was thronged with onlookers who had begun gathering early that morning, capping the frenzy of anticipation and press coverage that Alva had once again orchestrated. When Consuelo stepped out of the carriage, leaning on her father, the entire crowd roared, held back by a line of policemen who struggled to keep a pathway clear. The noise was deafening, and eager hands reached out to grasp a flower from the bride's bouquet or brush a fingertip along the satin of her dress.

Those hands reminded Consuelo of the trip she had made two

years before, to India. It was at the beginning of her debutante year, and her family had traveled aboard their yacht across the Atlantic to the Mediterranean, through the Suez Canal, the Red Sea, and into the Indian Ocean, and then had traversed India in a private sleeping car attached to a regular train. At Ahmedabad, Jaipur, Delhi, and Benares, as the train idled in the station, a crowd of people—Consuelo thought of them as "natives"—pounded on the doors to the Vanderbilts' private car looking for seats, trying to beat their way inside, making a din loud enough that Consuelo cowered, sleepless from fear. She had never seen such teeming masses of humanity. The memory of those people in India made her think of the taste of thin tea, toast, and marmalade eaten miserably in a private rail car as screaming strangers banged on the windows inches away, wanting something from her.

Just the previous week, the police had seized a man calling himself Sir Oliver de Gyarfas, Baronet of Leczfalva of Hungary, who traveled to New York from Baltimore and publicly professed a violent desire to marry Consuelo. He announced to authorities that his plan was to supplant the Duke in her affections, which he would do by throwing a bomb at the wedding party. He was obviously insane, but looked, by all accounts, like any other person. The papers described him as well dressed, about twenty-five, wearing a regular suit, striped shirt, and patent leather shoes. Any of the regular-looking crowd of curious onlookers thronging about the church now could be plotting something similar, or worse.

"I am pursued by astral bodies, and I want protection. They want me to commit a crime, and I am not strong enough to resist them alone," de Gyarfas told the police. The madman said it was his duty to rescue Consuelo from a match made only between his title and her fortune. Even a ranting lunatic from Baltimore could see the truth, Consuelo thought.

Consuelo wasn't the first of the "million-dollar duchesses," but she was the most spectacular. Many American heiresses in the Gilded Age had taken their massive, newly minted fortunes to Europe and hunted for husbands who had fancy titles with no fortunes to go with them. One of them, Consuelo's namesake and her mother's best friend, Consuelo Yznaga, would even go on to inspire the character of Conchita Clossen in Edith Wharton's unfinished novel of transatlantic husband hunting, *The Buccaneers*.

Reporting on the exchange of her millions for the Duke's title and some property of uncertain value and encumberment, the *Chicago Daily Tribune* wrote that "the item of prospective happiness does not cut any figure in the transaction. Perhaps it was taken for granted that the possession of a coronet is the highest possible standard of female happiness as well as ambition. There is some doubt, however, whether such is actually the case."

In the tower room of the church, the bride hung back on the arm of her father, who had been invited to walk her down the aisle and then disappear. Consuelo had barely seen her father all year, Alva had made sure. And of course, she had heard the gossip; it was impossible to avoid it. Officially, the court transcripts and complaints, the terms of the divorce, the money, and all the other details were sealed. Unofficially, though, everyone in New York—indeed, everyone in the world, it sometimes seemed—knew what had happened.

Some years earlier, Willie had met a lovely blond woman named Nellie Neustretter at a racetrack in France and had installed her in apartments in Paris and Deauville. He'd not only kitted her out in finery and servants, but he carried on with her publicly and didn't even have the decency to deny it when Alva confronted him. Nellie was twenty-five with a toddler and a weeks-old baby. No one said anything outright; there was no need. She was, as the papers said, a woman "notorious in Europe." And rumor had paired her with Consuelo's father, this man on whom Consuelo now leaned, as she followed the whispering skirts of her brides-maids and approached the start of the nave, from which all of New York waited to watch her be married.

Alva had forbidden her daughter from having any interaction with the Vanderbilts at all since the divorce. Consuelo wasn't allowed to accept any gifts from that side of her family, and none of them, save her grandmother, Maria Louisa Kissam Vanderbilt, Billy's widow, was even invited to her wedding. Because the others weren't invited, though, her grandmother had refused to come.

Of course, Alva had been keeping some secrets of her own, not the least of which was a budding relationship with Willie's best friend, Oliver Hazard Perry Belmont, the son of the financier and horse breeder August Belmont. Now that she was divorced, she no longer had to conceal it. Short, more pleasure-loving even than Willie, Belmont had been the subject of rumors, with regard to Alva, since 1888, but this hadn't seemed to bother Consuelo's father much. If anything, Willie seemed to view the gossip as tacit license to conduct his own private affairs with Nellie, or with whomever. Upon reflection, Consuelo couldn't say she understood why her parents had ever been married. They certainly didn't seem to love each other. They didn't have anything in common. They didn't even seem to like each other very much. Maybe that wasn't the point of marriage?

"He's only marrying you for your money," Consuelo's younger brother Harold had said when he learned of her engagement to the Duke. Leave it to a ten-year-old to say out loud what everyone else was whispering. If Consuelo had harbored any illusions about her fiancé's motivations, the financial negotiations between the two families before her marriage had laid them to rest. Her father reportedly settled on the Duke the princely (dukely?) sum of $3 million. They'd both receive a promise of $100,000 a year for life, provided she went through with the wedding. The Duke and his lawyer and her father and an ex-judge had met the day before at her mother's house to settle the money. The Vanderbilt lawyer had reviewed the deeds from Blenheim, and a memorandum of Consuelo's settlement from her father was read aloud—as at an auction.

No one would comment publicly on the amount, but it almost didn't matter. A London newspaper had printed a cartoon headed "The Duke's Return from the Land of Dollars," with a drawing of him in the stern of a fine yacht, squiring Consuelo to Britain on a mountain of dollar bills. At least the future of Blenheim would be assured, as the walls could be shored up and papered over with layer upon layer of fresh American money.

The day before the settlement, Consuelo and her mother had supervised the wedding rehearsal so that all eight bridesmaids knew their order and all the ushers knew what to do. Afterward, they all repaired to her mother's house for tea. The Duke, thinking the American custom of a rehearsal vulgar, had declined to attend, instead passing the day with his cousin at the Plaza Hotel. Few prospective American husbands would have considered their attendance optional. Apparently, the Duke found nothing vulgar about showing up for the financial settlement meeting.

Consuelo hesitated in the tower room in the vestibule of the church. The nave of Saint Thomas's yawned before her, the chancel near the altar festooned with riots of lilies, ferns, and white and pink azaleas. The La Farge murals on the church's walls were nearly obscured by enormous palms, and vines draped the ceiling in trailing profusions of the rare and perfumed, in defiance of the snap of New York City autumn outside. A whole tropical botanical garden, it seemed, had been snipped and cut and now filled the church to overflowing. The end of each pew featured a floral flambeau, ten feet high, spewing pink and white roses and tied with pink and white satin ribbon trailing all the way to the floor. A hundred-year-old palm tree branched out of the pulpit.

The Bishop of New York and the Bishop of Long Island waited in the chancel, dwarfed by three towering Gothic arches of bride roses and lilies, along with the Duke, who was accompanied by his cousin as best man. Thousands of invitations had been sent out, and every seat and gallery in the church was filled with women dressed in expensive silks, satins, and laces, with feathers waving from hair and hats.

The audience—that is what they were, really, rather than intimate guests gathered for a family event—who'd begun to file into the church as early as ten in the morning, basked in the splendor of the surroundings. They wanted to see everything: What was Alva wearing? Where was Caroline Astor seated? (At the front, lest anyone have any doubts. Yes, her power was waning, but one did still have to invite her and show her proper deference.) People craned their necks to take in the costly flowers, the dresses and hats, the jewels glinting on the bodices and ears and throats of the other guests. And of course, they all wanted to see Consuelo, the bride who would become a duchess.

The organ struck up the Wedding March from Wagner's *Lohengrin*, and Consuelo's bridesmaids started out in twos, proud heads high under thousands of admiring eyes.

Consuelo was grateful that the veils covered her face. Even so, newspapers would later report that it was obvious she had been crying.

Dark and meek, she was praised in the press as having nothing of the "new" woman about her disposition. She detested divided skirts (a recent invention designed to give women greater freedom of movement for riding and sports), had no opinion on women's suffrage or women's rights or the Irish question. Attractive in her presentation, a success in society, quiet in her gowns, democratic in her ways, and (depending on the newspaper) either addicted to or completely uninterested in the bicycle habit—indeed, to the public, Consuelo seemed to have no opinions of her own whatsoever.

The preceding year had been dizzying. She knew she would face more scrutiny from the press and the public after she came out into society, but nothing could have prepared her for the level of coverage she'd received. Sometimes it seemed to her that random members of the public knew more about the specifics of her mother's plans for her than she did. That July, for instance, the *Washington Post* had published a roundup of the most eligible millionaire girls on the scene in Newport and Bar Harbor, shamelessly pointing out that it was Consuelo's mother's ambition driving her daughter's rumored engagement to the Duke, and not the young lady's own heart. The *Post* also made sure to mention that the bride would have $15 million upon her marriage (not true) and the white marble palace on Fifth Avenue where she was born (she hadn't been born there). The paper dared to hope that she would come to her senses and, instead of "gilding the walls of Blenheim with more American gold," would have a change of heart and marry an American. But what they didn't understand was that the Duke was a prize. Consuelo didn't have any money of her own. What she had was her mother, Alva, and Alva's ambition.

Consuelo tightened her grip on her father's arm. When things became irreparable between her parents, Consuelo had been designated to deliver messages from her enraged mother to her diffident father, and the memory of how venomous the messages became was a difficult one. Willie kept to himself and didn't share Alva's penchant for the public and the dramatic, for entertaining on a lavish scale and making sure the press was there to document it. He loved private pleasure—though, too well, Consuelo could admit. But her mother loved combat, loved holding dominion over just about anyone—her husband, her three children, the slaves she had grown up abusing for fun. Once, Consuelo had dared express her own opinion about the clothes her mother had chosen for her. Alva informed her that she had no taste, and so, her opinions weren't worth considering.

"I thought I was doing right," Consuelo said.

"I don't ask *you* to think. *I* do the thinking, you do as you are told," Alva countered.

Consuelo moved at the prescribed stately pace up the nave, bouquet heavy in her left hand, conscious of thrums of activity along the packed pews on either side of the aisle as guests shifted in their seats to get a look at her wedding costume. The pressure of eyes on her, the weight of the silks and laces and beading on her body, the train dragging at her shoulders—it all pressed in on the teenage girl. The church aisle seemed to stretch on forever, the Wedding March never to end. The air in the church was scented with lilies and perfume and the heavy breath of the thousands of onlookers. Consuelo drew even with the pew where her mother sat flanked by Consuelo's two brothers, who'd been buttoned uncomfortably into their wedding clothes. Her mother appeared in a dress both severe and breathtakingly expensive—rich blue satin, the same blue as the sashes on the bridesmaids' dresses, trimmed in sable, with sea-green oval pearls on the bodice. She stared at her daughter from beneath the sable-trimmed blue satin toque on her head, and Consuelo could tell that her lateness to the ceremony had made Alva worried that her daughter had seriously disobeyed her for the first time in her young life. Consuelo was too cowed to defy her, though. All she could do was march silently, inexorably, toward the future that her mother had orchestrated for her.

Alva, watching her dark, swanlike daughter about to accept her marital fate before the admiring eyes of all the best of New York society (her former in-laws notably excepted), glowed with cool triumph, which wasn't exactly the same as pride, or love. Did Consuelo's mother love her? Certainly, she had given her daughter every advantage. There was some evidence, here and there, of love. One time, when she was a girl, Consuelo's pony bolted and would have run her cart straight into a fire hydrant had Alva not leapt forward and placed herself between the pony and disaster, seizing him by the bridle and bringing him to heel.

But Alva could be a hard mother. She had, at times, when Consuelo was young, resorted to beating her daughter with a riding crop to make her points. Consuelo didn't like to think back on the riding crop.

Newspapers called the debutante attractive, but Consuelo was never entirely convinced of her own beauty, perhaps because Alva used to discuss the unfortunate upward curve of her nose with her friends while the girl stood nearby. Consuelo dressed as she was supposed to dress, with high whalebone collars and tight-laced corsets cinching her waist to eighteen inches. When she was a child, Alva had made her wear a brace to force her posture to be straight and ladylike—a literal iron vise of Alva's will molding Consuelo's pliable young body into the image Alva preferred. Consuelo felt she was always being watched, observed, and judged, which made her anxious and hypersensitive. How could it not?

"How full of tedious restraint was this artificial life!" she would think to herself later about the end of her childhood, which greeted her with sickening finality at the altar of Saint Thomas's. Her brothers had more freedoms as they grew older, to run and play sports, just as the parameters of Consuelo's life tightened: no picnics, no flirtations. Her governess was to report to Alva on

Consuelo's thoughts and inclinations. Everything in Consuelo's already narrow life was winnowed down to make her perfectly presentable to the Duke of Marlborough. She was, Consuelo reflected, "hallmarked like precious silver."

Consuelo's ultimate fate was sealed the way Alva sealed everything—at tremendous expense, with the maximal amount of attention. On August 28, 1895, after weeks of preparation and speculation, and after their tour of Europe during which she had first met the Duke, Consuelo was officially presented to society at a triumphal debutante ball hosted by Alva at Marble House, their summer house in Newport. It was nominally a ball designed to present Consuelo to the world of fashion and society, but the real guest of honor was the Duke, of course. Or maybe it was Alva? The papers reported that with this ball's success, she reestablished herself, triumphing over the Vanderbilt clan that would have seen her pushed out and humiliated after her divorce.

The Duke lived at Blenheim, but was spending the season in New York and Newport at Alva's invitation, and so he passed the afternoon before the ball playing tennis at the casino grounds. He was spotted around Newport dressed in a grayish suit, with a dark shirt, white detachable collar and cuffs, a straw hat, and a necktie of "gaudy colors," according to tittering Bostonians who observed him. He completed his costume with tennis shoes.

Alva certainly understood how to offset her daughter most beautifully. The ball that night was given for three hundred guests, and the whole of Marble House was alit with small, multicolored globes dotting the pathways, marble terraces, and cliff face like fairy dust glowing in the night. She decorated the terrace with a bronze drinking fountain, its basin overflowing with blooming lily pads, lotus flowers, pink and white nymphal blossoms, and water hyacinths. Butterflies and bees hovered at the lips of the flowers, brought in specially by the florist. All the supper tables were heaped with pink hollyhocks tied in pink satin ribbon. Alva's affection for all things French, irrespective of their actual background, was evidenced by the French flags all the way up the grand staircase. A maypole strung with lanterns stood sentinel at the center of the lawn.

Consuelo led the cotillion, decked out in white satin and jewels, the center of hundreds of admiring, and often envious, eyes. Three bands, two dinners—one at midnight, another at 2:30 in the morning—and the favors! The most celebrated dancers would be gifted with exquisite Parisian toys chosen specially by Alva: real bagpipes handcrafted by French peasants, silk sashes, mirrors, watchcases, and white lanterns in the design of Marble House itself. Everyone fawned over the Duke, whose official proposal was expected at any moment, and the evening echoed with rising peals of laughter and the tinkling of glassware and the music for the quadrilles booming off the marble surfaces of the house, drowning out the murmuring and shushing of fine satin as women moved. Diamonds glinted in the soft evening lights, and the air was thick with the aromas of perfume and rich food and summer blossoms nodding in the August night. It should have been perfect. It was perfect—with the sole exception that the man Consuelo *really* loved was not there.

His name was Winthrop Rutherfurd, and he had grown up in the same fast and rich universe of New York as Consuelo. He was thirty and handsome, and he thrilled her so deeply that she was powerless to conceal it. On her eighteenth birthday, March 2, he sent her a single red American Beauty rose. He didn't attach his name, but she knew it was from him. She'd already received heaps of roses that day, sent from admirers all over, but his was the only rose she wanted. The afternoon of her birthday, she'd contrived to meet him while bicycling in Riverside Park, and he had proposed marriage in a moment when Alva and the others in their group had fallen behind, huffing and puffing. Consuelo and her mother were due to leave for Europe the next day, but she readily agreed to a secret engagement, her head buzzing, thrilled with his love for her, with the secrecy, and with the unfamiliar bliss of doing something her mother knew nothing about.

Winthrop planned to follow her to Europe, and when they were reunited in America, they would elope. Consuelo knew she could never tell her mother about their engagement, lest she jeopardize it. Though Winthrop was from a prominent New York family, and was a member of the Four Hundred like the Vanderbilts were (now), Alva had determined to marry Consuelo into royalty. No American man would be good enough. Consuelo was a chip, a token that Alva would play in her never-ending quest for social influence and rank.

When they got to Europe, Alva could tell that her teenage daughter was unusually happy—at first. They passed five months, doing rounds of parties, luncheons, teas; getting fitted for dresses in Paris; visiting museums; going to the theater. But then Consuelo's glow began to fade. The fine lunches turned to ash in her mouth. Her color drained. In all that time, Winthrop hadn't appeared. He didn't write. He had vanished. Only later did she learn that he had in fact followed her to Paris as he promised, but he'd been refused admittance when he attempted to call on her. His letters had all been confiscated and destroyed. Hers to him, the same. It was Alva. Alva would let nothing come between her and her plans for Consuelo.

As their time in Europe dragged on, Consuelo's mood grew increasingly dark. She withdrew; Alva noticed, and it irritated her.

"When one is young and unhappy," Consuelo would write later in her memoir, *The Glitter and the Gold*, "the sun shines in vain, and one feels as if cheated of one's birthright. I knew that my mother resented my evident misery, and her complaints about what she satirically termed my 'martyrdom' did not improve our relations."

Consuelo felt herself slipping further away from the person she had dreamed of being. She tried on clothes her mother chose. She moved robotically through museums and churches and lectures and concerts, each one more forgettable than the last.

"I went to a few of those deadly debutante balls which I no longer cared for and danced with men who had no interest for me. Then we moved to London, where events began to move rapidly, and I felt I was being steered into a vortex that was to engulf me," she wrote later. The vortex of Alva's ambition, combined with the outward pressures of money and attention and fame, was too much for one teenage girl to withstand.

When they returned to the United States near the end of the summer, Alva moved quickly to snuff out any possibility of Consuelo bucking her wishes. The Duke had been invited to visit them in August or September. Until his arrival, Consuelo was never to be out of sight of her mother or her governess. Friends called to see her in Newport but were told she was not at home. Locked away, Consuelo was unable to send word to Winthrop. She couldn't talk to him or find out what had happened. She didn't even know if he still felt the same way about her.

Late that summer, quite by happenstance, Consuelo ran into Winthrop at a ball in Newport. They had one dance together. One. It was long enough for him to assure her that he still loved her, that their plan could prevail. Consuelo was on the point of responding to him when Alva seized hold of her and dragged her away from their conversation.

Mother and daughter rode home from that ball in deadly silence. When their carriage arrived at Marble House, Alva told Consuelo to come with her to her private rooms. Once there, away from prying servants' eyes and ears, Consuelo marshaled all the fortitude she could muster. She had never dared challenge Alva before, not like this.

"I mean to marry Winthrop Rutherfurd," she said, steeling herself for the rain of fury that was surely to come. "I consider I have a right to choose my own husband."

Alva exploded in a blind rage even worse than Consuelo had imagined possible. Did Consuelo know what a ridiculous flirt her lover was? He was notoriously involved with a married woman, first of all. Secondly, everyone knew he only wanted to marry an heiress, and it didn't much matter who. He would never have children, Alva claimed, with no evidence whatsoever. Also, madness ran in his family like a Hapsburg lip!

Consuelo had no response to these bitter invectives dismissing the character of the man with whom she had fallen in love.

"My decision to choose a husband for you is founded on considerations you are too young and inexperienced to appreciate," Alva insisted.

"It's my life," Consuelo said.

She had never resisted Alva before. Alva was not someone to brook resistance.

"I would not hesitate," Alva hissed, "to shoot a man if I thought he might ruin your life."

The argument was endless, running in circles, impossible to win. Alva shouted. Alva threatened. Alva put her foot down. Finally, in the thin light of dawn, Consuelo fled her mother's room, feeling as if she had aged a decade. She hid in her bedroom, exhausted and afraid. She had no telephone of her own, so she couldn't reach out to Winthrop. Writing him was out of the question, as all the servants had been told to bring her letters straight to Alva. She passed that morning anxious and alone, but rumors thrummed through the veins of Marble House that Alva had taken ill, that a doctor was being summoned. Consuelo considered turning to her father, but he was away at sea on his yacht, and anyway, involving him would only upset Alva further.

After a time, a knock came to Consuelo's door. She opened it to reveal Mrs. William Jay, a houseguest and close friend of Alva's. Mrs. Jay told Consuelo matter-of-factly that her carelessness had caused Alva to suffer a heart attack. She also reaffirmed Alva's statement that she would never agree to Consuelo's marrying Winthrop, and if Consuelo dared to run away with him, Alva would hunt them down and shoot Winthrop dead.

"Can I see her? Do you think she will ever relent?" Consuelo pleaded with Mrs. Jay.

"Your mother will never relent, and I warn you there will be a catastrophe if you persist," Mrs. Jay told her. "The doctor has said that another scene may easily bring on a heart attack and he will not be responsible for the result. You can ask the doctor yourself if you do not believe me!"

Consuelo felt stricken. Her mother was dying, and it was all her fault! Tremulous, still shaking from the fury of their confrontation, she realized she was trapped. A tide of misery rose in her chest as she asked Mrs. Jay to please send word to Winthrop that she would not marry him.

Once her daughter's secret engagement was successfully broken off, Alva enjoyed a near-miraculous recovery.

There dawned a dreary end of summer for Consuelo as she waited out the term of her sentence. Alva's supposed ailment vanished—if anything but rage had ever truly ailed her—but she treated Consuelo coldly all the same. Willie was gallivanting off at sea, or wherever he was. Consuelo's brothers romped through their own pleasures and concerns. The same friends who had been turned away whenever they tried to call on her at Newport finally got the hint and stopped trying. There was nothing for Consuelo to do but swallow her loneliness and fear and anxiety into a sour little ball in the pit of her stomach.

By late August, Alva was hosting the Duke at the grandest debut ball ever held in Newport. The newspapers all promised that an official announcement of the engagement was imminent. Consuelo had resigned herself to never living her own life. And Winthrop had left Newport, possibly for good. At the ball, as revelers spun and danced and drank and ate and watched from under lowered lids for signs of drama, Mrs. Jay stood next to the Duke, guarding him like a Doberman.

Summer waned into early autumn, and Consuelo attended dinners and balls on the Duke's reedy arm, chaperoned at all times by Alva. They dined on the Astor yacht in Newport Harbor. The days passed leisurely, full of expensive pleasures. In the morning, Consuelo would drive with her mother to the Casino in a make of carriage called a "sociable" to visit with Astors and other scions of New York society, title-hunting buccaneers, like her. Alva dressed Consuelo in expensive Parisian fashions, and the Duke rode along in light flannels and a sailor hat, despite not being much of a sailor. Back at Marble House, Alva hosted luncheons, and Oliver H. P. Belmont would swing by and would sometimes drive them to the Polo Grounds to watch matches from carriages in the late summer sun.

One desultory evening, Consuelo found herself in the Gothic Room at Marble House. The room was Richard Morris Hunt's fantasia of the Middle Ages—multicolored stained-glass windows, a majestic, vaulted ceiling like what might be found in the passageways under a French cathedral. Rich, red upholstered walls offset a monumental stone fireplace. It seemed like the perfect setting for a sacrifice. In this room meant for display rather than for living, the Duke finally, officially, asked Consuelo to marry him. There was no expression of sentiment on either side.

He hoped, Sunny said, that he would make a good husband for her. As soon as it was done, Alva was immediately notified.

News of the engagement appeared in the papers the very next day, presumably by Alva's orchestration. The Duke left within the week to travel a bit around America, thinking he might as well see some of the land now, since he planned never to return after he had squired his new duchess and her new money back to Europe, where they belonged. When Consuelo told her brothers the news, she burst into tears.

In October, the Vanderbilts returned to New York, and plans for the wedding began in earnest. The days passed quietly. Consuelo was usually prevailed upon to accompany Alva to her new house on Madison Avenue, where the question of how to place furniture, tapestries, and pictures on the walls was forever pressing. She dined with the Duke and her mother every single evening, either in a private room at the Savoy or, on occasion, with Oliver Belmont at the Waldorf. The days ticked off, one after the other, with the newspapers counting down the passage of time before Consuelo would be made a duchess. And then, all at once, November 6 was here. Her wedding day.

When, at last, Consuelo arrived with her father at the chancel rail, Willie steered her into place before stepping aside. The Duke, dressed impeccably in a dark gray frock coat and trousers, white tie, and gloves, stepped forward and took her right hand, leading her to the chancel steps. The choir struck up the hymn "O Perfect Love, All Perfect Love Abounding." When Consuelo glanced hopefully at the face of her betrothed, she found him staring into the middle distance, at nothing.

The ceremony was over in what felt like the blink of an eye. Consuelo found herself led into the vestry on the Duke's arm, followed closely by Alva, her father, and her two brothers. The newlyweds signed the marriage register, witnessed by her parents, the bishops, and the British ambassador. Then they were hurrying together down the nave to the tune of Mendelssohn's Wedding March, and Consuelo allowed herself a smile. The beauty of the day, the pageantry, the music, the flowers, the fuss and attention—she wasn't immune to it all, even if she was the instrument and object of it.

When Consuelo emerged a freshly minted American duchess from the doors of Saint Thomas's on the arm of her new husband, the gawkers thronging the streets outside let out a tremendous cheer. Consuelo and Sunny hurried to the waiting carriage, which took them the twenty blocks from the church back to Alva's house, all the streets lined with people, who were cheering but also staring—mainly staring. Alva and her sons left the church by a side door, and Willie drove away alone.

The wedding breakfast passed in a blur, Consuelo's feet growing sore from her standing in the receiving line under a suspended bell of flowers. There were ancient, prehistoric palm trees standing guard in the windows overlooking the street, to thwart unwanted onlookers. There were toasts and a speech from the British ambassador and a speech from the Duke and laughter and food. The best man toasted the bridesmaids, but there was not a word from the ushers, all of whom had been thwarted in any pursuit of marrying Consuelo Vanderbilt and her millions.

Then it was time for her to change into her traveling outfit and depart with her new husband. She would finally get to leave Alva's house. As their carriage pulled away, Consuelo looked back to see her mother watching at the window, half-hidden by the curtains. To Consuelo's surprise, she could see that Alva was crying.

"And yet," Consuelo thought, "she has attained the goal she set herself, she has experienced the satisfactions wealth can confer, she has ensconced me in the niche she so early assigned me, and she is now free to let ambition give way to a gentler passion." What that gentler passion might be, Consuelo couldn't imagine.

She and Sunny rode the Thirty-Fourth Street ferry across the East River to Long Island City and then boarded a special train to Oakdale, on their way to Idle Hour, where they would begin their honeymoon. Consuelo wore a silvery gray brocade trimmed in sable, lace, and velvet, with fetching epaulets edged in sable and ivory lace. The outfit was finished by a green velvet hat topped with waving ostrich feathers that trembled whenever Consuelo moved. Some of her trousseau was intended for hunting and bicycling on their honeymoon, but most of the clothes packed in trunk after trunk on the train were designed for her to do nothing in but look beautiful.

Consuelo watched as the Duke passed the voyage reading congratulatory telegrams. He would hand them to her to read as well, and from his mien, Consuelo could tell whether she was supposed to regard the sender as worthwhile. The Duke reserved his greatest respect for the missive from Queen Victoria. It was a wonder, Consuelo thought, that her telegram wasn't presented on its own silver platter. For the first time, Consuelo began to understand that she had married into an ironclad social structure, one much older and deeper than the pretend aristocracy found in New York. She had thought she understood snobbishness, but she'd never seen it like this. The Duke explained to her that she would have to learn the lineage and rank of some two hundred families to which the Spencer-Churchills were connected, together with all the tenants of Blenheim, its employees, and its army of servants, all of them meticulously attuned to subtle shadings of rank.

As the Duke droned on, Consuelo looked at him, reflecting that she was now essentially ruled by a man who seemed completely indifferent to the fact that they were setting out together on their honeymoon.

When they arrived at the treasured country house of Consuelo's childhood, she was overcome with a sharp sadness. She thought back to times spent there when her parents were still married, when she'd romped in the comparative wilderness of Long Island with her garrulous brothers. Now she was here without them—with a stranger, essentially. Her mother's room had been prepared for her, and her old room had been made ready for occupancy by the Duke. All at once, Consuelo saw with utter clarity how naïve she was. Was this what marriage was?

She was seized with a miserable longing to be safe with her family again. She burned with resentment that that family was gone, a fiction perhaps from the very start. Everyone around them was content to let Nellie Neustretter be the stated reason that Willie and Alva could no longer stand to be in the same room with each other. But a dalliance with a pretty young thing, even an entanglement as expensive and indiscreet as Willie's, would hardly have been enough of a crime by the standards of the day for Alva to launch the greatest divorce case that society had ever seen. The risk to Alva had been prodigious. Women in New York society simply did not get divorced. They looked the other way. They enlisted other men as husband substitutes, walkers like Ward McAllister and Harry Lehr, who were content to dress up and go to parties and gossip and snipe. Or they recruited lovers like Oliver Belmont, the kind of men who would be invited on cruises in the Mediterranean, where flirtations could simmer to life under the hot sun glinting over deep, blue European water. Or, as in Alva's case, they contented themselves with both walkers and lovers, and leaned on their husbands for money and status only, letting them scamper off to dinners at Delmonico's and evenings at the Metropolitan Club free of prying, wifely eyes. Why would Alva have taken such a risk? She was generally confident that society would back her in whatever she did, but there was always the chance that she was too far before the fashion. She could have been left with nothing.

Consuelo knew the reason her mother had insisted on divorce. It wasn't Nellie.

Now here was Consuelo Vanderbilt, standing at the door of her mother's old bedroom at Idle Hour, staring into the rooms where she would spend her bridal night: newly married, an American girl, the new Ninth Duchess of Marlborough, mistress of Blenheim. She had sailed the high seas to Europe, hunting titles with her fortune as her lance, and had bagged the biggest one there was.

She had won.

"In the hidden reaches where memory probes," Consuelo would write, much later in her life, "lie sorrows too deep to fathom."

Part II

FALL

1

Failure Is Impossible

May 4, 1912

*It is only the shallow and silly who ever return from the divorce
courts in a carnival frame of mind, desirous of public celebration.*

—Amy Vanderbilt's Complete Book of Etiquette,
Part VI, "The Family and Social Education of Children"

The women had begun arriving early that afternoon, dressed
in smartly fitted suits of white serge or linen. They gathered in
Washington Square and lined the nearby streets and as far north
as the Twenties, sporting thirty-nine-cent straw hats trimmed in
veils and ribbons of green and purple and carrying yellow banners onto which were sewn phrases like "The Right to Follow
Duty Far and Wide, to Live as Nobly as Our Men Have Died,"
"All This Is the Natural Consequence of Teaching Girls to Read,"
and "Never Will Peace and Human Nature Greet 'Till Free and
Equal Man and Woman Meet."

No one knew how many marchers to expect, but it was rumored to be almost ten thousand. Carriages and automobiles had
been organized to carry the oldest suffragists, women in their
eighties and nineties who had been marching for decades. The
youngest were tiny girls pushed in perambulators, sticky-cheeked

and squalling. In between these two extremes could be found every imaginable stripe of woman from New York City: factory girls, skinny and exhausted; respectable matrons; seamstresses, milliners, laundresses, and clerks. A coalition of Black women had chosen black frocks with yellow sashes and carried yellow-and-black pennants with American flags. A band of women from Chinatown rode in their own automobile decorated with a saffron-yellow dragon, to spare their feet, broken by binding. There were women on horseback, women in academic robes with hoods lined in the satin colors of Vassar and Columbia, women whose seamed faces betrayed a lifetime of hard use. One woman was costumed as Joan of Arc, but much less finely than the Joan of Arc who appeared at an 1880s costume ball. And there, barking orders, leading a division of young uptown shopgirls flying blue banners, her money the invisible backing of their purple-and-green sashes and their suffrage slogan tea sets and even their hats, stood Alva Erskine Smith Vanderbilt Belmont.

Crowds thickened on the sidewalks that traced the more than two-mile-long parade route from Washington Square to Carnegie Hall. Some onlookers were there to jeer, carrying cabbages concealed in their coats to chuck at the fresh, white dresses of the marchers, but most were coming to gawk and cheer. Interspersed between the various battalions of women shuffling their feet and talking excitedly, marching bands honked their horns in quick scales to warm up, horses stamped their hooves, and automobiles and carriages idled, covered thickly with yellow buttercups, their wheels creaking as women helped each other in and out.

Activists had been drumming up interest in the march for weeks, sending earnest young girls schlepping news bags full of suffrage magazines behind a hand organ as they tromped across parks or coquettishly twirled parasols decorated with suffrage mottoes to ward off the springtime sunshine. Now actresses, Quakers, Socialists, trade unionists, and even some men waited for the stroke of five, when the greatest parade in favor of women's suffrage was set to begin.

When the signal was finally given, the brass bands pulled together, and slowly the line of marchers began to wend its way up Fifth Avenue from Washington Square, with successive waves of marchers merging into the crowd from the adjoining side streets and the whole mass of people moving like a white-clad tidal wave washing up the central artery of Manhattan. Alva knew as she proceeded in the throng that she was essentially demonstrating in her own neighborhood. She would be parading past the open windows of houses where she had often been a guest, passing before the silent, judging eyes of people whose favor she used to curry. But by 1912, she was past caring about the opinion of New York society. She had flouted the rules before, and now she would thumb her nose at everything that society stood for. The Gilded Age was over, and Alva—the most gilded of them all, the wearer of Catherine the Great's pearls, the hostess of the most fantastic and expensive costume ball ever given, plotter of the most spectacular royal marriage for her daughter—was ready to burn it all to the ground.

"It may be interesting and gratifying for Mrs. Belmont to know that after a group of prominent members of the Union Club had expressed their approval of her march on Saturday by clapping and cheering, they furthermore denoted their esteem by proposing a toast and drinking her health," reported the usually jaundice-eyed gossip rag *Town Topics*. "The windows on the ground floor of the club were filled, and the balconies on the floor above were crowded . . . But Mrs. Belmont looked neither to the left nor right. Like a real general she marched stolidly on. . . . Cornelius Vanderbilt stood at one of his windows . . . Mrs. Reggie Vanderbilt stood all alone in one of the windows of the great house in Fifty-seventh street . . . Every mansion along the route of the procession was wide open and the windows crowded with feminine members of the families . . . [I]f the movement has not won universal approval it has wrested universal interest."

Initially, it feels impossible to reconcile the Alva of the Veblenesque costume ball of 1883 with the Alva of the women's suffrage march of 1912. How does a woman go from being a society figurehead, famously prodigious spender, and publicity maven in her early life to being a leader in the first wave of Progressive Era feminism in her later years? How does that trajectory make sense?

The answer begins to form itself in her sensational divorce from Willie K. Vanderbilt in 1895, the same year she married off her daughter, Consuelo. Alva splashed into society with gusto when she married a Vanderbilt in the first place, but she ripped it all asunder when she had the temerity to divorce him twenty years later. This divorce would forever alter the landscape of New York society, just as it remade the trajectory of Alva's life. Within her understanding of her marriage to Willie and its end can be found the seeds of Alva's later activism, as well as one woman's experience of nineteenth-century perspectives on gender and conditions of freedom—or lack thereof.

Maybe no one was surprised that the Vanderbilt marriage wasn't a happy one. Many society marriages weren't especially happy, as a cursory review of the blind-item pages of *Town Topics* proved. Even Caroline Astor, society's supreme queen before Alva's successful siege on her domain, lived a life notably separate from that of her husband. A man of the period was almost expected to have mistresses—well-appointed yachts could be very convenient for just such an intimate rendezvous—and a canny society woman might even get away with keeping a lover of her own, if she was especially careful. But no one—and I mean *no one*—expected the William K. Vanderbilts to get divorced. The plot of Edith Wharton's novel *The Age of Innocence* turns on the social impossibility of divorce for a certain class of women. But then again, Alva never was one to do what was expected of her.

"I always do everything first," she said, according to her friend Elizabeth "Bessie" Drexel Lehr, wife of Harry Lehr, the society walker who stepped into Ward McAllister's shoes. "I blaze the trail for the rest to walk in. I was the first girl of my 'set' to marry a Vanderbilt. Then I was the first society woman to ask for a divorce, and within a year ever so many others had followed my example. They had been wanting divorce all the time, but they had not dared to do it until I showed them the way."

In her 1935 memoir of life in Gilded Age New York, *"King Lehr" and the Gilded Age*, Bessie Lehr paints a dramatic picture of Alva as a "valiant warrior to whom opposition was the breath of life. Nothing made her happier than the knowledge that she was pitting herself against the rest of the world. She loved to see herself as a pioneer, to make others bend to her will, to have them follow her in the end, meek, sheeplike." But even she couldn't have anticipated what was to come.

When the curtain rose on the 1890s, Alva Vanderbilt was still in the thick of consolidating her hold over what had, until recently, been Mrs. Astor's New York. Alva's sense of herself and her self-worth revolved around two primary spheres, or so she told herself—the maternal and the constructive. By "constructive," she was being literal: her obsession with architecture and her friendship with architect Richard Morris Hunt were two of the defining aspects of her life as a queen of society. She fed her desire to build and to dominate by acquiring the plot of land next door to Beechwood, Mrs. Astor's Newport "cottage," and setting out with Richard Morris Hunt to build a summer house that would stagger anyone who set eyes on it.

"The Vanderbilts must have homes which represent original-ity, art, and beauty," Alva insisted. She was confident in her taste, which she had developed during a girlhood in France, and she was especially proud of the Petit Chateau that Hunt had built for her at 660 Fifth Avenue. "My house was the death of brown stone fronts," she boasted. "I wanted to put my whole soul into the con-struction of the house on 52nd street."

She found her perfect match in her preferred architect. "Mr. Hunt's temper was very fiery," Alva remarked. "We had terrific word battles. Turning to me[,] he said[,] Damn it, Mrs. Van-derbilt, who is building this house? And I answered[,] Damn it, Mr. Hunt, who is going to live in this house? Our friendship was most beautiful . . . When they buried him, I felt he had been the most resourceful and cherished friend of some of the saddest years of my life."

Alva's instinct for drama led her to hide the construction of her new summer house behind a wall, as five hundred thousand square feet of marble imported from Italy was slowly assembled into the mock Petit Trianon palace that would come to be called Marble House. It may have had fewer rooms than Mrs. Astor's, but the whole shebang cost $11 million in 1890s money ($310 million today), and its levels of ostentation left Beechwood in its dust. Construction lasted from 1888 until 1892, when Alva cel-ebrated its completion by throwing—what else?—a ball. The guests all gathered on the lawn one August evening, the house shrouded in darkness. When Alva gave the signal, the lights were thrown, illuminating a tremendous glittering temple to her taste and ambition. The triumph was so complete that within the next year, Alice Vanderbilt, Alva's sister-in-law and rival, would begin work on The Breakers so as to not be so utterly shown up.

But while Alva was enjoying architectural and social triumph, by 1892 her private life was starting to show cracks. Willie wanted a quieter life than she did—or at least one further out of public view. She had married him largely out of social ambition and financial necessity rather than love per se, a fact that was not lost on any of their children. And instead of the children bringing them closer together as a couple, Alva and Willie had grown further and further apart.

One indication that her divorce fueled Alva's later activism is that in the summer of 1917, she hired a young suffragist named Sara Bard Field to make notes for her second attempt at a memoir. Alva, after all, was as aware as anyone of the unique contours of her life. Over the course of several afternoons that July and August, she mused aloud while Sara scribbled detailed notes in pencil and green ink. At several points in her reflections, Alva shifted from the personal to the general, though it's evident that she was still speaking about her own experience. The promised book never came to fruition, but the notes and typescript that Sara made, which reside in the Huntington Library, offer a unique window onto Alva's interior life.

From Sara's hasty green scrawls we learn that, over time, Alva's view of marriage sharply soured. She spared no detail when reflecting on the institution in general and on her unique experience of it. For a reader accustomed to implication and delicacy and elision in Gilded Age accounts of the separate spheres of men and women in the nineteenth century, Alva's perspective is bracing.

"The man in my class married a young and pretty woman from whom he asked nothing more than good looks, careful grooming and a readiness to serve his desires," she told Sara. "By no chance did he turn to this petted creature for mental stimulus. He would as soon have thought of expecting wisdom from his wife as professorial dignity in a butterfly.

"To speak frankly," Alva continued—and one wonders what color Sara's ears turned as she listened—"in most cases they wanted a woman for one purpose only and that was the gratification of their sex passion. If she was of a man's own class he could not gratify this desire for her without marrying her. So long as the woman was young and pretty[,] she was the object of her husband's selfish interest. Then[,] when love, founded as it was on the sands of mere passion, had died, I noticed with surprise and indignation that this woman"—Alva shifted here to talking about some hypothetical woman, rather than herself, but hypothetical women don't brave public scandal with a divorce; only real women do that—"was set aside, relegated to a stupid domestic sphere. Still young and attractive, she found herself with Romance an illusion, with affection taken from her, with the freedom of contact denied her. On her devolved that dull task of maintaining the family's prestige and respectability, of observing the approved moral code as a cloak for the sins of the husband."

Alva had certainly done all those things, and in spades. In fact, she had done them perfectly. Only through her own cunning and social instincts had the Vanderbilt clan achieved the social prominence they craved. She had also created the scrim of prestige and respectability behind which Willie was free to entertain anyone he wished, on his yacht or wherever he chose.

"And I noticed," Alva continued, "that the women grew stupid and morbid, that, like unpicked sweet peas, they went to seed while it was still blooming time and their great cry, midst all their luxury and material satisfaction, was 'I am so lonely.'"

Beneath Alva's evident contempt for the women of her set, the women who lacked the strength of character she believed herself to have, was a plaintive cry for help. The separate spheres of the era were stifling, at least for the women imprisoned within them, and empty.

It's hard to imagine someone as surrounded by people and attention and wealth as Alva Vanderbilt as "lonely." But the word
comes up in her recollections of her first marriage again and
again. Think of Alva, still a young woman at thirty, all bedecked
in her diamonds and jewels and faux-Venetian princess tiara, posing stock-still with stuffed doves in her hands as she waited for
the photographer to snap her picture for her grand fancy dress
ball in 1883, her stare vacant from her keeping her eyes open long
enough for the exposure to take. Her mother had died when she
was a child, an abrupt erasure of what Alva called "the governing
and controlling influence in my rebellious life." Her father had
died penniless two weeks into her marriage to Willie. Willie's father, Billy the Blatherskite, had always liked Alva and had urged
her to think of him as her father after she suffered that loss. The
Commodore had liked her, too—he admired her grit—and enjoyed the weekly calls that the junior Vanderbilts paid to him in
his later years.

Even so, Alva had never felt particularly assured of her own father's love. His devastation over the death of her brother when she
was eight left Alva with the stinging impression that her father
preferred a dead son to a living daughter. As the moisture drained
from her eyes while she posed for her party photograph, her palatial house was crammed full of over a thousand people, eating her
food, drinking her champagne, marveling at her taste, dropping
hints to the reporters she had invited. How many of them were
her friends? Her *real* friends? Did anyone actually love her, other
than her children?

"I know that material Poverty is a mother of crime and disease and wretchedness and that it must be abolished on the earth,"
Alva admitted to Sara. By the time of their conversation, Alva's
involvement with women's suffrage had brought her in contact
with some women who actually knew something about poverty.

In 1917, as part of her political work, she had established a soup kitchen in New York City that catered to desperate women and streetwalkers, and had been shocked when some of them came with newspapers for petticoats, their dirt-blackened toes sticking out of battered shoes, owning nothing but their coat and a dented straw hat, complaining that the war had robbed them of all their work. "But I also know that Spiritual Poverty produces as great evils even among the rich. The idle useless lonely woman of the leisure class is a thing spiritually dead."

By the early 1890s, Alva looked at the women surrounding her in New York and Newport, women trapped in base and manipulative marriages like her own, and found herself loathing what she saw. She called the Newport women "uneducated, parasites, frivolous, self centered" and compared them to lap dogs.

"All their standards are of wealth," she complained to Sara Field, conveniently overlooking her own magnificent expenditures in the course of her two decades as Mrs. Vanderbilt. Then again, her famous ball appears nowhere in the notes for her memoir. She took particular pride in her architectural projects and in the education of her children, and she is full of justifications for Consuelo's forced marriage to the Duke of Marlborough. But she skips right over her Gilded Age social excesses. "I have never met a lower type of women in general attainment, than those [at Newport]," she sniffed.

Alva tried vainly to revive her spiritual self as Willie withdrew from her. Around the time of her Marble House triumph, she began her affair with Willie's best friend, Oliver Hazard Perry Belmont. In 1888 he joined the Vanderbilts for a cruise on the *Alva*, Willie's 264-foot diesel-powered yacht. It is likely that cruise was when the dalliance with Alva began. Tongues started wagging almost immediately, with blind items bubbling up in the gossip papers. But even though Willie seemed to know about the affair—some whispered that he'd come home one day and found Belmont hiding in his closet!—it didn't seem to bother him all that much. Alva's extracurricular entanglement gave Willie license to conduct his own affairs. Even knowing Oliver's rumored relationship with Alva, Willie invited Belmont to join them on a cruise to Europe, the Mediterranean, and India on his yacht the *Valiant*, successor to the *Alva*, in 1893. Oliver breathed new life into Alva's gasping soul, but it wasn't enough. She watched Willie gallivanting around, away from the judgment and censure of the public, and her rage began to burn.

"Meanwhile during these lonely, uninteresting years of women, what was happening to the husband?" Alva asked Sara rhetorically. "Stepping over the confining threshold of his home whose respectability he left in the hands of his discarded wife, like a young colt in a meadow[,] he kicked up his heels and was off for a romp in the wide world field.

"If he was merely sensual[,] he had all the mistresses and other self gratifications he could procure," Alva complained. "If he was irresponsible in his nature, he met his obligations as a husband and father by merely signing generous checks." Of course, checks bought many things in the Gilded Age society marriage—not only grand houses and gowns from Worth, and education for children, and phalanxes of servants, but also freedom . . . for the husband, not the wife.

And what's worse, the wife, Alva, knew perfectly well what was happening, and was powerless to stop it. "Younger and more attractive women would patronize her," Alva said to Sara, still speaking of herself in the third person, as was her wont when discussing painful topics. "And often before her very eyes, without even the thinnest veil of decency being drawn over the act, she would see others being given her place."

But being replaced wasn't the only thing that kindled the fires of Alva's rage. What truly set her aflame was Willie's exercise of power over her. "They held wives in subjection through their money rule," Alva said, "and through the more subtle method of holding up to them the chaste submissive slave as their ideal while in reality they sought the demi monde with her easy virtue and her free living. If a wife, hungering for love and with more spirit than most of her sex, asserted her right to a lover or to contacts with the outside world, the husband declared she was ruining his reputation along with her own and with the power of the bank resources at his command bade her retire to the obscurity of respectability."

A few telling details bubble up through Alva's narration of a hypothetical society woman struggling within a hypothetical society marriage that is clearly an account of her own life. First, the passage suggests that she tried to assert her right to take Belmont as her lover and that Willie batted her down. Alva, without naming names, implies that Willie used the power of his money to compel her to give up Belmont by making appeals to her responsibility for maintaining the family's respectability, but that he did this while pursuing, with impunity, whatever extramarital sexual relationships he desired.

The second, and related, salient detail we can derive from this passage is that Alva was utterly unable to conceal her sense of rivalry with, and contempt for, other women.

Third, and perhaps most jarring, is her choice of the word *slave*. Alva's objection to marriage, ultimately, was that she felt owned by her husband—like a slave, robbed of authority, robbed of personhood. Slavery was the most debased condition Alva—once a slaveholder, born into a slaveholding family, who had played "North and South" the way other children played cops and robbers—could possibly conceive of.

Hinted at here, too, is the suggestion that one of Willie's romantic distractions was someone close to Alva. While Willie's involvement with the notorious Nellie Neustretter was the public face of his infidelity, the truth was more appalling to Alva and everyone she knew. His most shocking lover was none other than Consuelo Yznaga—Alva's best friend, namesake and godmother of her daughter, and sister-in-law of Alva's sister Virginia. The rumor was everywhere; even the New York *World* hinted at it. Such a betrayal would certainly fuel Alva's rage, Consuelo's wantonness in boldly taking up with the husband of her closest friend.

Whatever freedom Alva grasped for within her foundering marriage to Willie, it wasn't enough. In the midst of the ill-fated Mediterranean cruise in 1893, with Oliver along, Alva abruptly quitted the ship. Willie and all the guests on board could no longer pretend that the Vanderbilt marriage was a happy one. Alva broke the first rule of being a society wife: she cast aside concern for appearances and laid bare her grievances.

In Alva's world, appearances were everything.

Back home in New York, she determined that she would sue Willie for divorce. Her decision ushered in a period in the family that her daughter, Consuelo, would later characterize as one of "dread and uncertainty." Willie moved out of the Petit Chateau at 660 Fifth Avenue and installed himself at the Metropolitan Club, and Alva engaged Mr. Joseph Choate as her attorney.

The first thing Choate tried to do was talk Alva out of a divorce. It was impossible, he said. A defenseless woman, without wealth in her own name, whose influential friends would certainly side with her husband, could not possibly take such a drastic step. How could she hope to stand up against the combined forces of wealth, social position, and public opinion? Choate had a man's mind and knew that the situation would be governed by the rules of a man's world. Men controlled the law. Men controlled the government. Men controlled the money. "Looking behind him," Alva said of her attorney, "he saw only the beaten track, and looking ahead, he saw a rocky wilderness."

But Alva felt that there was more at stake than her own happiness. What about all those other empty-eyed Newport society women—the cowed ones, the ones as miserable and controlled as she was, but who lacked her sense of her own power? After all, marriage was a cover for a great many miseries for women. Alva characterized the institution more than once in the notes for her memoir as legalized prostitution. One wonders if she knew she was echoing Marxist organizer Emma Goldman, who wrote in 1911, "The wife who married for money, compared with the prostitute, is the true scab. She is paid less, gives much more in return in labor and care, and is absolutely bound to her master. The prostitute never signs away the right over her own person, she retains her freedom and personal rights, nor is she always compelled to submit to man's embrace."

Alva put it slightly more delicately to Sara Field: "If marriage is a protection for the woman against many wrongs," she said, "divorce is also an escape from many degrading evils."

Alva embodied a curious contradiction in that she felt she cared deeply for women as a class while nursing venomous contempt for the women she actually knew. A society woman in New York was a creature of "envy, jealousy, and her eternal resort—the lie," Alva said. "For centuries her competition with other women has made it impossible for women to stand together. Her object was to beat her rivals off. This has made it necessary for women to fight each other and criticize each other."

Of course, Alva had proved quite adept at this gendered gamesmanship. But the single-mindedness of her social ascent and triumph had left her feeling isolated and alone, and if she cast away her marriage, the source of much of her power and influence, she knew that women would be the first to condemn her. "This is why

I have found so little companionship in women," she reflected to Sara. "Women [are] dwarfed not developed by competition. . . . What men did not want to do, they said was women's sphere. If a woman is natural[,] a man does not want her. This makes of woman a liar and a pretender. A woman is an actress who plays to an audience of men. They know what will be applauded and what will be hissed."

Though Alva understood better than most people the impossible position in which women found themselves in Gilded Age society—the necessity of conforming to men's expectations to assure themselves economic and social security—she felt bitter contempt for women for, in her view, allowing themselves to be put in such a position. It's hard not to read her rage as rage at herself. She was Alva Erskine Smith. If she, an ungovernable and rebellious child grown into a powerful and influential woman, felt this trapped, this hobbled, this *owned* by her marriage, what about the weak and pitiful creatures around her?

"If no woman meant much to me at that period," Alva put it to Sara, "women as a mass[,] by some inexplicable contradiction, did."

Her attorney, Mr. Choate, argued the point with her over and over again. But Alva wouldn't be moved. She was going to get her divorce—not only for herself, but for other women like her. She would blaze the trail. The others would follow, like sheep. "I had Right with me," she told herself. Moreover, and crucially, "the race would never progress if women were to eternally sacrifice themselves to a person or to a power."

The divorce trial began in January 1895 and was over by March. The New York *World* called it "the biggest divorce case that America has ever known." Alva understood why there was so much hungry interest in the press. "Gilded sin is so much more interesting than ragged sin," she reflected. "Scandal dressed in ermine and purple is much more salacious than scandal in overalls or a kitchen apron."

Willie willingly served as the party at fault, rumors about Oliver Belmont notwithstanding, and admitted to keeping a mistress in Europe to whom he gave a handsome allowance of $200,000 a year, as well as homes in Paris and Deauville. Consuelo Yznaga was nowhere mentioned. Willie's taking the blame allowed Alva's reputation to remain unsullied, in spite of the open secret of her affair. She was granted a decree of dissolution, together with a settlement of $2.3 million, alimony, and custody of their three children. Alva kept her architectural prizes, too: Marble House and 660 Fifth Avenue. But the latter would be too expensive for her to maintain; she had to let the Petit Chateau go.

"I got my divorce," Alva said, describing the aftermath. "And just as [when] in childhood days I accepted the whipping my mother gave me for asking the forbidden liberty, so I bared my back to the whipping of Society for taking a freedom which would eventually better them as well as myself. And they put on the lash, especially the women, and especially the Christian women."

The Sunday after her divorce was finalized, when Alva appeared at Trinity Church in Newport, all the women cut her. Alva moved through the church the target of cold stares, dogged by the whispers of women gossiping in groups. She was invited to dinner parties where no woman would speak to her except the hostess. She was a pariah, but it didn't last forever. As time went on, Alva's force of will proved stronger than the culture in which she found herself.

Alva married her lover, Oliver Belmont, on January 11, 1896, in her temporary home at 24 East Seventy-Second Street. She locked up Marble House and moved into Belcourt, Belmont's Newport mansion up the street, which was famous for its stables.

(As one might surmise from the name, the Belmonts were avid breeders and racers of horses, and their influence lives on in the Belmont Stakes, one stage of the famed Triple Crown of horse racing.) Alva's friend Bessie Lehr visited her one afternoon as the tour omnibuses were rumbling up Bellevue Avenue. Even then, people paid to come gawk at the well-heeled of Newport. "Oh, here's that dreadful man with the megaphone," Bessie remembered Alva saying over the tea table. "He's going to tell all the tourists about our staircase. Do listen to what he says, it really is too funny for words." Then Bessie heard an amplified voice cry, "Here you see before you the new home of a lady who is much in the public eye, a society lady who has just been through the divorce courts. She used to dwell in the marble halls with Mr. Vanderbilt. Now she lives over the stables with Mr. Belmont."

With her divorce and remarriage, Alva had gotten what she wanted most of all, other than love: she had gotten control—ownership, if you will—of herself.

"At last free, my own mistress, the great power within me to love claimed my whole being and all willing, I married the man who for a few short years completed for me a life in its perfection in every sense," she sighed to Sara Field. "Few, alas, I believe have realized . . . that neither man or woman were intended to live ununited. Any imperfect result of their union, was of their own making either because of the wrong mate selected or by the moral imperfection of one or more likely both of the participants."

Alva posited to Sara that any couple desiring to be married should have to submit themselves to a board for approval. She claimed that her reasoning for pushing Consuelo to marry the Duke lay in her belief that marriages were more successful in Europe because greater thought was put into them. Young people in Europe were guarded from making foolish mistakes out of ephemeral passion. That's what she told herself, anyway. But for Alva, all these questions and justifications dissipated before her great, ever-present need for control.

Despite his rather plush background, Oliver Belmont actually pushed Alva in a more politically progressive direction. He published a liberal weekly called the *Verdict*, which railed against corruption and was doggedly antitrust. When Belmont died in 1908, Alva found herself in a new stage of life. Her daughter was brilliantly married off, though desperately unhappy, and already living a life largely separate from that of her husband. In fact, Consuelo wrote that by 1906, "the nervous tension that tends to grow between people of different temperament condemned to live together had reached its highest pitch," so she and the Duke officially separated, and Alva traveled to Europe to support her. Alva's two sons were away at college. Alva had money to bestow, but she was uninspired by the charities she saw, which seemed arbitrary and ineffective. The House of the Good Shepherd for Wayward Girls, a popular charity for ladies of her set, one designed to aid the moral and religious instruction of "fallen women" by putting them to work in a laundry, "dealt with spoiled material," Alva thought. "Why not find out what spoiled them? These girls did not want to be reformed and nine times out of ten were not."

She began lavishing her considerable fortune on soup kitchens, affordable and healthful housing experiments, the promotion of birth control, and most important: the vote for women. In 1909 she founded the Women's Political Equality League, and she opened Marble House, whose furniture was still shrouded in dust covers, to suffragist planning meetings. Purple-and-gold banners unfurled in the grand summer house bearing a quote from Susan B. Anthony (whom Alva would later disparage as insufficiently radical): "Failure Is Impossible." A stint in Europe left her believing that American suffragists were being too meek in their demands. The time had come to stop asking men to give them favors. The time had come to remake entirely how men saw women.

"Woman's emancipation means education of men as well as women," Alva insisted. "The mating of the future which will be a success will be founded on the truth of being. We are not only making a new woman—we are making a new man. We are not only bringing forth the truth in women but making men desire the truth." In these remarks, the signal importance of Alva's failed marriage to her activism is hard to miss, but so, too, is her ongoing contempt for other women. "I predict that just as now[,] the men look back to the women of the Victorian Era[,] who fainted away and wept on all occasions[,] and think what wretched companions they would now make, so the men of tomorrow will look upon the stupid doll of today who may not faint but cannot think."

As it happens, the wreck of Alva's marriage only partially explains her turn to activism. To fully understand why her marriage imploded, to locate the source of her deep and abiding contempt for women who were not as eager to dismantle a sexist power structure as she was, we must look further back—to Alva's childhood, which began in the antebellum South and continued in New York City just as the Civil War broke out.

"I remember the terrible discussions at the dinner table," Alva told Sara Field. "My Father did not believe slave holding was wrong. Even in New York we had our household slaves who would not have taken their liberty if we had given it to them . . . My father disbelieved in the Secession Movement yet all his love and sympathies were with the South. I sat next to my father[,] always staying in the room after dinner when the women left to hear the discussions. My father went to Liverpool. . . . [and] sent for the family to come to Europe on account of war conditions making it impossible for him to live either North or South. So we went to Paris to live."

The mother whom Alva so revered, whose death so devastated her, was also completely unable to control her when she was young. As Alva referenced when describing the experience of her social ostracism after her divorce, she was often whipped as a child for being too headstrong. In fact, she notes almost with pride that her mother whipped her every single day for an entire year for being too rebellious. But of course, while Alva describes herself as "baring her back" to be whipped while wishing for her freedom, one cannot forget her own treatment of the enslaved people forced to work in her childhood home. In fact, when Alva proved too difficult for her mother or any governess to manage, she was turned over to an enslaved man named Monroe Crawford, who had been presented as a gift from Alva's maternal grandfather to her mother on the occasion of her marriage.

"I was an impossible child," Alva admitted. "I could not stand any restraint. I did not want the routine of a woman's life from the beginning[,] and with Monroe, I got it. I bossed him. It was a case of absolute control on my part."

Alva's nostalgic account of Monroe Crawford is straight out of the Lost Cause book of Reconstruction-era racist characterizations: "He was one of those unique characters, a combination of childlike simplicity and wisdom, superstition and knowledge found nowhere except among the negroes of that slave period," she said to Sara Field.

Alva claimed that Monroe used to enlist her help to write love letters for him to a woman he had met "up North." Whether he truly needed help with writing because he was illiterate, or whether he simply hit upon an effective method to keep his otherwise impossible charge quiet and seated on the back stairs for longer than five minutes at a time, one cannot say.

Recalling her relationship with slavery and enslaved people in her childhood, Alva also waxed nostalgic about Sundays spent at her godmother's house, during which she and her godmother's son "tyrannized" over the enslaved children in the household. "I don't believe I was ever cruel to them in the way of doing them physical harm," Alva mused, "but I was conscious of my superiority[,] and I think even then I despised submission and lost no chance to assert my masterful position." She forgave herself, though, for her childhood excesses. "I was too young to know that the Negro race was a race in its infancy, and as infants[, they] submitted to any authority that was superimposed upon them. I am very sure it was that quality of meek submission that I then despised as I still do today[,] in women who are wives of tyrant husbands or who live under tyrannous laws."

There it is: the source of the contempt. Alva could not stand to feel owned herself. But even more than that, she could not stand people who, she believed, allowed themselves to be owned. It is impossible to think about Alva's feminism without looking squarely at her virulent racism. Her contempt for women who allowed themselves to be subservient to men aligned directly with her contempt for enslaved Black people for, in her absurdly simplistic view, allowing themselves to be enslaved. (Alva was hardly alone in espousing these views in 1917. Two years before, the Ku Klux Klan–glorifying film *The Birth of a Nation* was released with a glowing endorsement from President Woodrow Wilson.)

"In this connection," Alva continued, "I remember my eager admiration for the Indians who used to come at times into [Mobile] selling herbs and hand made trifles. The straight, upstanding character of their physical bearing and the moral bigness of their self ownership and independence as contrasted with the servile frailty of the negro people and their possession by the white race was a contrast that either consciously or unconsciously my childish mind made in the Indians' great favor."

It's true that in the 1910s, Alva made moves toward integrating the push for women's equality and helped establish a suffrage settlement house in Harlem. She even urged Black feminists to form a "negro branch" of her Political Equality League, the organization she had founded to further the reach of suffrage activism in disparate neighborhoods of New York City, and at the head of which she was marching that balmy May afternoon in 1912, as Vanderbilts and Astors looked down at her from their elegantly open windows and as the occasional egg or tomato went sailing by overhead. Nothing would stop Alva from gaining a point once she was decided upon it—not even her own deeply entrenched racism.

White women got the vote in 1920, and Alva spent the remainder of that decade living principally in Europe, to be closer to her now-divorced daughter, Consuelo. Alva died in France in January 1933, shortly after her eightieth birthday. Her life was celebrated at a lavish funeral in New York City marked with female pallbearers and politically themed eulogies.

Never one to shy away from publicity, Alva appeared again in the press not too long ago. In 2016, on April 12, Equal Pay Day, the Sewall-Belmont House and Museum, in Washington, DC, which had served as the DC headquarters for the National Woman's Party since 1929, was finally named a national monument. The Belmont-Paul Women's Equality National Monument, as it is now called, was intended to serve as a living repository for the history of the women's suffrage movement and was named to jointly honor the founder of the National Woman's Party, Alice

Paul, and its principal benefactor—perhaps she would have preferred "benefactress"—Alva Erskine Smith Vanderbilt Belmont.

The woman whose single-minded drive to work for women's equality and who was motivated by her deep-seated, unapologetic contempt for Black people was enshrined in American history by the country's first Black president, Barack Obama.

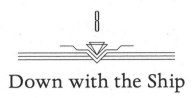

Down with the Ship

May 1915

Congenial people usually introduce themselves to one another in short order aboard ship, but it should be kept in mind that shipboard friendships, like shipboard romances, usually end when the boat docks, despite many protestations to the contrary.

—Amy Vanderbilt's Complete Book of Etiquette,
Part IX: "Travel Etiquette at Home and Abroad"

Up until that morning, the passage from New York had been utterly uneventful: clear air, smooth seas, the usual rushes to friendship and rehashed discussions at dinner. Passengers on the Cunard line to Liverpool had enjoyed sunny and mild weather since May 2, the day after their departure, and though the elegant ship had traveled at only eighteen knots for much of the journey, rather than its top speed of closer to twenty-three, no one thought the voyage had been anything other than completely ordinary.

The current head of the Vanderbilt family, a married man of thirty-seven traveling with his valet, was no different. If anything, the trip, a quick jaunt to London to see about contributing to the Red Cross's wartime ambulance service, had been somewhat boring. He strolled the decks to stretch his legs, went to dinner, and spent time with a friend or two from New York, including Thomas Slidell, a desultory young man who lived at the Knickerbocker Hotel. He was also taken up by the Thomases, owners of a lucrative coal mine concern in Wales, and he passed pleasant evenings mildly flirting with their daughter, Lady Mackworth. All very routine. One could almost imagine the European continent wasn't at war.

It was cool and foggy off the coast of Ireland on the morning of the seventh. The Cunard line flagship, one of the "Monarchs of the Sea," dropped its speed slightly because of the poor visibility, from around eighteen knots to fifteen, and sounded its foghorn at regular intervals to advertise its location—the mournful blast booming through the mist, echoing strangely off the surface of the ocean. Fog can do funny things with sound and space and light. Ships can loom into being out of nowhere, almost as if they have risen up suddenly from the depths—even ships as massive and elegantly appointed as the R.M.S. *Lusitania*.

On board, a rill of anxiety rippled through the passengers when the foghorn first groaned over the water. Steerage for that journey, as was typical of ships bound for Europe from New York, was barely filled. Second class, however, was full to overflowing, so much so that some second-class ticket holders had been stashed in first, which was not quite a third full. First class on this voyage featured the usual cast of characters: a couple of actresses, the occasional novelist, scions of business, entrepreneurs, a suffragette viscountess, a baronet, a noted theatrical producer . . . and Alfred Gwynne Vanderbilt, heir to the greater part of the Vanderbilt fortune. Though he preferred to be known as a sportsman active in horse circles, and though he sat magisterially on various railroad boards, it was the fortune that made him famous and the subject of constant notice among his fellow passengers as the otherwise tiresome miles of ocean swelled past their porthole windows.

While it was true that newspapers all over the country had

posted notices from the German government on their date of departure, warning that ocean liners could not expect to be safe from the flourishing war in Europe, nobody on board had taken the warning as anything other than grandstanding. In any case, everyone knew that the Cunard ships could outrun torpedoes— provided they kept up top speed, of course, and didn't advertise their position.

Alfred had never expected to be the head of the Vanderbilt family. He was, after all, the third son of Cornelius II and Alice of The Breakers, and so the mantle of head of family should rightfully have fallen first on his oldest brother, William Henry II. Sadly William came down with typhoid fever while an undergraduate at Yale and died in 1892, at the age of twenty-one. Alfred was still in high school at the time, at St. Paul's, where his two older brothers had gone before him, the first generation of Vanderbilts to enjoy an elite education.

The mantle should then have settled on the shoulders of Alfred's next-oldest brother, Cornelius Vanderbilt III, called Neily, who even shared a name with their legendary great-grandfather. Neily had stubbornly insisted on marrying Grace Wilson, a Southern upstart from an ambitious social-climbing family, against the express wishes of his parents. Neily was hardly the first Vanderbilt man to have a taste for upstart Southern women. If anything, a taste for upstart Southern women might, by Alfred's generation, have qualified as a persistent family trait, like slightly almond-shaped eyes or high foreheads or an inclination for marble in interior décor. But Grace was too independent even for the Vanderbilts, and when Neily defied his parents' wishes and eloped with her, he was disinherited.

And so, in 1899, after finishing at Yale as a Bonesman (a member of the elite Skull and Bones secret society), Alfred had set off on a grand jaunt around the world with a party of his friends.

He'd just gotten to Japan when word arrived of his father's abrupt death, and Alfred found himself most unexpectedly the head of the Vanderbilt family at only twenty-two years old. He hurried home from Japan to take the reins of the family business, assume control of the family fortune, and step into the public eye as the leader of the next generation of Vanderbilts.

When Cornelius II died, he left an estate valued at roughly $70 million, according to the *New York Times*. That's about $2.2 billion today. What the papers called his "favored" children—nineteen-year-old Reginald, Gertrude (by then Mrs. Harry Payne Whitney), and Gladys—each came away with an estimated $7.3 million. Neily was "cut off" with only $1.5 million. The vast lion's share, estimated by the *Times* at around $35 million, fell to Alfred, who gave a further $6 million to Neily so he would be equal with the other siblings. Alfred also was awarded the gold medal given to the Commodore at the conclusion of the Civil War, with the request that it be passed to his eldest son. A clearer marker of the head of the Vanderbilt family could scarcely be conceived. Upon the reading of his father's will, Alfred found himself the richest young man in America.

Rich young men have rich young tastes, and Alfred was no exception. He took his place as a director at the New York Central Railroad and had controlling interests in several other railroads as well as the Pullman Company. He also had a nose for real estate. Back in 1864, the Commodore's son Billy, Alfred's grandfather, had acquired a portion of the block between East Thirty-Third and Thirty-Fourth Streets, west of what was then called Fourth Avenue, near the Grand Central railroad depot and just around the corner from the home of J. Pierpont Morgan. In 1867, Billy gave a portion of that parcel to his son Cornelius II, Alfred's father, who erected a comfortable, elegant house there for his growing family.

Murray Hill in the 1870s was a polite, respectable enclave of upper-middle-class houses, stables, and churches, but by 1880, fashion had flowed northward, and the Vanderbilts followed wherever fashion went. Particularly as Alfred's mother, Alice, felt the need to outspend and out-consume her sister-in-law Alva, Murray Hill would no longer do. The Vanderbilts went to upper Fifth Avenue and didn't look back.

The neighborhood around the old Vanderbilt house grew more urban, with office buildings and city clubs and apartment houses gradually replacing the society palaces. Alfred started buying up the remaining land in the city block adjacent to the house in which he had grown up, finally succeeding, by 1907, in owning the entire block. He erected the twenty-one-story Vanderbilt Hotel on Park Avenue and Thirty-Fourth Street and lived there in sumptuous comfort in a fifteen-room penthouse apartment.

For all his interest in the development and design of the hotel, however, Alfred's chief joy and passion lay in horses—the breeding of horses, the showing of horses, and the rather arcane sport of coaching, which consisted of driving horse-drawn coaches along the same routes traveled in the early nineteenth century. He spent much of his free time—and he had copious amounts of it—gadding about the English countryside driving coaches with like-minded friends, staying at scenic inns along the way. In 1901, he'd married his sweetheart from his days at Yale, Ellen French, a dear friend of his sister Gertrude, in Newport. At the end of that year, they had a son, William Henry III. Alfred passed his twenties ably discharging his duties as head of the family, which consisted of living well, marrying well, and spending money beautifully.

But as often happens, Alfred's passion for fine horses was only one of his areas of refined preference and expertise. In 1903, the equine circles of New York City took notice of the arrival of the elegant wife of Don Antonio A. Ruiz y Olivares, attaché of the Cuban Legation at Washington, DC. Mrs. Ruiz, born Agnes O'Brien, the daughter of a farmer in Missouri, had gone on the stage using the name "Ruth Hilton." Despite her theatrical bent, Alfred knew that Mrs. Ruiz could be discreet; she kept her birth name and background a secret even from her husband until several months after her marriage. In New York she passed much of her time at the riding academies or driving in Central Park. "Her acquaintance with Alfred Gwynne Vanderbilt," the newspapers would report later, "is said to date from an act of courtesy on his part one morning in Central Park, when he found her tugging helplessly at an obstinate saddle buckle. He asked her if he might assist her, and the offer was accepted."

Agnes Ruiz accepted many offers from Alfred—so many, in fact, that by 1906 she had separated from her husband, and rumors of marital problems began to circulate around Alfred and Ellen. As the whispers began to intensify, Agnes lived quietly, but in excellent style, in a richly appointed apartment at 596 Lexington Avenue, which Alfred likely supplied for her. She didn't entertain, but she drove handsome horses and automobiles. In October 1906, she traveled with Alfred in his private rail car across Virginia and met several of his associates. The public was largely unaware of or indifferent to the fact of the beautiful former actress stashed in a respectable but unfashionable part of Midtown. In 1907, Alfred Vanderbilt's stable manager, Harry Brenchley, was even tasked with procuring for her a prized automobile that was rumored to cost $11,000—or around $310,000 in 2020 money.

Shortly after he bought Agnes that car, Ellen sued Alfred for divorce.

From there, the affair went, for lack of a better term, off the rails. The newspapers swarmed around Agnes, Alfred, and Ellen like flies. Despite his relative professional successes, 1907 was a horrid year in Alfred's personal life. One of the only bright spots was the time he spent on his yacht with Thomas Slidell, when they watched this very Cunard liner, the *Lusitania*, pull into New York Harbor on her maiden voyage and saluted her with a dip of their burgee, the flag that yachts carry to identify themselves to one another.

But if Alfred thought 1907 was bad, 1908 was even worse, as the seamy details of his divorce leaked to the press. Ellen Vanderbilt charged Alfred with "misconducting himself with an unknown woman while traveling on his private car, the Wayfarer, from Richmond, VA to Norfolk VA on or about Oct. 17, 18, 19 or 20, 1906," the papers drooled. Alfred denied his wife's charges, but it was no use. The principal witness against him was Harry Kempster, his own British valet. Another witness, a banker named Thomas Benedict Clarke Jr., "told of Mr. Vanderbilt introducing him to a woman named Ruiz." With news of the divorce dominating gossip columns, Alfred fled to England to ride out the storm among the safety of friends and fine gray horses.

In March 1908 the papers feasted on reports of Ellen Vanderbilt packing everything she owned, even the dogs and little William Henry's toys, in stable carts outside their Newport estate, Oakland Farm, and heading off to her brother's house in Tuxedo Park, New York. Alfred was still hiding out in England, avoiding the wagging tongues of Newport and New York, driving his coach, *Venture*, between London and Brighton. Their divorce was granted in May 1908, with Alfred found legally at fault. On the *Lusitania*, unsurprisingly, Alfred was accompanied by a different valet.

The frenzy of publicity didn't touch only Alfred. Agnes's husband, Don Antonio, resigned his Washington post in shame after their separation and sued Agnes for divorce in the summer of 1908. The courts granted it to him handily, which meant that, legally, the fault was hers. Mr. Ruiz then, instead of slinking off into obscurity, installed himself in the Waldorf Astoria, and a whisper campaign began against Agnes Ruiz throughout New York society. She was already isolated, but now she was even being closed out of the horsing circles she loved, the ones that had brought her together with Alfred in the first place, and she couldn't avoid notice wherever she went. Alfred packed Agnes with him off to London, a city to which he often traveled to oversee his coaching interests and pursuits and to run riot with horses in the countryside with his coaching friends.

But tastes change. On June 10, 1909, the *New York Times* reported that Agnes Ruiz, "the former actress," whose name was mentioned in connection with Alfred's divorce, had been found shot to death in bed in her home on Grosvenor Street the month before. As if her mode of death weren't shocking enough, the papers reported that the shot had been delivered "evidently by her own hand." She had been secluded in London, her isolation deepening, "practically her only caller being Mr. Vanderbilt," the papers said, "and at the inquest it developed that she had become depressed when the visits ceased." On the day her suicide hit the news, Alfred participated in a meet of the Coaching Club, "driving his famous team of grays," but he had been spending less time in his horsey circuits in the preceding months. Perhaps he was avoiding Agnes Ruiz. In any event, if Alfred's vast fortune hadn't been enough to guarantee the breathless attention of the public, the spectacular implosion and sordid end of his marriage and his extramarital affair sealed the deal.

Two and a half years later, Alfred remarried in England, this time to Margaret Emerson McKim. His ex-wife, Ellen Vanderbilt, still moved in their same social circles, passing the holidays in Newport at her estate, Harborview, which had belonged to her mother, together with their son William Henry, but also spending part of each week in her apartment in New York, at the Ritz-Carlton. Alfred's new wife was herself a wealthy divorcée, an heiress whose marriage to the former surgeon on her father's yacht had also ended in a haze of scandal. She and Alfred had two children together, Alfred Junior and George Washington III, and as the *Lusitania* drew near the coast of Ireland, slowing its speed and groping forward in the heavy morning fog, she was back in New York with them.

By the time of this voyage, Alfred was inured to publicity and attention. Everyone on board, and certainly everyone in first class with him, would have read about his divorce and remarriage. Eyes would have followed Alfred as he strolled the decks, affecting not to notice. People with the remotest claim of acquaintanceship would have found an excuse to chat him up. Anonymity would not have been available to Alfred. Perhaps it never had been.

The R.M.S. *Lusitania* was a very fine ocean liner, to be sure, but not the finest Alfred had ever seen. As on most Cunarders, the first-, second-, and third-class passengers were all separated from each other completely, lest any untoward mixing of the classes occur. The Cunard and White Star ocean liner companies competed for the prestige of transatlantic passengers like Alfred G. Vanderbilt, who had booked himself two rooms complete with a private bath and another nearby room for Ronald Denyer, his current valet. For comparison, first-class passenger George Kessler's cabin, on A Deck, had cost him $380. Alfred's small suite of rooms was on the more sumptuous B Deck, so we can expect his ticket to have cost appreciably more.

Rich guests expected rich accommodations, and the *Lusitania* did not disappoint. The grandest space on the ship was the first-class dining saloon. It was designed to maximize the opportunity for fashion, display, and intrigue, and stood two decks high, with seating arranged around an open circular well topped by a twenty-nine-foot dome decorated with frescoes. The saloon was furnished in a neoclassical faux–Louis XVI style, with white and gilt mahogany walls, and the cupola overhead supported by soaring Corinthian columns. Only one detail set this space apart from the most well-appointed hotel or restaurant of the day: all the furniture was bolted to the floor.

First-class passengers also enjoyed access to the boat deck for promenading and could while away a week's voyage across the Atlantic between a lounge, a reading and writing room, a smoking room, and a veranda café that could be opened up to permit dining al fresco in the soft sea breeze. (The fact that a journey across the North Atlantic was almost always too cold or inclement for passengers to enjoy dining al fresco didn't stop the company from advertising its uniqueness.) Each public room in first class was done up in a different historical style. The lounge, for example, was Georgian, decorated in mahogany, greens and yellows, and crowned with a monumental green marble fireplace. The library was a symphony in gray and rose, with Rose du Barry silk curtains, a nod to Louis XV. The smoking room was Queen Anne style, paneled in Italian walnut with red upholstery. A grand stairway linked the six decks of passenger rooms, opening off spacious hallways, and for those whose hobble skirts didn't allow for so many steps, passengers could avail themselves of two different elevators.

The real moneymaker for Cunard and White Star, however, was third class, as the grand ocean liners ferried successive waves of immigrants from Europe to North America. If steerage was often undersubscribed on the passage to Liverpool, the fares in the other direction, to New York, more than made up for it. The *Lusitania* was especially popular for immigrants to North America, as her steerage accommodation was considered an improvement over most other options available. Third class typically consisted of large spaces where hundreds of people shared open berths, with a small portion of outdoor deck space for fresh air, but on the *Lusitania*, it was toward the front of the ship, and boasted a seventy-nine-foot-long dining room on the saloon deck, with a smoking room and a ladies' room on the shelter deck. Meals in third class were held at long communal tables outfitted with swivel chairs, in two sittings, and steerage passengers also had access to a piano, for raucous singing and dancing parties. Instead of the open berths usually found on ocean liners at the time, the *Lusitania*'s steerage boasted two-, four-, six-, and eight-berth cabins, offering more privacy for families traveling together. A family of five traveling third class on *Lusitania*'s final voyage paid $122.50 for their fare, so the steady ferrying of immigrants was quite profitable for the Cunard and White Star liners.

The R.M.S. *Lusitania* didn't impress Alfred, though. He had traveled on the R.M.S. *Olympic*, one of the White Star line sibling ships to the *Titanic*. The sinking of the *Titanic* only three years before had shocked every level of American society, but members of the Vanderbilt set had felt the loss with special keenness. The scale of the tragedy beggared the imagination, for one thing. More than fifteen hundred people had died on the maiden voyage of a ship that was meant to be the very pinnacle of maritime technology and sophistication, and widely believed to be unsinkable. But the R.M.S. *Titanic* commanded the world's attention also because of the fame of the passengers traveling on board. Among those lost were Isidor Straus, the owner of Macy's department store, and his wife, Ida, as well as New York industrialist Benjamin Guggenheim, who was only ten years older than Alfred. And the *Titanic* took John Jacob Astor IV, who had been—along with Alfred—one of the wealthiest men in the world.

"Jack" Astor was only a few classes ahead of Alfred at St. Paul's, though he had gone on to Harvard instead of Yale. At the time of his death, Jack was traveling with his second wife, Madeleine Force Astor. He and Alfred divorced their first wives within a year of each other and remarried around the same time, but Jack's wife was only eighteen years old, which had set some tongues wagging and put the press on high alert. Jack and Madeleine had decamped to Europe on an extended honeymoon to dodge the attention and were taking the *Titanic* home to New York after the worst of the furor had died down. Madeleine, at least, had been saved.

After the *Titanic* sank, all the ocean liners plying the transatlantic route reevaluated their safety equipment and practices. Before the *Titanic*'s loss, it was common practice on ocean liners not to carry enough lifeboats for everyone on board. The thinking was that the liners would capsize only in shipping lanes, where help was always close by. And in any event, no one expected an ocean liner to sink. Regardless, the *Lusitania* was equipped with a further six wooden lifeboats. Despite the upgrade, the pall of the *Titanic* fell heavy on the passengers of the *Lusitania*, and in response to the disquiet circulating on board following the torpedo warning, several of them urged the captain, William Thomas Turner, to run practice drills so that everyone would know which lifeboat they should head for in the event of an emergency. Turner, who'd stepped in on this voyage to replace the *Lusitania*'s previous captain, Daniel Dow, who had collapsed from nervous exhaustion brought about by piloting a civilian ship in a war zone, didn't think drills were necessary.

George A. Kessler, a friend of Alfred Vanderbilt's from New York, knew about the warning the Germans had run in the newspapers the day of their departure, as did everyone on board. On the afternoon of May 7, he idled with Captain Turner, smoking and chatting, gossiping about the torpedo scare. "Neither of us regarded it with any moment," Kessler said later of the German warning. The captain explained that they would slow to about eighteen knots until they reached the war zone, a radius of five hundred miles out to sea from Liverpool, and at that point, they would go full steam ahead, which should put their speed ahead of that of any torpedoes. Kessler smirked to himself when he heard this tidbit, as it gave him the inside advantage on the daily betting pool among the passengers over how many miles the ship had covered the previous day. He hurried to put down a hundred dollars on his guess, and was pleased as punch when he won.

About the same time that George Kessler was collecting his winnings on May 7, Kapitänleutnant Walther Schwieger of the Imperial German Navy ordered his submarine *Unterseeboat-20* to the surface of the water off the southern coast of Ireland, near Fastnet Rock. Schwieger was thirty-two years old, a steel-eyed twelve-year veteran of the German Navy who had been piloting U-boats since 1911. The morning fog had complicated his mission, which was to form part of a German blockade of the British coast in retaliation for the British blockade of the North Sea. As of February 1915, Germany had declared any vessel within the zone of the blockade between Ireland and France a legitimate target, even a passenger ocean liner. Before February, the rules of war stated that a U-boat should warn the crew of any ship before an imminent attack or sinking. But now, warnings were no longer required.

The *Lusitania* was in fact officially listed as an auxiliary ship of war, and her manifest on this voyage stated that her cargo included more than 4 million rounds of rifle cartridges, 1,250 empty shell casings, and 18 cases of fuses. Not that Schwieger knew this, but he had his orders, and those orders were to maintain the German blockade in the waters south of Ireland through which all shipping had to pass to reach the English Channel. Trolling around in the fog had depleted U-20's fuel reserves, and she had only three torpedoes left in her arsenal. Schwieger was almost ready to order the submarine to return to port.

The fog finally burned away by around ten in the morning, and the *Lusitania* picked up speed, back to eighteen knots, gliding easily over a glasslike sea. They would be in Liverpool in no time.

U-20 broke the surface at around 12:45, fresh sunlight glinting on the water pouring off the sides of her deck. At around 1:20, Schwieger was summoned to the conning tower, the superstructure of a submarine that contains the periscope. Over the horizon, the submarine crew had spotted what at first seemed to be several ships grouped together, but presently the grouping resolved into the four funnels and two masts of a grand ocean liner plowing proudly through the zone of war. Though the funnels had been painted a duller black than their usual eye-catching red, and though the ship flew no flag, the profile of the R.M.S. *Lusitania* was unmistakable.

At 1:25, Schwieger ordered U-20 to submerge to periscope depth, about eleven meters, and set a course to intercept the ocean liner. The submarine, which was capable of traveling at about nine knots, crept slowly toward her prey, drawing nearer to the oblivious ship. When both vessels were only about two miles apart, the *Lusitania* shifted course, and Schwieger was disappointed, certain that his quarry would escape. But then she changed course again, fortuitously, bringing herself onto an irreversible collision course with destiny.

On board, most of the first-class passengers, probably including Alfred, were enjoying luncheon in the grand dining saloon. The meals in first class were typically long, drawn-out affairs. One first-class menu from the *Lusitania* in 1911 lists such elegant offerings as oysters on the half shell, consommé Renaissance, halibut in sauce Orléans, broiled sea bass, veal cutlets in tomato sauce, noisettes de pré-salé, and celery-fed duckling. The dining

The statue of the Commodore, which he himself commissioned,
still stands today at Grand Central Terminal.

The Castello Plan, a map of New Amsterdam, circa 1660

Cornelius Vanderbilt, "The Commodore"

William H. Vanderbilt

Cornelius Jeremiah,
or "Cornie," the Commodore's
namesake

William Henry Vanderbilt,
known as "Billy," the oldest son
of the Commodore

Cornelius II, the son of
Billy and Maria Louisa Kissam

William Kissam Vanderbilt,
or "Willie," his brother

The Breakers in Newport, Rhode Island, built by Cornelius II and his wife, Alice

Alva Vanderbilt in costume for her famous ball,
dressed as a Venetian princess

660 Fifth Avenue, the "Petit Chateau," where Alva
and Willie hosted many of their grandest parties

Caroline Astor, the doyenne of
Gilded Age New York society

An 1895 magazine issue featuring
"The Late Ward McAllister"

Miss Kate Fearing Strong wore a costume
made from real cats to Alva's costume ball.

A young Consuelo Vanderbilt

One of the only known images from Consuelo's wedding day

Consuelo, the Duke, and their children,
as painted by John Singer Sargent, 1905

Alva Belmont in her later years

The New York Times.

VOL. LXIV...NO. 20,921. ..... NEW YORK, SATURDAY, MAY 8, 1915.—TWENTY-FOUR PAGES. ONE CENT

LUSITANIA SUNK BY A SUBMARINE, PROBABLY 1,260 DEAD; TWICE TORPEDOED OFF IRISH COAST; SINKS IN 15 MINUTES; CAPT. TURNER SAVED, FROHMAN AND VANDERBILT MISSING; WASHINGTON BELIEVES THAT A GRAVE CRISIS IS AT HAND

SHOCKS THE PRESIDENT

Washington Deeply Stirred by the Loss of American Lives.

BULLETINS AT WHITE HOUSE

Wilson Reads Them Closely, but Is Silent on the Nation's Course.

HINTS OF CONGRESS CALL

Loss of Lusitania Recalls Firm Tone of Our First Warning to Germany.

CAPITAL FULL OF RUMORS

Reports That Liner Was to Be Sunk Were Heard Before Actual News Came.

SOME DEAD TAKEN ASHORE

Several Hundred Survivors at Queenstown and Kinsale.

STEWARD TELLS OF DISASTER

One Torpedo Crashes Into the Doomed Liner's Bow, Another Into the Engine Room.

SHIP LISTS OVER TO PORT

Makes It Impossible to Lower Many Boats, So Hundreds Must Have Gone Down.

ATTACKED IN BROAD DAY

Passengers at Luncheon—Warning Had Been Given by Germans Before the Ship Left New York.

Only 650 Were Saved, Few Cabin Passengers

The Lost Cunard Steamship Lusitania
X Where the First Torpedo Struck.   XX Where the Second Torpedo Struck

The sinking of the *Lusitania* made headlines all over the world.

Alfred Gwynne Vanderbilt
on the *S.S. Olympic*

Harold Vanderbilt defended
the America's Cup three times.

Gloria and Thelma,
the "Marvelous Morgans"

Reggie with Gloria Morgan
before their marriage

Reggie with his baby daughter Gloria

Gloria with her aunt, Gertrude Vanderbilt Whitney,
during the time of the trial

Gloria returning to her mother's apartment,
escorted by her chauffeur and a bodyguard

Gloria as photographed by Horst P. Horst in 1966

Gloria out on the town with Truman, attending the
New York premiere of *Caligula*

Gloria with her husband, Wyatt Emory Cooper,
attending the Black and White Ball in 1966

Truman Capote as painted by Gloria

Gloria in her studio. Art was a passion and career that brought her great joy.

Gloria with Carter and me at Studio 54 in 1978 for a party
celebrating the success of her line of jeans

The Vanderbilt mausoleum in New Dorp, Staten Island, New York

room would have been busy with the sounds of talk and laughter, clinking cutlery and glassware, excited murmurings of passengers knowing they were within a day's journey from Liverpool. Shipboard flirtations would have acquired a special urgency, as time was growing short. Everyone knew they were steaming through the war zone, everyone wondering with excitement or anxiety about the torpedo warning.

The afternoon was sunny and mild, and some passengers would have risen from lunch to stroll the decks, enjoying a smoke in the fresh air and scanning the horizon for other ships, or for a glimpse of Fastnet Rock. One of those was George Kessler, who was idling on the upper deck, staring out over the sea. The *Lusitania* was still about 380 miles from Liverpool, running at eighteen knots. The fresh breeze would have felt cool on George's face, and he would have had to squint against the sun glinting off the smooth surface of the ocean.

At 2:10 p.m., stalking the *Lusitania* from a distance of two miles, Kapitänleutnant Schwieger ordered a single gyroscopic torpedo fired. The torpedo boomed out from U-20, running at a depth of three meters. Schwieger watched through the periscope as the seconds ticked by while the torpedo bubbled through the water toward its unsuspecting mark.

Kessler, leaning on the railing of the *Lusitania*'s upper deck, later told the papers that he "saw the wash of a torpedo, indicated by a snakelike churn of the surface of the water. It may have been about thirty feet away. And then came a thud."

At the same time, a young lookout on the bow, Leslie Morton, spied the wash of a torpedo streaking along the surface of the water and screamed through a megaphone, "Torpedoes coming on the starboard side!"

Schwieger watched through the periscope as the torpedo slammed into the hull of the *Lusitania*, just behind the bridge, spouting a plume of water and bits of shrapnel into the sky. Almost immediately, a second explosion ripped through her, rocketing debris high overhead. Schwieger wrote in his wartime diary that "an extraordinarily heavy detonation followed, with a very large cloud of smoke (far above the front funnel). A second explosion must have followed that of the torpedo (boiler or coal or powder?)"

The boom of the second explosion—later erroneously reported to have been a second torpedo, but more likely the ignition of the boiler, as only one torpedo was fired—ripped through the riveted metal of the *Lusitania*. Everyone in the first-class dining saloon screamed and rushed outside to the deck. The passengers crowded together in a panic, shouting, demanding to know what had happened. Crew leapt to their stations to lower the lifeboats— and then things began to happen very quickly.

The *Lusitania* groaned slowly to a halt as an immediate SOS beeped out over the wireless. The liner's position was given as ten miles south of Old Head of Kinsale. Then, at 2:14, only four minutes after impact, the electrical power on board failed, and the interior of the ship plunged into darkness. Elevators full of passengers stopped short. Bulkhead doors refused to open, trapping many passengers and crew as fifty-two-degree water rose in the starboard hold, then lapped into steerage. By now, the *Lusitania* was leaning at a fifteen-degree angle.

Schwieger watched the aftermath of the impact from a safe distance, noting in his diary, "The ship stopped immediately and quickly listed sharply to starboard, sinking deeper by the head at the same time. It appeared as if it would capsize in a short time. Great confusion arose on the ship; some of the boats were swung clear and lowered into the water."

The sharp list meant that the lifeboats on the port (or left) side were useless, as they couldn't be lowered; if they had been, they would have landed on top of passengers on the lower decks. Similarly, many of the lifeboats on the starboard side were useless as well, swinging too far out to be accessible as the deck tilted away under the passengers' feet. A few lifeboats dropped successfully, but the pandemonium on board meant some of them plunged into the sea and capsized on impact; or were released from too high up; or went into the sea with only a few people on board; or went into the sea perfectly but without the boat plug, thus instantly filling with water. Twenty-six of the new lifeboats added to the *Lusitania* after the *Titanic* disaster were never deployed at all; they were collapsible, made of hollow wooden bottoms and canvas sides that required assembly before use, assembly there was no time for. There was no time for anything.

Schwieger was still watching through the periscope of U-20 as the *Lusitania* settled, the surface of the ocean water lapping inexorably closer to the starboard deck. "Many people must have lost their heads," he speculated in his diary. "[S]everal [life]boats loaded with people rushed downward, struck the water bow or stern first and filled at once. . . . The ship blew off steam; at the bow the name *Lusitania* in golden letters was visible. The funnels were painted black; stern flag [was] not in place. It was running 20 nautical miles. Since it seemed as if the steamer could only remain above water for a short time, [I] went to 24 m[eters] and ran toward the Sea. Nor could I have fired a second torpedo into this swarm of people who were trying to save themselves."

As U-20 disappeared into the depths, chaos reigned on board the grand ocean liner. Dr. Owen Kenan of Wilmington, North Carolina, trying to elbow his way onto a lifeboat, spied Alfred Vanderbilt leaning against a gateway door.

"They've got us now!" Alfred shouted at him. He was wearing a large overcoat with a lifebelt buckled around the outside. Nearby, theatrical producer Charles Frohman stood passing out lifebelts, saying, "Why should we fear death? It is the greatest adventure man can have!"

After he was saved, Oliver O. Bernard, a scenic artist at Covent Garden, told the *New York Times* that he last saw Alfred Vanderbilt standing at the port entrance to the grand saloon. "He stood there the personification of sportsmanlike coolness," Bernard said. "In his right hand was grasped what looked to me like a large purple leather jewel case. It may have belonged to Lady Mackworth, as Mr. Vanderbilt had been much in company of the Thomas party during the trip, and evidently had volunteered to do Lady Mackworth the service of saving her gems for her. Mr. Vanderbilt was absolutely unperturbed. In my eyes, he was the figure of a gentleman waiting unconcernedly for a train. He had on a dark striped suit, and was without cap or other head covering."

If it's true that Alfred had been charged with safeguarding Lady Mackworth's jewels—unlikely, given the speed at which the sinking occurred, but who knows how quickly a motivated lady can retrieve her valuables after lunch—he unfortunately failed in this charge. Lady Mackworth and her father both went into the water when the *Lusitania* went down. Both of them were stranded in lifeboats for three hours before being rescued, and she was still recovering from shock and exposure on May 10. Her father, David Alfred Thomas, told the papers that he had a relatively easy escape, all things considered: a lifeboat was being lowered on the starboard side when an officer ordered him to take one of the empty seats. The boat got away without mishap and was one of the first to be picked up by rescuers a few hours later. The man ostensibly in possession of Thomas's daughter's jewelry, however, was not so lucky.

Thomas Slidell, Alfred's friend from the Knickerbocker Club, spotted him moments before he himself abandoned the ship. "He was standing with a lifebelt in his hand," Slidell told the papers after his own rescue. "A woman came up to him, and I saw him place the belt around the woman. He had none for himself, and I know that he could not swim."

Slidell, too, remembered the afternoon in 1907 that they had spent together on Alfred's yacht in New York Harbor. "Only the day before we had been talking of a day and a dawn some years ago when we went down the bay at New York in his yacht and waited to welcome and dip our flag to the *Lusitania* on her maiden voyage," Slidell marveled. "We saw the first and last of her."

Being Alfred's friend, Slidell could be expected to offer a heroic account of Alfred's final moments, just as Bernard, a stranger, might be expected to offer an account of Alfred's end that was tinged with a hint of scandal. But of the two versions of Alfred's death, Slidell's has some corroboration. Norman Ratcliffe, an Englishman traveling on the *Lusitania* as the last leg of a long return voyage from Japan, was rescued from the ocean after clinging to a floating box for three hours with one of the ship stewards. The steward told him that he had seen Alfred G. Vanderbilt on deck, after the ship was hit, wearing a life belt, which he took off and gave to a passing woman who was "trembling with fear of the fate she expected to meet." The steward told Ratcliffe that Alfred turned back as if to look for another lifebelt, but then disappeared.

In one version of Alfred's heroic last act, the woman he gives his lifebelt to is carrying a baby, though that assertion has proved difficult to support. Some think the beneficiary of Alfred's largesse might have been second-class passenger Alice Middleton, perhaps one of the overbooked second-class members who had been put into first class due to lack of space. She was twenty-five years old, British, and heading home after living in Seattle for several years. Alice Middleton survived, but no record exists of her confirming the story.

The *Lusitania* sank in only eighteen minutes, its bow disappearing under the soft afternoon waves, its stern groaning upward until the propellers emerged dripping from the ocean, then heaving down into the depths, taking more than 1,100 people with it. Of the 139 U.S. citizens traveling on board, 129 were lost, including Alfred Gwynne Vanderbilt.

The outcry was swift and immediate. The *Lusitania* was a British vessel, bound for Britain, and so public feeling was particularly strong across the British Empire. Debate raged over the legitimacy of targeting a passenger ocean liner full of noncombatants, including women and children, which nevertheless was classed as an auxiliary cruiser and was carrying munitions. Germany claimed that it had issued a warning to all vessels flying a British flag not to travel in the zone of war, and that the classification of the vessel and the cargo meant the sinking was legitimate. But the tremendous loss of life, and the failure of U-20 to give passengers an opportunity to abandon the ship before it sank her, caused widespread outrage in Britain and the United States. President Woodrow Wilson found himself under increasing pressure to declare war. Though two years would pass before the United States did officially join the war against Germany, its entry was partly in response to the resumption of unrestricted submarine warfare in the waters around Great Britain. "Remember the *Lusitania*" was used as a rallying cry, printed on posters in the United States and Great Britain to encourage men to enlist.

The dawn of the morning after the *Lusitania*'s sinking, newspaper headlines blared in rage and horror about the attack in broad daylight, with no warning, and Alfred Vanderbilt's name as often as not appeared before the lede. The wealthy playboy, head of the richest family in America, whose life up to that point had been remarkable primarily for his passion for horses and the scandalous nature of his private life, beamed the harsh light of

his fame on international affairs through the astonishing circumstances of his death. Coming so soon on the heels of the *Titanic*,
the loss of the *Lusitania* staggered the American and British public not only for the number of lives lost, but for the fame of some
of those lives, Alfred's chief among them. No hand-wringing appeared in the press about the last moments of the cook whose job
it was to make the beef consommé on the *Lusitania*. But Alfred
Vanderbilt, rendered untouchable up to that point by his wealth
and influence—wealth and influence that began waterborne, on
ferries trolling up and down New York Harbor three generations
earlier—went down with the ship. When he did, the eyes and
outrage of the world went with him.

Alfred's fame never sat easily with him, not in the way that it
had with other members of the Vanderbilt family. He didn't deploy the press to his own purposes like the Commodore or Alva.
But, in a way, the fame and attention that followed him in life and
in his death meant that the impact of the *Lusitania*'s loss was felt
even more keenly than it otherwise would have been. The private
Alfred was loved by his family, by his gray horses, and by Agnes
Ruiz, but the public Alfred was loved by enough people that they
would not stand for his loss. When the water closed over his lips
and the last bubble escaped his nose, Alfred Vanderbilt could not
have known that his death would play a part in a remaking of the
world.

Standing in a Cold Shower, Tearing Up
Hundred-Thousand-Dollar Bills

September 15, 1934

If you smoke on a sailboat, flip your ashes or discard your ciga-
rette on the side the sail is on, so the wind won't blow sparks or
ashes or butts back into the boat.

—Amy Vanderbilt's Complete Book of Etiquette,
Part II: "Dress and Manners"

No wind. In September, off the coast of Newport, Rhode Island. It didn't seem possible.

The ten thousand spectators in more than 750 motor yachts, steamers, battleships, and all manner of pleasure craft couldn't believe it. Nor could the newspapermen jotting notes aboard a Coast Guard cutter tooling along in the wake of the sharp-bowed beasts fighting for the highest glory known to international yacht racing: the America's Cup. The newspapermen bent low against the chill, raw day, many of them sporting Block Island swordfish-ermen's caps, prized for their long, eye-shading visors. Not all the spectators knew enough about yacht racing to understand how to tell who was ahead, or which direction the boats were supposed to go, and more than a few evinced confusion when one yacht headed northwest from the starting line while the other tacked off northeast. But they all did know one thing: for a yacht race to happen, you had to have some wind—and there was none.

After all the preparations, all the money, the designs, the bitterly fought trials, building the syndicate—seventeen millionaires coming together to back the American defender, *Rainbow*, ensuring, through means both nautical and social, that *Rainbow* was chosen by the New York Yacht Club as the defender, and not *Yankee*, despite *Yankee*'s superior performance at the trials and the widespread belief that it was the superior yacht. (The New England sailors were still grumbling about this.) The professional crew, the jockeying at the start—all of it, for this, the greatest yacht racing series in the world, to have no wind.

Harold Stirling Vanderbilt, Consuelo's younger brother by eight years, a great-grandson of the Commodore, stood at the helm of the J-class yacht *Rainbow* simmering with frustration. The racing machine under his hands thrummed with thwarted ambition. Its perfect curves, designed by Starling Burgess for maximum speed over the water, were idled by absent wind. The sails slopped in the dead air, as empty as ghosts. The twenty-five men in the crew were as eager to win as Harold was. They had five and a half hours from the starting gun at 11:40 that morning to finish the thirty-nautical-mile race. It was now 1:12 p.m. Their challenger, *Endeavour*, skippered by Sir Thomas Octave Murdoch Sopwith, of Sopwith Camel fame, drifted a mere eight boat lengths behind them.

The silence of a sailing yacht is eerie in the absence of wind. The only sound to be heard on *Rainbow*, other than the murmurings of the crew as they kept an eye on *Endeavour*, was the irritating buzz of the airplanes overhead carrying newsreel crews and, in one instance, a trailing banner advertising a brand of beer as both mellow and refreshing. There was also the constant chugging of spectator boats swarming about the two contenders like seagulls trying to steal from a picnic and the occasional irritated horn blasts from the Coast Guard, keeping the boats from interfering with the race.

"If you don't want to pay a five-hundred-dollar fine," the Coast Guard blared to a cruiser whose flags indicated it carried the vice commodore of the Newport Yacht Club, "get back where you belong and get there quickly!" The cruiser obeyed.

Harold Vanderbilt couldn't allow himself to be distracted. *Endeavour* was widely considered the superior boat. It had an eighty-three-foot waterline to *Rainbow*'s eighty-two, and conventional wisdom held that the longer the waterline, the faster the boat. Before the races began, when asked how *Endeavour* compared to *Rainbow*, Sopwith had drily responded, "How long is a piece of string?" By this, he meant that there was no comparison, as a piece of string can be infinitely long. That's how confident he was in *Endeavour*'s superiority.

Sopwith's professional crew went on strike for higher wages right before the boat's delivery across the Atlantic, so he fired them, and hired a mix of professional and amateur sailors at the last minute. Usually, America's Cup yacht owners used professional skippers as well, but Tom Sopwith was owner and skipper both, with a solid track record racing twelve-meter yachts as well as designing airplanes. Harold Vanderbilt was convinced he was the superior sailor, though, with his lifelong thirst for speed and relentless drive to compete. If only there were a breath of wind.

Harold could already congratulate himself on a far better start than Sopwith's. The trick in any yacht race is to cross the starting line at top speed at the very moment the race begins and to head in the most efficient direction according to wind and tide. The starting line is set between a committee boat, with officials keeping time and watching for any illegal maneuvers, and a mark,

usually a government buoy like a gong or a bell. Timing the boat
speed, distance, wind, and tide for an optimal start is such a vital
and complex task that it can sometimes effectively end a race before it even begins.

Harold's timing up to this moment had been impeccable. In
the first race of the Cup, which would be won in the best of seven
races, *Rainbow* had begun her defense at the starting line a full
minute ahead of the challenger. But now, nearly an hour and a half
later, as the wind died, Harold's determination became grim. If
the breeze didn't pick back up, they could lose the ability to steer
the boat. Sailboat rudders require the pressure of moving water
to work. A becalmed boat is an unsteerable one. Harold couldn't
risk making a half-million-dollar, 126-and-a-half-foot racing
machine into little better than a hunk of driftwood. Just before
the wind disappeared, at 1:05, *Rainbow* had tacked to starboard—
"tacking" means moving the bow of the boat across the wind,
one way for a sailboat to change direction—and *Endeavour* immediately followed her. Harold had watched closely as the crew
thrummed about the deck of *Endeavour*, setting up to tack back
to port again. The bow of *Endeavour* moved left, and *Rainbow*
did the same, to keep *Endeavour* behind her, controlled by her
superior position. But it was a fake-out. Whether Sopwith pulled
the maneuver to trick *Rainbow*, or whether he tried to tack but
realized his boat didn't have enough headway to make it, *Endeavour* fell off back to the starboard direction just as the last stirring
breath of wind finally faded into nothingness.

At ten past five in the afternoon, their time was up. *Rainbow*
had held a decisive lead from the beginning, but now she lan-
guished two miles away from the finish line, and the race was
over. The first race of the America's Cup would be rated "no contest," meaning there was no winner. The fact that *Endeavour* was
a half mile behind mattered not one whit. The whole race couldn't

have averaged more than six knots of speed, a fact that would be enraging to a weekend sailor and that would make a yachtsman of Harold's caliber nothing short of apoplectic. Nothing—not Harold's ambition, not his yachting or piloting experience, nor his hunger for competition at the card table or on the automotive race course or in any of the other socially sanctioned avenues for a gentleman of means to exert his relentless desire to win—could make the wind blow.

Harold Vanderbilt wasn't used to not winning. When interviewed later on board his own yacht, the *Vara*, he was tight-jawed. "There's nothing to say," he replied.

Sopwith was more loquacious, remarking to reporters on his waffling about which headsail to use, considering how his choice had affected the start. "With the weight of the wind today, I should say that *Rainbow* was very slightly superior to windward," he conceded. When pressed to share what he thought of Harold as a skipper, he smirked and said, "I don't think. I know he can sail a boat."

That night, the whole of Newport was alight with festivities. Harold's cousin Neily and Neily's wife, Grace, were hosting a party at their home, Beaulieu, and would give a dinner the following night. Harold's brother, William K. Vanderbilt II, had arrived in town on his motor yacht, named the *Alva* for their mother, to watch the festivities. Goelets, Astors, Delanos, and even President Franklin D. Roosevelt himself thronged the parties. The entirety of the American elite in the fields of wealth and government was spending the week in Newport to watch Harold Vanderbilt defend the Auld Mug, as they called the America's Cup.

The United States had never lost the America's Cup, ever, and Harold would be damned if it lost now. He had developed his taste for speed early. While an undergraduate at Harvard, he was arrested for driving too fast and eventually pleaded guilty to the lesser charge of driving without his headlamps. If Willie and Alva thought this would slow their younger son down, they were mistaken. He continued racing while at Harvard Law School and even after joining the New York Central Railroad. In 1930, Harold successfully defended the America's Cup in the J boat *Enterprise*, a feat that landed him on the cover of *Time* magazine.

A strapping man of fifty, Harold looked ten years younger. He was tall, wiry, hard, and browned by the sun, with curly hair and a weathered face. Handsome in a sailorly way, he also had a sailorly reserve and didn't much like giving a window onto his thoughts. He was more comfortable barking curt orders on shipboard, a man of action rather than words, of mathematics and efficiency and planning. Off the water, his talent for calculation gained him fame and notoriety as a bridge player. Harold, who'd also served in the navy during the Great War, deployed military discipline to his expensive pursuits of pleasure.

On *Rainbow*, Harold had instituted specific tasks for every member of the crew, be it sail trim, rigging, or course plotting, and put two men on tactics who were told to confer out of his earshot so he would have no distractions. Harold and his crew already had frayed nerves. He knew of the rumor that *Rainbow* had been chosen over *Yankee* for the defense based on undue influence, but the truth of that matter was that he had beaten *Yankee* in six of the seven last determining races. Still, the *New York Times* reported the strain the yachting season had had on him already. "The amiable Vanderbilt of other seasons has become more taciturn and more likely to show traces of the temperament which he frankly admits," the paper wrote, and also quoted an Englishman about Sopwith: "He is a good sailor, with the gall of the devil, and lucky. And it is time we had a little luck."

Sailors are, as a whole, a superstitious lot. Maybe it had been premature, Harold being gifted a set of plates depicting all the successful Cup defenders when he and his new wife hosted their dinner at Bluebird Cottage the night before the first race. Well, it was too late now. *Rainbow* had work to do.

The year before, Harold had married Gertrude Lewis Conaway, a sporty young sailor from Philadelphia, and she went on to compete alongside him in both his 1934 and 1937 America's Cup campaigns, one of the first women to do so. By the opening race of the 1934 challenge, Gertrude and Harold—formerly considered the "most eligible bachelor" by the press—had been married for exactly a year.

That Sunday, September 16, Gertrude and Harold were received, together with Sopwith and his brain trust, by President Roosevelt on board the Astor yacht. Also present was Governor T. F. Green of Rhode Island. In addition to the finer points of yacht racing, the party discussed the governor's "hard week worrying about mobs of strike rioters and looters," per the *New York Herald Tribune*. Green assured the president that conditions had improved, and he didn't think federal troops would be needed to restore order.

The next morning dawned more to Harold's liking, with twenty-two knots of wind—a fine day for yacht racing. In the minutes before the starting gun, *Rainbow* and *Endeavour* danced for the position, speed, and timing that would allow each to cross the starting line at top speed at exactly the right moment. The start was delayed by fifteen minutes, however, when *Endeavour* plunged into the trough of a heavy swell, causing one of Sopwith's sailors, who was tied in a bosun's (boatswain's) chair at the dizzying top of the mast, struggling to clear a snarled halyard, to be slammed into a spreader and knocked unconscious fifteen stories up in the air. It took some time to lower him safely back to deck and move him out of the way. The ocean that day was heavy with rollers, the wind high enough that the spectator fleet was only a third of Saturday's crowd. The weather on the open water hovered just this side of dangerous, with passing rain squalls needling into the skin and eyes of every sailor and spectator. Just to Harold's liking: fewer spectators meant fewer distractions, and big wind meant fast boats.

The starting flag ran up on the committee boat, and *Rainbow* tore off like a shot, heeling far over in the southeasterly wind and tacking off to starboard. *Endeavour* was close behind, but had to head into the wind a bit to clear the stern of the committee boat, costing herself valuable seconds as *Rainbow* peeled away. *Rainbow*'s bow sliced through the wind exactly as it had been designed to do, lifting high off the peaks of the rollers and crashing into the troughs, flinging explosions of spray along the deck, but *Endeavour* followed her on every tack she made, snapping close at Vanderbilt's heels.

At 11:04, Harold tacked; Sopwith stayed on top of him. Within eleven minutes, *Endeavour*, able to carry a higher point of sail into the wind, was making up the distance between the two boats. But by 11:40, *Rainbow* held a commanding lead. Harold would have been smelling victory on the wind, but there was plenty of race still to fight.

Rainbow came roaring down on the windward mark at 12:59:09, with *Endeavour* only 23 seconds behind. *Rainbow*'s feather-light spinnaker sail ballooned out before the bow, filling in with the breeze. Hot on her heels, Sopwith steered *Endeavour* to try to blanket *Rainbow*, maneuvering so that *Endeavour*'s billowing spinnaker might block *Rainbow*'s wind. But Harold was familiar with this elementary yacht-racing trick. He steered *Rainbow* to the north, past the point where the spinnaker could hold, then doused it and threw up his genoa jib. Harold could feel the wind softening. Following a hunch, he sent *Rainbow* downwind, tacking after the slight breeze to the north, leaving *Endeavour* to wallow

her way back along the route they had just sailed, with the wind
directly on her stern.

But Harold had made a fatal tactical error in judgment.

The breeze softened further, to fourteen knots, but *Endeavour's*
new style of spinnaker cupped perfectly around it, lifting her elegantly back to the finish line. Harold jibed—changing the boat's
direction by bringing the stern across the wind instead of the
bow—and commanded the crew to put the spinnaker up again,
but the pressure on the fragile sail was so great that a rip opened
along its foot. The crew on *Rainbow* grew frantic. Harold's mind
tripped over the necessary calculations, desperate to find the perfect arrangement of sails to harness the fading wind. They were
still a mile out from the finish, but it was all over.

Endeavour's proud blue prow crossed the finish line a half mile
ahead of white-hulled *Rainbow*, a lead of more than two minutes,
and Sopwith waved at the committee boat with elation. The assembled spectator fleet went crazy, blowing horns and cheering,
with someone even producing a set of bagpipes. The strains of
the British national anthem drifted ignominiously over the waters
of the coast of Newport. That night, the bookmakers shifted the
odds to favor the challenger for the first time.

Endeavour had beaten him. Sopwith, the Brit, had beaten him.
Harold might be the first American skipper ever to lose the America's Cup. It would have been a sullen and bitter tow back to the
mooring in Newport for *Rainbow*, with no one feeling the sting of
defeat more keenly than Harold.

"This was one of the grandest races I have ever sailed," Sopwith crowed to the press that night.

Reporters asked Harold to weigh in on what had happened.
"Too many minor accidents," he replied, tight-lipped.

And what was going to be done about the spinnaker problems
they'd had?

"It's being fixed now" was all Harold would say. He allowed himself more time speaking with the press than usual. All right, so he had been beaten. But now he had seen how Sopwith handled *Endeavour* in heavy weather. Harold knew what *Rainbow* could do. At least, he thought he did.

The next race would also be thirty miles long, but in a triangular course, rather than the out-and-back windward/leeward they had fought today. Harold knew he could outsail Sopwith. He just knew it.

Race day three: Sopwith headed out to sea at the helm of *Endeavour*, playing the steering wheel back and forth with a feather-light touch, pipe in his mouth. The pipe might never be forgotten, as it had been clenched in Sopwith's teeth during *Endeavour*'s victory. But the British public worried for the pipe, as it was already half bitten through.

The day was perfect: smooth seas, a breeze at around thirteen knots, nothing like the near gale of the previous day and certainly nothing like the windless doldrums that started it all. The triangular course would take them reaching offshore, then beating to windward toward Point Judith, followed by a short leg back to the finish. Harold had a few ideas for improving their performance. He would have *Rainbow* towed to the starting line, rather than sailing her from Newport and wearing out the crew. He would also change out the main sail for one he had used on *Enterprise*, his triumphant defending boat in 1930.

Once again, *Rainbow* had the start to envy, but *Endeavour* clung hot to her heels. Sopwith steered the challenger through the defender's lee, the side away from the wind, a move that should have been madness. Instead, *Endeavour* slipped into the lead. The pressure from the wind caused the corner of her headsail, the big genoa jib, to rip, but the sail held together. By the time the two yachts approached the first turning mark, *Endeavour* held the slimmest of leads, about sixteen seconds. Harold would have been watching every move of his crew with narrowed eyes. But after the first mark, as the boats beat into the wind, *Endeavour*'s sliver of a lead opened to two fifths of a mile. Harold couldn't understand it. By the mark off Point Judith, *Endeavour* was a full minute and a half ahead. After that last turn, *Rainbow* shook off her frustration and started screaming for the finish, picking up speed and gaining forty seconds on her elapsed time. The racing machine under Harold's hands knifed through the dark Atlantic water, tossing spray from each dip of the bow. Perfectly tuned, on her fastest point of sail, the defending yacht started to hum, touching 11.1 knots of speed, the fastest time yet clocked in the race for the America's Cup.

It wasn't enough.

The early autumn afternoon exploded with whistles and horns, the flag of the New York Yacht Club committee boat proclaiming the challenger's victory as soon as *Endeavour* crossed the finish line. Harold would have been livid. Not only did the challenger now lead in the standings by two races to zero—something almost unheard of in the America's Cup—but Sopwith had finished the course in only three hours, nine minutes, and one second: a new record.

"Naturally, we are much pleased," Sopwith told the papers later that day. He thought they'd had two of the finest races ever sailed in the series.

The defending skipper refused to be discouraged. Lighter air, Harold decided, was what *Rainbow* really needed. They had been well in the lead on the first no-contest race day. Would Harold be sure of winning if he got up the next morning with merely a light wind stirring? reporters asked.

"I would not be sure," he said, "but I think we would do better." He didn't give the newspapermen much else.

"How did you find the race today?" pressed one reporter.

"About the same as yesterday," Harold answered drily.

The *Hartford Courant* saw through Harold's reserve, however, reporting that he leaned on the rail of his own yacht, *Vara*, in the fading light over Newport Harbor that evening, peering into the settling dusk, trying not to look downhearted, and failing.

September 19 dawned with the promise of the soft wind that Harold had hoped for. If Sopwith won two more races, the Cup would go to Britain. *Rainbow* and *Endeavour* sailed out early to the starting line, set for a starting time of 10:40 a.m., accompanied by a somewhat diminished, but persistent, spectator fleet.

And then they waited.

The sky was heavy with clouds, and the air was perfectly still. No sound could be heard at all, other than the gentle slopping of water against boat hulls and the mournful "groaner" government buoy that defined one end of the starting line. Harold couldn't believe it. The sea was motionless as an oil slick. Ten miles away from shore, butterflies drifted along near the surface of the water, their wings the only movement in the lifeless air.

Rainbow and *Endeavour* both hoisted sails, but there was no wind to catch. The two racing machines couldn't even pace back and forth behind the starting line. They bobbed instead, their sails hanging slack.

At 1:20 p.m., the New York Yacht Club committee boat admitted that there was no way a race could be held that day. A whistle blasted, and they hoisted the flag for postponement. A race of a sort broke out among the spectator fleet, who went tearing off for Newport Harbor. Gentle swells and no breeze make a potent recipe for seasickness, as some of the newspapermen had miserably discovered.

President Roosevelt's holiday aboard the Astor yacht ended in disappointment, as he spent three hours waiting with the rest of the spectator fleet but was then obliged to return to his summer White House at Hyde Park, New York, where he would deal with the ongoing textile strike. It had begun in the South, but while the yachts had battled for supremacy on the East Coast, the strike had caught fire and spread through the mid-Atlantic and into New England and was acquiring national urgency. For Harold's part, the postponement meant that he was back in port in time to play a game of tennis.

The next race, the following day, was another windward/leeward, thirty miles, out and back. And finally, at long last, Harold had his wind. The breeze was soft, an easy six knots out of the northeast, and the ocean smooth. This would be *Rainbow*'s day. Harold could feel it.

This time, Sopwith beat him to the start by half a boat length, and *Endeavour* quickly pulled three lengths ahead. But Harold was undaunted. The crew hoisted *Rainbow*'s spinnaker, and Harold blanketed *Endeavour* with his sails, stealing her wind. *Rainbow* edged into the lead, but then *Endeavour* unfurled her own massive parachute spinnaker. To Harold's horror, *Endeavour* passed them as quickly as if someone had turned on a motor.

By the time *Endeavour* reached the turning mark, she was running a full six minutes and thirty-nine seconds ahead of *Rainbow*—an eternity in yacht-racing time. After they rounded the mark, Harold stepped away from the helm, out of either frustration, pragmatism, or shame. In his place, he slotted C. Sherman Hoyt, a famous skipper in his own right, whose usual job on board *Rainbow* was managing the headsails. Hoyt took control, and directed all the crew to the lee, or downwind, side of the boat, to increase her degree of heel (how far tipped over in the water the boat is) and make her go faster—a small-boat racing method being brought to bear on a giant international racing yacht.

Rainbow got into the slot and held it. At last, the white-hulled

J-class yacht was humming. She climbed on *Endeavour*. Then she climbed higher. Then she was breathing down *Endeavour*'s neck. *Endeavour* tacked, crossing *Rainbow*'s bow. But *Rainbow* sailed on straight through *Endeavour*'s lee, stealing her wind again and never giving it back. When all was said and done, *Rainbow* sailed in triumph over the finish line.

The two-hundred-boat-strong spectator fleet went wild at the American defender's finish. Air horns, foghorns, flares—all manner of noise burst forth from the decks of the assembled vessels, and news of the finish was beamed immediately by radio all over the world, as far away as Shanghai and Australia. Back on shore, automobiles lined the oceanfront drives of Newport two and three deep, even though the racers weren't visible from land. *Rainbow*, now figured as the underdog, was even cheered by the crew of *Endeavour* as the two magnificent yachts were towed back to Newport Harbor. Harold had triumphed.

Only one detail marred the perfect racing afternoon: The race had been won with Hoyt at the helm. Perhaps that's why, the following day, Harold made a decision that nearly cost sixty-two men their lives.

On race day four, *Endeavour* swept over the finish line just one minute and fifteen seconds behind *Rainbow*, and to the shock of the spectator fleet, *Endeavour* could be seen flying a red signal flag. Snapping in the twelve-knot breeze, this flag was code for the letter *B* and signaled that *Endeavour* wished to file a protest. Such a flag had not been seen in America's Cup racing since 1895, when *Valkyrie III* collided with *Defender*, bringing down her topsail. That protest was sustained, and ended in the race being awarded to *Defender* on the grounds that *Valkyrie* had committed an unforgivable foul. As it happens, *Defender* was co-owned by Willie K. Vanderbilt, Harold's father. The red flag's appearance now suggested that Sopwith believed Harold to have committed a similar foul. It was a shocking allegation.

The fourth race had been thirty nautical miles, in a triangle shape. At the first turning mark, *Endeavour* was in the lead, with *Rainbow* barreling down on the mark twenty-three seconds behind. Both yachts bore off for the second mark, with the wind essentially perpendicular to them, which is a very fast point of sail. At this moment, it was like a horse race, both yachts optimally heading in a straight line to the next mark. *Rainbow* picked up speed. *Endeavour* was within her rights to try to keep the defender from overtaking her, essentially elbowing her off to the side, since it's the responsibility of the overtaking boat not to hit the leading one. But this time, when Sopwith attempted, by minute adjustments to his course, to block *Rainbow* and hold on to his lead, Harold didn't budge. He held his course, aiming for the second mark.

The spectacular yachts drew closer together, and closer—close enough that the crew on *Endeavour* could hear the crew on *Rainbow* screaming, "Luff her, for God's sake, luff her!" But Harold ignored them, refusing to divert *Rainbow.*

The two yachts were on a course to disaster; one of them would have to alter course to avoid a collision. Sopwith had the right of way, but if he carried on his course, as was his right, and Vanderbilt didn't give way, *Endeavour* would plow straight into the middle of *Rainbow*, smashing both yachts to splinters and plunging more than sixty members of the two crews into the deep. At the last possible instant, Sopwith's nerve broke, and he altered course, falling off the wind, which allowed Harold to pull into the lead. (One wonders what befell Sopwith's famous pipe at that moment.)

When *Rainbow* crossed the finish line in triumph, it was clear to Sopwith that the battle of wills as they raced for the second mark had cost him his victory. He had no choice but to lodge a protest, sending shock waves through the sporting world.

Writing from the motor yacht *Vita*, Sopwith appealed to the New York Yacht Club race committee. He complained first of a maneuver at the starting line, in which Harold had arguably been more aggressive than he should have been. Sopwith went on to say, "I further protest against *Rainbow* under Rule 30, Clauses A and B. After rounding the first mark, *Rainbow* was overtaking *Endeavour* to windward. *Endeavour* then luffed, but *Rainbow* did not respond[,] and *Endeavour* was forced to bear away to avoid a very serious collision."

Later, recalling the near miss, Sopwith admitted of Harold, "His nerve is magnificent."

The night of September 23, silence hung over Newport Harbor as the race committee huddled over Rule 30, Paragraph B. The meeting took place on the *Wilhelmina*, the New York Yacht Club's motor yacht, her running lights glowing well after dusk. The committee consisted of an architect, a broker, and a manufacturer, and the *New York Herald Tribune* noted drily that their "brows furrowed in creases that a bear market, a skyscraper in construction or a factory strike probably never produced." The writer would go on to compare Rule 30, Paragraph B, to Woodrow Wilson's Fourteen Points, and the parsing of the rule to be worthy of "Einstein, Long John Silver, and Noah Webster combined." (It's just possible that the *Herald Tribune* reporter didn't take yacht racing as seriously as the NYYC did.)

The race committee acknowledged Sopwith's protest and asked that he clarify exactly when after the alleged incidents he had raised the protest flag.

"I hoisted my protest flag immediately. I had decided to make a protest and at the first opportunity that it could be visible to the race committee," he responded.

The race committee replied that the rules stated that the protest flag must be flown "promptly," and that as two hours had elapsed between the foul and the flag raising, the protest was not legally lodged, and so, would not be heard.

Rage rose hot in the ranks of the British challenger and her skipper. Fine if he lost the protest on a point of sailing, but to not even be heard? To be dismissed on some flimsy technicality? Observers quickly picked sides, with Sopwith partisans saying, "What a pity, that any question should arise to suggest that Vanderbilt took advantage of his rival by a bold move which perhaps violated one of the rules of the sea," and Harold's contingent countering, "What a shame, that Sopwith should fall back on a technicality in an effort to rob *Rainbow* of a well-earned victory." No one made much of the fact that Sopwith wasn't known to act in bad faith or out of pique, or that Harold was a prominent member of the New York Yacht Club. In fact, for several years he'd been its chairman—or, as they called it, commodore.

Sopwith wrote to the NYYC race committee, "Dear Sir: I acknowledge your letter of last evening. I regret to note that your committee refuses to hear *Endeavour*'s protest of yesterday owing to my not having complied with a very trivial technical formality regarding the time my protest flag was flying. Yours truly, T. O. M. Sopwith." In his understatement, anyone who knew Sopwith could only hear anger and frustration.

With the race committee's decision, the contest stood tied, 2 to 2. Journalists eagerly filed their reports, sending 120,000 words a day over wireless telegraph services all around the globe. But a haze of dishonor now hung over the proceedings, one that couldn't be dispelled.

The fifth race was as flawless as any Harold could have designed. All right, so the spinnaker pulled apart like ribbons on the wind, but they jibed and doused it at the perfect moment, ballooning up a replacement and losing almost no time at all. And they nearly lost a man, Ben Bruntwith, who got swept off the deck by the boom on another jibe. He clung wriggling to the topping lift twenty-five feet out in the ocean before the rest of the crew dragged him, wet and coughing, back on board. And a good thing, too. The racing rules of sailing were very clear that a yacht must end the race with the same number of crew on board as at the start.

The wet and somber clouds peeled back, the sun sparkled through, and the wind was a fine fourteen knots with puffs to twenty, just the speed to make *Rainbow* fly under Harold's control. They won, handily, four minutes ahead, with none of this bellyaching from Sopwith about fouls. Harold felt his confidence swell. Three victories now to *Endeavour*'s two. So what if the spectator fleet had fallen from more than 550 vessels at the outset of the races to fewer than 100 now? It was as much due to the wet and chilly weather as to worldwide grumbling about the race committee's refusal to hear Sopwith's case. And his cousins, Neily and George Vanderbilt, were still in attendance, watching from their own yachts. In any event, with one more win, the Cup would be theirs, secure, defended. Harold felt calm, secure, ready.

Onlookers pressed both Sopwith and Harold for their thoughts on the protest drama even after the fifth race was decided. "I am bitterly disappointed with my treatment in Newport," Sopwith confessed that night. He wouldn't go into specifics, but he indicated that he would leave town as soon as the racing was over.

Harold was willing to talk about some aspects of the race, but when asked for his thoughts on the protest controversy, he declared, "I can't say a word about that."

The sixth race arrived, with Harold determined that it should be their last. At the finish, the sky was painted in shades of pale green with opalescent clouds drifting lazily along the horizon.

The sun had finally broken through, warming the shoulders of the yacht crews and spectators, setting the ocean water afire with gold. *Rainbow* was in the lead. Harold had picked up three minutes along the course, after a botched start. *Endeavour* pushed hard, dipping and riding over the swells. Both yachts made straight for the finish line, the blue-hulled British challenger just behind the white-hulled defender. *Rainbow* crossed the line to a siren call of celebration, with a few lackluster toots of air horns from other spectator yachts. If Harold could tell that the sentiments of the onlookers lay with *Endeavour*, he didn't show it.

As they sailed over the finish line, past the New York Yacht Club committee boat, both yachts were flying protest flags in the shrouds.

Everyone agreed that the disagreement happened in the maneuvering just before the start. No one knew who had protested whom first. Later, on *Vara*, Harold refused to discuss it in detail, saying, "I don't know definitely. I am not sure, but it is my impression that I protested first."

Both yachts had been behind the starting line waiting for the signal, maneuvering to be in the best possible position. *Endeavour* had jibed and headed for the line on port tack, with *Rainbow* bearing down on her on starboard. Harold had expected Sopwith to yield, as he had the right of way. But Sopwith, perhaps nursing some resentments, hadn't done so, and Harold had had to luff to avoid a collision, bringing *Rainbow* nearly to a standstill and losing fifty seconds at the start. But as the race unfolded, Sopwith made an error in choosing his sails, and further errors in his tactics. To all observers, it was apparent that Harold was the superior sailor—as he had known all along.

Ultimately, Sopwith withdrew his protest, and *Endeavour* conceded the loss. The America's Cup would stay in America.

"My protest concerned a violation at the start," Sopwith said later. "Inasmuch as I won the start and lost the race fairly, I feel that I should not go along with the protest." His disappointment was obvious as he went on to say that he would never again challenge for the America's Cup.

The British press pointed out that the race was run in waters familiar to the Americans, with a professional crew against the British crew of half professionals, half amateurs. (Of course, Sopwith had fired his professional crew when they'd gone on strike.) The press also singled out Hoyt, the crewmember who steered *Rainbow* to her first victory in the series, for his helmsmanship. "Mr. Hoyt is the backbone of the successful direction of *Rainbow*," the British dispatches claimed, "rather than Mr. Vanderbilt." A correspondent for the *Daily Mail* pulled few punches in the characterization of Sopwith: "He seemed distraught and highly indignant at the treatment he alleged he had received at the hands of Mr. Vanderbilt and the race committee. . . . Mr. Sopwith looked a complete mental wreck and I feel that he was prevented from saying much more only by magnificent self-control."

The same month that Harold S. Vanderbilt defended the America's Cup for the second time in the waters off Newport, Rhode Island governor T. F. Green was ultimately forced to send the National Guard to Saylesville, only forty-five miles away, to put down armed conflict between the strikers and the scab laborers barricaded inside the factory. Governor Green declared martial law in the state on September 11, just four days before the first race was called for lack of wind, following a thirty-six-hour riot in which guards armed with machine guns clashed with strikers who fought back with flower pots, stones, and broken headstones taken from a nearby cemetery. The next day, a picketer was shot to death in nearby Woonsocket while trying to storm a rayon plant. Governor Green minimized the scale of the violence in his meeting with President Roosevelt on the Astor yacht.

Instead, Mr. Roosevelt had enjoyed his vacation and cheered on Harold S. Vanderbilt, the great-grandson of the Commodore, who had made his first fortune plying sailboats in New York Harbor in a never-ending loop between Staten Island and Manhattan, as Harold skippered his million-dollar racing yacht in a hotly contested series of thirty-mile circular races to nowhere. *Rainbow*, the magnificent racing machine, the pinnacle of maritime engineering and Vanderbilt money, would be scuttled by 1940.

Living a Roman à Clef

November 21, 1934

Children are much more realistic than we believe. They can accept all kinds of economies and deprivations if they are told quietly and sympathetically why they are necessary.

—Amy Vanderbilt's Complete Book of Etiquette,
Part VI, "The Family and Social Education of Children"

F. Scott Fitzgerald probably had no idea how deeply the opening lines of his 1925 short story "Rich Boy" would resonate: "Let me tell you about the very rich. They are different from you and me. They possess and enjoy early, and it does something to them, makes them soft where we are hard, and cynical where we are trustful, in a way that, unless you were born rich, it is very difficult to understand." How else are they different? Sometimes the most harrowing, difficult passages of their childhood are dramatized in TV miniseries starring Angela Lansbury, Bette Davis, and Christopher Plummer.

The TV version of *Little Gloria, Happy at Last*, tells the story of my mother, Gloria Vanderbilt, and her sort-of kidnapping and then the ensuing vicious custody battle between her aunt Gertrude Vanderbilt Whitney and her mother, Gloria Morgan Vanderbilt. It is less documentary than parody, despite having racked up some Emmys. The miniseries plays fast and loose with some facts—the *Lusitania* was not still plying the seas in the 1930s, for instance, and it was odd they'd make that mistake, given that she took one of the main characters' brothers down with her— and dispatches a surprising volume of exposition while the actors box-step around a set that looks like a Gatsby-themed costume party. Also, Christopher Plummer is much more handsome and debonair than Reggie Vanderbilt was toward the end of his life.

Pictures of the actual Reggie from the time of his second marriage, which is detailed in the miniseries, show a rather doughy-cheeked good-time boy, aging blurrily. His slightly slanting Vanderbilt eyes recede behind heavy lids; his hair is parted in the middle, in 1920s fashion. Reggie was the baby son of Cornelius Vanderbilt II and Alice of The Breakers; little brother of Alfred, who died on the *Lusitania*; great-grandson of the Commodore. He partied his way through Yale, got kicked out but was allowed to graduate, and enjoyed fast horses and fast cars. Reggie was fortunate to live at a time when rich kids could mow down pedestrians in the street with their automobiles and get away with an apology, as he killed at least two. He once ran over a seven-year-old boy, who fortunately survived. The papers suggested it was the little boy's fault for getting in Reggie's way.

When Christopher Plummer sneaks a nip from his pocket flask in the midst of a glittering party peopled with revelers, we know we are supposed to understand that in a few short years, he will have drunk himself to death. That is, after all, what Reggie Vanderbilt did, and his death arguably laid the groundwork for the first "trial of the century," which would consume the newspapers in the early years of the Depression and leave one small child indelibly marked for the rest of her otherwise very long and notable life. But Christopher Plummer looks nothing like a man about to die from cirrhosis of the liver. If only the real Reggie had been more like Christopher Plummer.

For a very long time, Gloria—often called "Little Gloria" as a child, to distinguish her from her mother, with whom she shared a first name—didn't discuss this period of her life. She was horrified when journalist Barbara Goldsmith published the book *Little Gloria . . . Happy at Last* in 1980, and then, needless to say, not thrilled when it was turned into a television spectacle. When she was ninety-one, I asked my mom why she had never talked about the unique traumas of her childhood with my father, and with my brother and I when we were growing up, and she reflected that "trying to explain my feelings exhausted me, and all that emerged was a brief encapsulation, nothing that got to the heart of the matter. If it was too complicated to lay it out for the man I loved, how could I even begin to translate it for my children?" Also, it was perhaps difficult to reconcile a narrative that is a battle for custody—two women, each wanting legally to take care of her—with the lived reality of emotional abandonment. No one wants to confess to feeling abandoned, afraid, and alone as a child, especially not to one's own children.

Gloria refused to be interviewed for Goldsmith's book and never read it or watched the television version. I knew how much it upset her and, out of allegiance, refused to watch it when it was broadcast as well. A few years later, however, my mother did write her own bestselling and critically acclaimed memoir about her childhood, called *Once Upon a Time*. The custody trial was, after all, a defining—perhaps *the* defining, for a time—experience of her life. We can see a small window into the trial's importance in Gloria's life seven years after it was all over, when a teenage Gloria was living in Los Angeles with her mother, Gloria Morgan Vanderbilt, and her mother's identical twin, Thelma. Her fame—the fame of her name, about which there was nothing to be done, and her fortune, but of the custody case, too—was now burnished by her exquisite youthful beauty and her emergence in society on her own, eager for adventure. When Howard Hughes came calling, at first Gloria Morgan thought he was calling for *her*. She'd been just a teenager herself when her famous heiress daughter was born, and by 1941, she was an elegant international socialite widow only in her mid-thirties, eminently pursuable by powerful men. But it was seventeen-year-old Gloria whom Hughes was after, and she leapt at the chance to date such a powerful and distinguished Hollywood change maker. She dreamed that he would touch her with a magic wand, as she put it, granting her wish to be famous for her talent and vision rather than her name.

Gloria hemmed and hawed over what to wear on their first date, consulting closely with her maid, wanting to be taken for a sophisticate rather than a kid, wanting to be thought as beautiful as her mother. She planned to talk to Hughes about becoming an actress; she wanted to step through the glittering doors that he seemed willing and able to swing open for her. But when she and Hughes were finally alone together on their date, tooling along the coast toward Malibu with the radio playing softly, in that first flush of wanting to feel fully seen by a new lover, what did Gloria want to talk about?

"I tried to tell him about my aunt and my mother," she wrote later, "and how I felt about what happened, but since I didn't really know myself[,] I'd get lost in a maze of confusion and end up saying, 'Oh, I'll tell you another time,' and I'd end up sitting silently on the seat beside him, looking out at the Pacific Ocean rolling by."

So, what happened? We could start with Little Gloria waking up screaming in the dark in the Sherry-Netherland Hotel in New York City, pleading with her nurse, "Don't let me die!" Or we could open with her aunt Gertrude Vanderbilt Whitney, a woman living two almost entirely separate lives: the society grand dame on the one hand, respectable, pearl-laden, bored by the polo matches her late husband so adored; and the downtown art goddess on the other, a sculptor who took whatever lovers she wanted, men or women, and who championed American art at a time when the Metropolitan Museum kept it hidden in the basement. Or we could begin with the "Marvelous Morgans," the glamorous, elegant identical twins Gloria and Thelma Morgan, members of the international jet set before jets were invented. They'd been christened with their "marvelous" moniker by Maury Paul, who reported under the alias "Cholly Knickerbocker" for society gossip columns. At the time, a hungry readership followed the doings of high society as breathlessly as the public today follows the Starbucks runs of pop stars, actors, and athletes. (Maury Paul serves as the voice of exposition in the tacky TV version of this story.) By the first decade of the twentieth century, due in part to the hunger for publicity and the manipulation of the press shown by Alva and her contemporaries, society was being made in part by its reporters.

Everyone in this story wants something. So, we might as well begin back with Reggie, a man who could at one time buy almost anything and who discovered in the winter of 1922 that what he really and truly wanted was his daughter's seventeen-year-old friend Gloria Morgan.

Some women are bred from the beginning to be perfect specimens for men, like prized orchids that are snipped and cultivated to appeal to the collector of rare plants. Maria Mercedes "Gloria" Morgan was just such a specimen. Born in 1904—later, her mother led everyone to believe it was 1905, surmising that if an eighteen-year-old brings excitement in a society marriage market, a seventeen-year-old whips up something close to a frenzy—

in a Swiss hotel to a minor American diplomat father and an aristocratic half-Chilean mother, Gloria and her twin, Thelma, grew up in New York, Berlin, Amsterdam, Brussels, and Cuba, amid a swirl of international society and opulence. They moved constantly, following the fashionable seasons in places like Paris, London, and Biarritz, and spoke five languages before they were teenagers, but they could barely do math. At age sixteen or seventeen, depending on how you count, they moved into their own, unchaperoned apartment in Manhattan, which they called "Chez Nous," and launched themselves on glittering careers as what would today be called "celebutantes." Their cream-white complexions, rich mahogany hair worn in low chignons even before they were fashionable, and glamorous, slightly lisping international accents gave them both an air of romance and exoticism. British portraitist Cecil Beaton memorably noted that "they should have been painted by Sargent, with arrogant heads and affected hands, in white satin with a bowl of white peonies nearby." They even scored bit roles in the movies, appearing as extras behind Marion Davies in *The Young Diana*, in 1922, the same year Reggie and Gloria Morgan would meet.

Things move fast in a fast crowd, and very quickly Thelma ran off and married a man named James Vail "Junior" Converse. When they returned from their honeymoon, they gave a smart dinner in a private room at the Café des Beaux Arts, with good food and beverages provided by a good bootlegger. Gloria Morgan was late arriving at the dinner, having been at a debutante tea at the Plaza and a light dusting of snow on New York City having caused all the cabs to evaporate into thin air. She had to walk to the dinner, a shawl clutched around her cream-white shoulders. When she finally arrived at the gay table, full of noise and drinks and warm light and merriment, a heavyset man with graying temples and lidded eyes introduced himself.

"I'm Reggie Vanderbilt," he said.

Reggie had left his first wife and daughter in 1912. That's why, when the press reported on Mrs. Reginald Vanderbilt watching Alva Belmont lead the suffrage march up Fifth Avenue that same year, it noted that she watched alone. For several years, Reggie lived his life indulgently, showing horses and ignoring his wife and daughter, both named Cathleen, until his wife finally divorced him, uncontested, in 1920. He also gambled, spent, and drank his way through the $7.3 million inheritance he'd received from his father, in addition to half a million dollars that had been left to him by his brother Alfred after the *Lusitania* went down. By the time he cast an appraising eye on "glorious Gloria" of the Marvelous Morgans at Thelma's 1922 dinner party, Reggie was a confirmed alcoholic, and he was broke. The press didn't know this, of course. To them, Reggie was a Vanderbilt, and they took note of his fast cars and his fast horses and his sprawling farm and called him the most eligible bachelor in New York. Gloria Morgan, hothouse flower that she was, believed his public image. He droned on about his horses, and she managed to fake interest long enough to net an invitation to come out to the farm one day to see his favorite, Fortitude. Gloria Morgan was seventeen; Reggie Vanderbilt, forty-two.

In Gloria Vanderbilt's later years, a passage from the 1981 Mary Gordon novel *The Company of Women* acquired special significance for her as she grappled with her feelings about her childhood and the twists and turns of her adult romantic relationships, many of which were, like her mother's with Reggie Vanderbilt, with significantly older men. She referenced the passage repeatedly in her recollections and writings over the last two decades of her life. "I suspect that being fatherless," Gordon writes, "leaves a woman with a taste for the fanatical, having grown unsheltered, having never seen in the familiar flesh the embodiment of the ancient image of authority, a fatherless girl can be satisfied only with the heroic, the desperate, the extreme. A fatherless girl thinks all things possible and nothing safe."

This description certainly applies to Gloria, left fatherless by Reggie's death before she could even remember, but it could easily apply to Gloria Morgan as well. Her own father, Harry Morgan, carried on his diplomatic career in Brussels and, later, Buenos Aires, seeing his children and wife less and less. At one point during the custody trial over his granddaughter, he would be called upon to fill out an affidavit attesting to his daughter's lack of fitness as a mother, and he proved unable to list her birthday. In contrast, here was Reggie, smiling and attentive. He had cars and horses and Sandy Point Farm and family and connections. He had a life, well established, one that would be easy for Gloria Morgan to enter, she could be forgiven for assuming. He seemed to offer all the sophistication and security that Gloria Morgan's life alone risked lacking. Reggie, of course, was also old enough to be her father. Twice during the custody trial, Gloria Morgan would accidentally refer to him as her father, causing her lawyer to gently correct her for the record.

Reggie had left his first marriage when his daughter Cathleen was eight. She was eighteen the winter of 1922, invited to many of the same deb parties and balls as Gloria Morgan, in a season culminating in a ball given by Reggie's mother, Alice, at 2 West Fifty-Eighth Street. Cathleen looked a lot like her father, with the same doughy face, the same hooded Vanderbilt eyes. (Later, she would die of the same disease that took him.) She thirsted for Reggie's attention, and for most of her life, she had been unable to get it. So, it was a happy turn of events for her both when she was befriended by the glamorous and popular Gloria Morgan and when her father began showing glimmers of interest in her company. For several months, the gossip pages took note of the three of them out and about in New York City, Cathleen and Gloria Morgan eating ice cream while Reggie threw back stingers with absinthe.

Reggie and Gloria Morgan finally settled their engagement in the winter of 1923, under the encouraging push of her ambitious mother, Laura Morgan, who had swept into the city to get the deal done. Laura Morgan patterned herself after Napoléon Bonaparte and always slept with a well-underlined biography of the military mastermind by her bed. On January 20, Reggie hosted a costume ball for Cathleen at which Gloria Morgan appeared as Marie Antoinette. On the following afternoon, he broke the news to his daughter that he and Gloria were to be married. It apparently didn't go well. Though Gloria Morgan triumphantly informed the press that Cathleen would be her bridesmaid, when the day of their wedding arrived on March 6 of that year, Cathleen was nowhere to be found. When she herself married the following summer, Reggie and Gloria Morgan weren't invited. Cathleen wouldn't meet her baby half sister until Little Gloria was fifteen years old.

Cathleen wasn't the only Vanderbilt dismayed by Reggie's nuptial plans. His mother, Alice, always a walking contradiction with her extravagant consumption and her Puritanical comportment, worried that Gloria Morgan had "been around." When the latter arranged to be examined by Alice's private physician, who then attested in writing to her intact virginity, Alice's veneer of icy disapproval dissolved completely. In the TV version of this story, Alice is played by Bette Davis, who conveys this moment with magnificent, almost incredulous laughter. The revelation was shared with the press, too, for good measure.

On February 20, 1924, Gloria Morgan gave birth to a baby girl, whom they named Gloria Laura Morgan Vanderbilt.

Reggie was delighted. "It is fantastic how Vanderbilt she looks," he crowed. "See the corners of her eyes, how they turn up?"

Photographs from Little Gloria's early months show Reggie holding her and smiling. In one image, a nine-month-old or so Gloria, in a crisp, white ruffled dress and socks, seems transfixed by Reggie's shiny tie pin. He laughs down at her, a large, fatherly hand holding her securely against his chest.

Reggie would be dead in a matter of months. When Christopher Plummer as Reggie pretends to die, he still looks handsome, though he coughs very hard, so we know what's coming. Reggie, in contrast, hemorrhaged blood so explosively out of his mouth at the moment of his death that when his wife arrived two minutes too late to see him, Alice wouldn't let her in the room. It was painted with Reggie's blood.

After he died, Gloria Morgan was faced with some sobering truths. When Reggie and Gloria Morgan restaged the scene of their proposal for the benefit of Maury Paul, Reggie had been honest with Gloria about the state of his finances. Had he outlived his mother, Alice, he could have counted on another inheritance to squander for a few more years. But he didn't. When he died, he left an estate in tatters, owing money all over town to creditors who had been all too willing to give him notes because of his famous name. In an age when a newspaper cost pennies, he owed $269 to his local newsstand. He owed almost $4,000 to B. Altman booksellers; $712 to a woman who did his laundry; nearly $9,000 to Tiffany and Company. And none of this includes what he owed in back taxes. To cover his debts, his town house in the city, his Sandy Point Farm, all the horses, all the cars, the furniture, the linens, and even a stuffed elephant belonging to the baby had to be auctioned off.

The only value left in his estate, the sole source of cash that profligate and self-indulgent Reggie had been unable to touch, was the $5 million trust fund that Cornelius II, Reggie's father, had established for the benefit of Reggie's children. Baby Gloria would now share equally in this fortune with Reggie's daughter Cathleen, who was twenty-one years old by then. (History does not record how Cathleen might have taken the loss of $2.5 million to a baby half sister she hadn't met, born of her father and her estranged friend, but we can imagine the answer is also "not well.")

Gloria Morgan was left with nothing—well, almost nothing. She did have dower rights over a portion of the proceeds from the sale of her home and all its contents. At the auction, Alice bought up items of special sentimental value, like Reggie's horse show trophies, to keep them from falling into the hands of strangers. She also bought back two portraits, one of the Commodore and another of Billy the Blatherskite, willed by Cornelius II to the head of the House of Vanderbilt. In the days following Reggie's death, Gertrude Vanderbilt Whitney's husband, Harry, dropped off a check for $12,000 to help tide Gloria over—that's about $180,000 now. But in the course of her marriage, Gloria Morgan had learned to live as Reggie had: too well.

Further complicating matters, Gloria Morgan was still, legally speaking—and likely emotionally, too—a child herself. She was only twenty when Reggie died, which meant that she could not serve as her own daughter's legal guardian, and in fact needed a guardian herself. She barely had experience running a household. Most of the day-to-day management of her and Reggie's life had been handled—if you can call it that—by his alcoholic butler, Norton. She herself admitted that she was out of her depth.

It was left to Justice James Aloysius Foley, surrogate of the New York courts, to determine how best to administer the strange arrangement of a minor mother left with nothing of her own, in whose care lay a baby child in sudden possession of $2.5 million.

Gloria Morgan engaged a lawyer, George Wickersham, to file a petition with Surrogate Foley requesting that an allowance be allotted from her daughter's trust to cover the "monthly expenses necessarily incurred for the maintenance and support of said infant" and the home where they were living. These expenses amounted to $4,165—about $60,000 today—every month, and included $925 for servants, plus another $250 for the servants' food. Baby Gloria was now the piggy bank for her entire household, and she couldn't even talk.

When Little Gloria was three weeks old, her grandmother Laura Morgan had moved in with the Vanderbilts to make herself useful and had appointed herself responsible for engaging a nurse to look after the baby's day-to-day needs. Entrusting the care of infants and children completely to nurses and governesses was not unusual at this time and in this social set, in part because of the desire of the American would-be aristocracy to ape the practices they observed in the Old World. Such staff also enabled society figures to maintain their mind-scrambling social schedules. In the spring of 1924, when their baby was only a few months old, Gloria Morgan and Reggie hotfooted it to Europe for three months, leaving her at Sandy Point Farm with "Naney," as Laura Morgan was known, and the nurse. They returned in time for the Newport Horse Show, naturally, and the family spent the summer in Newport, before Gloria Morgan and Reggie zipped back to Europe on the R.M.S. *Mauretania* while Naney Morgan, the nurse, and the baby repaired to the town house on East Seventy-Seventh Street.

The nurse whom Naney Morgan hired for $125 a month, Emma Sullivan Kieslich, was thirty-three years old, pigeon busted and wide hipped, with the narrow-lipped mien of a woman of authority. Her society references could not have been better: trained in Switzerland, she had been engaged by the daughter of President Grover Cleveland for two years. Nurse Kieslich, whom the baby would come to call Dodo, moved into the child's room and, from then on, never left her side. (In the TV miniseries version of this story, Dodo is played by Maureen Stapleton, who was a friend of my mother's. After she agreed to take the role, the two never spoke again.)

Near the end of her life, my mother recalled Dodo with the impressionistic memories of a child. "Sometimes she is a mountain of soft sheep's wool for me to sink into," she wrote. "Other times, a tree rooted so deep in the earth that no thunder, wind, or rain, no storm of day or night, could rip my arms from her." She would come to believe that, as she was born by caesarean section, Dodo's voice was the first she heard in her life. This isn't true—Naney Morgan was present when Little Gloria was born, and Dodo didn't start working for the Vanderbilts until after baby and mother were home from the hospital thirteen days later. But what matters is the feeling. Over the course of her childhood, my mother would come to feel that Dodo was her real mother. Gloria Morgan she would characterize as "a beautiful stranger, glimpsed only fleetingly."

After Reggie's death, with the finances temporarily resolved, and having promised Surrogate Foley that her daughter would eventually be educated in America, Gloria Morgan packed up her baby, her mother, the nurse, and her life and set sail for Europe. She wanted pleasure and freedom and to enjoy being the young and beautiful Widow Vanderbilt, with all the pursuant attention. They would spend baby Gloria's young childhood in constant motion, following the vicissitudes of fashion and Gloria Morgan's love affairs, often as not with the baby and Dodo in one country and Gloria Morgan in another. "I was not bound to any place," my mother would say later, "or any person." She would not return to the United States again for eight years.

Back in New York City, Gertrude Vanderbilt Whitney also wanted something. Three of her brothers and a sister were dead. One of her brothers, Neily, had been disinherited. Her mother,

Alice, the dowager empress of the Vanderbilt family, continued the same iron control she had always exerted, as when she had maneuvered Gertrude into making what was then universally called "a brilliant marriage," to Harry Payne Whitney. He, too, had died, in 1930, leaving Gertrude's financial and social position in New York unassailable. Gertrude embodied a curious contradiction. She was, by any measure, a society leader, a mother and grandmother, wealthy, privileged, maybe even a bit bored by her privilege, possessing all the authority and influence that her money and her prominence in society guaranteed her. But inside that person, behind the composed face, the eyes lidded like Reggie's, under the perfectly cut cream silk blouses and heavy pearls, beat another heart entirely—a tender, rebellious heart. Her TV movie self appears in the guise of Angela Lansbury, with a matronly coiffure unable to outweigh sharp, almost sexual eyes.

"It seemed to me," Gertrude wrote in her journal, "that there were two of me. One figure the sensible middle-aged woman with a family, with ties of the most ordinary and pleasurable kind," though, of course, nothing about her life was ordinary in the way we usually understand that word to mean. "A family whom she loved," she went on, "longed to make happy; a person well dressed, normal, healthy. But someone else was in the background, a restless person, a lonely, selfish, weak person with violent desires and wild dreams of impossible things." Gertrude had the sensitive soul of an artist. Not content merely to consume what others told her she ought to value according to her class prerogatives and wealth, as Vanderbilts had done for generations before her, Gertrude yearned to create, to express, and to change.

By 1931, some of Gertrude's wild dreams had come to fruition. After years working in her downtown sculpture studio, befriending contemporary American artists and championing their work,

Gertrude had realized her ambition of opening her own museum. She had initially offered her considerable collection to the Metropolitan Museum of Art—and been politely rebuffed. She wasn't satisfied with donating art just to see it molder in a basement unappreciated. Instead, she founded the Whitney Museum of American Art, the first collection of its kind, unique at a time when American art was considered the second-rate, discount version of its more accomplished European equivalent. Also, in 1931, her most important public sculpture, a memorial to the women who died in the *Titanic* sinking (from which director James Cameron got Rose's posture of an angel, arms outstretched on the prow of the ship, for his 1997 movie), was unveiled in Washington, DC. But making and championing art wasn't the only avenue for Gertrude's need to express herself.

Gertrude gave voice to some of her secret violent desires and impossible things in a roman à clef entitled *Walking the Dusk*, which she published under the pseudonym "L. J. Webb" in the autumn of 1932. The pseudonym couldn't hide the fact that all the characters moved through a plush, privileged, emotionally vacant world that was identical to Gertrude's own, or that, in many instances, they were clearly modeled on people with whom she was intimately acquainted. Maids and butlers, bathing suits and backgammon, bridge and boredom and marriages drained of passion—it was a shocking book, and also perhaps not a very good one.

"A very depressing lot of people roam the pages of this book," the *New York Times* said in a cursory review of *Walking the Dusk*. "Some of them belong to the class of the idle rich, and others are Bohemians of the more prosperous sort. All of them appear to spend most of their time in the pursuit of pleasure and to get very little fun out of it." A character named Mabel Randolph dies suddenly, a suspected suicide, but her dear friend Diana isn't convinced. Diana stops at nothing to prove that Mabel was murdered. Of course, the murder hides a shocking secret: that Mabel was the lover of rich and powerful society figure Katharine Osmund, who lives on a farm uncannily like Gertrude's own on Long Island. The *Times* dispatched the book by noting that "this is not so much a detective story as a study in morbid sex psychology."

Angela Lansbury, in a caftan with a cigarette holder in her hand, silkily offering to "warm up" a chilly seminude female model in her louche downtown artist's loft, does very little to convey the depth of Gertrude Vanderbilt's complexity. In fact, before Gertrude was married, her most passionate relationship was a three-year one with Esther Hunt, the daughter of the Vanderbilt family's favorite architect, Richard Morris Hunt. One of Gertrude's granddaughters, Flora Irving, would later write that Gertrude was "a true Bohemian. She believed that passion was the guiding nourishing force of life." But much of that passion remained hidden under the surface. Women of her class and position could not afford outward shows of emotion or loss of control. To the public, she had to remain smooth and unflappable— alienated, perhaps, from her own tender, beating heart.

When a sickly eight-year-old Gloria Vanderbilt arrived back in the States in the spring of 1932, Gertrude barely knew her. Gertrude guessed that she had seen her niece only a handful of times in her life. But Naney Morgan, together with Dodo, had been scheming for some time already to get Gloria away from her mother. They disapproved of Gloria Morgan's carefree, gallivanting life. Her twin sister, Thelma, whose first marriage had been a flash in the pan, had become, in Maury Paul's colorful lexicon, the "fast friend" and "favorite dancing partner" of Edward, the Prince of Wales, who collected around himself a cast of fast-living, decadent aristocrats and hangers-on called "the Palace set." (Thelma is also credited with, or blamed for, introducing the prince to Mrs. Wallis Simpson and asking her to "take care of him" while she was away.)

It was in this heady milieu that Gloria Morgan met His Serene Highness Prince Gottfried Hohenlohe-Langenburg, a land-rich, cash-poor European prince. They fell for each other hard and fast, but it would never work, as Hohenlohe was penniless. He owned a palace larger than Buckingham, yet made a salary less than what Gloria Morgan paid Dodo. It was a problem.

Gloria Morgan knew that Surrogate Foley was bound to reduce her allowance from her daughter's trust fund if he thought the money was going to support a second marriage. Little Gloria was already paying for their entire household, plus servants and travel and all of Gloria Morgan's considerable expenses. Why should Little Gloria underwrite a penniless prince, too? Naney Morgan took her suspicion of the prince one step further—deep down, she was afraid that he and Gloria Morgan might be capable of harming the child, just to get their hands on her money. It was a crazy worry, feverish almost, but Naney had in some respects become a professional worrier over the welfare of her granddaughter. Her worry, though born of love, also guaranteed her centrality to the story and placed her in a position of importance in the Vanderbilt world. And Naney Morgan wanted very much to be important.

She and Dodo treated Little Gloria like the American princess she effectively was. Nothing was good enough for their little Vanderbilt, not even the food at the Ritz. Gloria had to be protected at all costs—from what, they weren't sure: bad food, danger, drafts, illness, her mother's indifference. And above all, she must be protected from being spirited away to Germany in the event that her flighty young mother married her broke prince. Buried in the dense thicket of Dodo and Naney's concerns, Gloria grew weak and sickly, like an orchid overwatered, too well pruned, and kept too far from the sun.

When Little Gloria arrived in New York with swollen glands in her neck, the newspapers heralded her arrival, trumpeting her status as the richest child in America. The bright light of publicity shone on Little Gloria as she disembarked from the ocean liner (on board which Naney hadn't allowed her to play with other children) and followed her in the chauffeured car to the Sherry-Netherland Hotel. Barbara Goldsmith also points out in her book that, in addition to arriving in New York City during the depths of the Great Depression, Gloria disembarked a mere seven days after the kidnapping of Charles Lindbergh's namesake baby son from the supposed safety of his own crib. Abduction for ransom had become a moneymaking crime; since 1929, more than two thousand people had been kidnapped in America, resulting in the handing over of millions of dollars in ransom money. "The Lindbergh kidnapping was symbolically perfect for the Depression," argues Goldsmith, "for it demonstrated that an individual—no matter who he was—could not control his own destiny."

While Gloria Morgan set about renting a house on East Seventy-Second Street, Little Gloria was taken to see her pediatrician from infancy, Dr. Oscar Schloss. He inspected her swollen glands, recommended that the child have her tonsils and adenoids removed, and referred her to a specialist. Gloria Morgan decided that the best time for the operation would be that July, so she could enjoy the summer in Europe and Little Gloria would remain behind, spending June and July with her Vanderbilt cousins outside Newport. While these plans unfolded, Dodo and Naney, along with much of the country, hungrily followed the Lindbergh kidnapping in the newspapers.

Dodo was worried over her charge, too. All the newspapers

had identified the hotel where they were staying and had made a point of loudly counting Little Gloria's money, in a day when breadlines stretched around the corner. What if someone were to kidnap Little Gloria? How could they keep her safe? The TV version of this story is ham-fisted in drawing out this theory, between newspapers conveniently folded so that the camera can read the Lindbergh headlines and ample opportunities for Maureen Stapleton as Dodo to worry loudly within Little Gloria's earshot. But just because the movie beats this theory to death doesn't necessarily mean the argument is wrong. The Lindbergh kidnapping seized the imagination of America that year. Special prayer services were held all over the country, in which destitute Americans would beg God for the safe return of Baby Lindbergh. If it could happen to him, a famous and well-loved baby sleeping safe in his crib with his parents downstairs, it could happen to anyone.

Then the worst happened, or almost: an anonymous kidnapping threat against Gloria arrived in the mail. Dodo was frantic, and so was Naney. (Though, a jaundiced historian might wonder if Dodo herself had written it, as a way of proving her point.) The administrator of Gloria's trust, Tom Gilchrist, finally hired some Pinkerton detectives to keep watch over the child and urged Gloria Morgan to delay her departure until August.

She left in April anyway. Who stays in New York City in the summer?

The child's doctors were shocked that her mother had taken off. Gloria was sickly, malnourished, underweight, and racked with anxiety, and she had a perpetually sore throat. The operation couldn't wait. In fact, the doctors agreed it should occur as soon as the child was well enough to handle it.

The Lindbergh baby was found dead, beaten to death and decomposing in a shallow grave in New Jersey on May 12, 1932, around when Gloria Morgan's attorney cabled her to come back to New York for her daughter's operation. She booked a round-trip ticket on the S.S. *Bremen*, leaving for New York on the first of June and returning to Europe on the eighteenth. She got back just in time to take her daughter to the hospital, where the girl stayed six days and then went to the Sherry-Netherland to convalesce. The night of June 17, after Gloria was safely settled in her hotel bed, Gloria Morgan told her daughter she was leaving for Europe again the next day. Then she went out to dinner.

Late that night, after midnight, Gloria Morgan was still out, and Naney called Dr. Schloss in a panic. Something was the matter with the child, and they didn't know what to do; nothing she or Dodo did could help. The child seemed to be in terrible pain. Would he please come immediately? Dr. Schloss hurried to the Sherry-Netherland. When he got to Gloria's bedside, he found a fragile and frail child writhing in agony. In his most soothing voice, he asked her what the trouble was. Gloria clutched her stomach and screamed, "Don't let me die!"

Dr. Schloss was puzzled. He examined the child carefully. Nothing was physically wrong with her, and he suspected her pain was emotional rather than physical. Poor eight-year-old Gloria was clearly terrified, in fear for her life. But why?

Even late in her life, the word comes up again and again in Gloria's account of herself and how she felt as a child: *scared*. In talking about her freedom on that teenage visit to her mother in Los Angeles in 1941, Gloria said, "I was not equipped to handle it, and was scared to death of it, too." In reminiscing about her stilted relationship with her mother during her teens, she mused, "Maybe she was as scared of me as I was of her?" When, on that same LA sojourn, her mother called her up drunk and asked if she had been smoking marijuana, seventeen-year-old Gloria hung up and lay, as she wrote, "alone in the darkness of my room, scared to death." Little Gloria was scared of her mother. She was scared of other people. As she grew older, she was possibly even scared of herself and the lack of control she often felt over her life.

Maybe eight-year-old Gloria had imbibed the atmosphere of dread simmering in Naney and Dodo about the murdered Lindbergh baby. Maybe that dread built upon the already stressful possibility that Gloria Morgan would spirit her away to Germany. Maybe it's just enough to be a child, small and in pain, after a scary operation, with your mother far away and never there and ready to go far away again. Maybe it was all these things bound up together—the wild impermanence, the lack of safety, the loneliness, the pain.

Naney took her worries to Gertrude Vanderbilt Whitney, who visited Little Gloria and was appalled at the state in which she found her niece. The girl was pale, drawn, underweight, and as nervous as a baby fawn. Gertrude consulted the society pediatrician they used for her grandchildren and suggested that, instead of staying on in the city after the tonsillectomy, Gloria come back to her compound at Wheatley Hills and recuperate.

"That's very kind of you, Gertrude," a grateful Gloria Morgan said. Now she wouldn't have to postpone her return to Europe.

Once out on Long Island, in fresh air and sunshine, with stability and with Dodo, and with cousins to play with, Little Gloria began to improve, both physically and emotionally. When her mother returned from her summer in Europe expecting to take Gloria to winter with her in New York City, Gertrude dissuaded her, citing the opinion of her grandchildren's pediatrician. "She can attend Greenvale School with my grandchildren," Gertrude assured her, "and you can visit her."

Everyone agreed it was the right thing. Even Surrogate Foley, who, upon learning that it was Gertrude who was caring for Little Gloria, reduced Gloria Morgan's allowance from her child's trust fund from $48,000 a year to $9,000, with all the child's expenses being disbursed by an attorney. Very quickly, Gloria Morgan realized she had made a fatal error. By surrendering her child, she had surrendered her own financial freedom. It was like Little Gloria didn't even belong to her. "She belonged to the Vanderbilt name, and the Vanderbilt money," Gloria Morgan realized.

She consulted a different attorney, a showbiz lawyer named Nathan Burkan, who started to draw up the papers to have Gloria Morgan declared the sole guardian of her own daughter and the joint guardian of her property. While sitting next to her lawyer in the courthouse in downtown Manhattan on July 3, 1934, assuming that they were close to completing the legal process, she had no idea that the "trial of the century" was about to begin.

Burkan submitted the application, which should have been a routine step the judge would have seen many times before. Instead, a voice from the back of the courtroom broke through, shouting, "I object to the petition!"

Burkan was stunned. "On what grounds?" he demanded.

"On the grounds that Mrs. Vanderbilt is unfit," said the objecting lawyer, Walter Dunnington.

Gloria Morgan was baffled. What could this mean? Who could be alleging that she lacked the moral character to be a mother to her own child?

"I must refuse, Your Honor, to proceed in this case unless I am informed who is bringing the complaint objecting to the guardianship," Burkan insisted.

The judge insisted that Dunnington name his client.

The name was given, and the entire courtroom gasped. It was Little Gloria's grandmother—Gloria Morgan's own mother, Naney Morgan. She had joined forces with Gertrude Vanderbilt

Whitney. They wanted to keep Little Gloria away from her own mother. The trial would electrify the press and dominate their lives that fall.

By September 1934, Gloria was ten and still spending the bulk of her time with her aunt Gertrude. Gloria Morgan begged to have her daughter come visit her in the city.

"I don't want to go," Little Gloria said to Gertrude. "I don't want to see her. I don't feel happy with her."

"Gloria, you will be back by the end of the week."

"Are you sure?" Gloria repeated it over and over and over again, scared.

"Yes, I'm sure," Gertrude promised.

On that visit, Gloria Morgan told her daughter the good news that she had rented a house on Long Island. If the fresh country air was so salutary for her child, then she would move there, and Little Gloria could live with her. During that visit, Gloria Morgan also reprimanded Dodo for keeping a sloppy nursery, pointing to some shredded wheat that had been spilled on the floor for Gloria's puppy. Dodo was enraged that this flighty young woman, who seemingly just wanted her daughter's money, would speak to her in this way. She grabbed a carpet sweeper in a rage and roughly swept up the shredded wheat.

"You'll have to learn a thing or two about neatness, because starting tomorrow you'll be living with me," Gloria Morgan informed the recalcitrant nurse. "She's not going back to Gertrude Whitney."

Later on in that visit, Gloria overheard her mother in confidential discussion with her older sister, Consuelo, who was urging her to get rid of Dodo. Little Gloria panicked. They were going to take away her nurse, the only steady presence she had known for her entire life! When a hysterical Gloria told Dodo what she'd overheard, the nurse hustled her and her puppy out of the house and barked at the chauffeur to drive them straight to Aunt Gertrude's studio in the Village, claiming that the girl was suffering from a sudden onset of illness. She was taken to her aunt's city mansion for the night.

The next morning, Gloria Morgan, with her sister Consuelo, stalked straight to Gertrude Whitney's palace at 871 Fifth Avenue to demand the return of her daughter. They waited in the library with glasses of sherry, and Little Gloria came downstairs to greet them. Dodo was kept out of sight. After a time chatting uncomfortably, Gloria Morgan said, "Gertrude, don't you think Gloria had better go and get her coat on?"

"Oh, yes, Mummy," said Gloria, mindful of how Naney Morgan had instructed her to act—calmly, as if nothing were wrong. "I won't be long. May I be excused?"

Gertrude said she may.

Slowly, deliberately, her puppy in her arms, Gloria left the library where her mother and two aunts were sitting. Her aunt Gertrude's maid met her and silently escorted her into a waiting car.

After an unusually long period of time had elapsed, Gloria Morgan wondered aloud where her daughter was. The girl was probably dawdling, but they had better be going.

Gertrude rose from her seat with what seemed to Gloria Morgan to be a "faint slow smile of triumph." When Angela Lansbury re-creates it, she practically has canary feathers on her lips. "I'm very sorry, Gloria," Gertrude announced. "But Little Gloria is halfway to Westbury by now. I'm not going to let you have her."

That afternoon, Gloria Morgan's attorney served Gertrude with a writ of habeas corpus. The court date was set for September 25, 1934.

At all of ten years old, Gloria was now in the bizarre position of being fought over by two women who did not actually know her or how to love her. Her grandmother Naney Morgan coached her on how to appear affectionate toward Gertrude, whom Gloria certainly admired but also barely knew. Gloria Morgan wanted her daughter, but she also wanted the money. Gertrude no doubt felt she had to protect her niece, but she also wanted to win.

"The Matter of Vanderbilt" began in the New York State Supreme Court on October 1, 1934. The press crushed the cars of the arriving parties, hungry for a glimpse of the publicity-shy Gertrude Vanderbilt Whitney, the publicity-courting glorious Gloria Morgan, and the richest little girl in the world. The miniseries version of their courthouse arrival shows Angela Lansbury, in a sharply elegant hat and mink stole, protectively escorting a young girl in bangs and knee socks through a carefully attired throng of reporters, none as shabby as a Weegee photograph would suggest Depression-era reporters looked.

Dodo was the first witness called. Everyone in this story wants something. What did Dodo want? She wanted to secure the safety of her charge, but also, in a way, of herself. Emma Kieslich's entire self had been subsumed in her role as Gloria's nurse, always with her. In a decade, she had never taken a day off. She hadn't even left Gloria when her own mother died.

Dodo had been saving up for this moment. Years of bitter resentments and disapproval exploded to the surface. Gloria Morgan had despicable friends, all "night life people." Her shiftless brother lived with them in Paris off the largesse of the child's trust fund. Gloria Morgan was out all night and slept into the afternoon every day. And then there were the books.

"What kind of books did you see? You looked at them, didn't you?" the lawyer asked.

"Yes, I looked at them[,] and as I said, I had never seen anything like it."

"I move to strike that out!" Burkan cried.

"They were vile books!" Dodo screamed. It was pornography. Flogging, and nuns, and naked men with women's tongues—left out where the child could easily see them.

Nathan Burkan did his best to suggest that Gloria's antipathy for her mother was Dodo's fault and due to Dodo's judgmental influence. But if Dodo's evidence was hard on Little Gloria's mother's case, the evidence given by Gloria Morgan's French maid, Maria Caillot, was damning. Even though Burkan was able to get her to admit that she was being paid for her testimony, the maid offered something too salacious for the court to let go.

Recalling a trip to Cannes in 1929, Mademoiselle Caillot recounted that Gloria Morgan Vanderbilt called for her breakfast. "Then I served breakfast, and I take her things up to my room, pressing them, and a few minutes afterwards I come back in Mrs. Vanderbilt's room to bring back the clothes in the closet. Then when I came, Mrs. Vanderbilt was in bed reading a paper, and there was Lady Milford Haven beside the bed with her arm around Mrs. Vanderbilt's neck—and kissing her just like a lover."

Chaos broke out in the courtroom. Gloria Morgan stood publicly accused of lesbianism at a time when New York was retreating from having been the open city it was in the 1910s. Homosexual behavior was criminalized, and queer spaces were subject to increasing policing and violence. Seeing this accusation splashed across the newspapers, Little Gloria would discover another fear that would stalk her into adulthood. What if she was like her mother . . . in that way? What would that mean?

The judge cleared the courtroom and determined that he should speak with Little Gloria alone. She arrived at the courthouse all by herself, save for the bodyguards who battled a path clear for her up the courthouse steps. In the privacy of the judge's chambers, with only the lawyers and the court stenographer,

Gloria told the judge that she was afraid of her mother. "I don't like her," she insisted. When the judge asked her why she had sent her mother affectionate postcards over the years, she said, "Well, I had to, because I was afraid of her."

"What are you afraid of?" the judge wanted to know.

"I don't know," said ten-year-old Gloria, in her bangs and her slipping socks, with the exhortations of her aunt and her grandmother ringing in her ears. "I'm just afraid of her.

"In England," she continued, "they hardly ever used to pay any attention to me. They used to go out to parties and things."

"When you grow up you will be able to go out to parties and dances," the judge presciently pointed out.

"She never even kissed me goodnight," said Gloria.

The judge released his opinion on November 21, 1934, granting Gloria's sole custody to her aunt Gertrude Vanderbilt Whitney. Her mother would have visitation on weekends, for a month in the summer, and on Christmas Day.

Gloria Morgan aired her grievances to the press, pointing out that in entrusting the care of her child to nurses and governesses when she was small and to private schools and summer camps when she grew bigger, she'd only done what any mother on Park Avenue would do. Gertrude Whitney herself had done the same with her own children, and was doing that with Gloria now, her mother contended. "But of course, I have very little and Gertrude Whitney has $78 million. And $78 million couldn't possibly be wrong." Except it was all wrong. And the only thing all parties, except the ten-year-old girl at the heart of the matter, agreed on was that Gloria's meddlesome nurse, Dodo, must be fired.

The made-for-TV movie version of Dodo's departure shows a sniffling Maureen Stapleton hugging the child actress playing Gloria, as the little girl screams, "Dodo, please don't go! Dodo!" and striding out of Gertrude Whitney's house with her gray head held high. The vintage car pulls away down a pebble drive, and Little Gloria runs after it while sentimental music swells. As the child wrings her hands in despair, the TV versions of Gertrude and Naney clink glasses of sherry.

"To Little Gloria," Naney declares, beaming. "Happy at last."

The fictional version of this story ends in an anticlimax of semi-hopeful orchestral music as Gloria rides a horse in desultory circles in a verdant field, while a flawlessly made up Gloria Morgan watches her longingly through the window of an elegant chauffeured car. A voice-over before the credits then suggests that when Gloria turned twenty-one, she had Dodo come live with her and gave her a living until her death. That would have been a nice ending, Gloria and Dodo both getting what they wanted. Too bad it isn't the truth.

In 1960, after fifteen years of complete estrangement and a therapy session involving LSD, Gloria reached out to try to rebuild a relationship with her mother. "My heart was pounding as I opened the door to her," she wrote many years later. "But standing there alone in the hall was a stranger: tentative, beautifully dressed, but hesitant, even fearful. Had we passed on the street, I would not have known who she was or given her a second glance."

Gloria Morgan was suffering from hysterical blindness at the time of their meeting, and her daughter mixed her a scotch and soda and lit her cigarette for her. Little Gloria was thirty-six years old by then, a mother herself. She hadn't seen her mother since she was twenty-one. "I took her hand in mine," she remembered, "but she pulled it away to pick up her drink."

"From the day she walked through the door until the day she died, we never discussed the trial or anything about my childhood," Gloria wrote near the end of her life. "Not once."

Between the ages of ten and seventeen, Gloria couldn't see

Dodo, but she did write to her. Then Gertrude finally let her visit Dodo before the fateful trip out to Los Angeles that would change Gloria's life. They fell on each other with relief, pledging never to be apart again. Gloria started to support Dodo monthly and would continue to do so for much of her life. Dodo lived with her in Kansas during her first, tumultuous marriage and came to New York to help out during her second marriage, to conductor Leopold Stokowski, when her first two sons were born. But during her third marriage, to director Sidney Lumet, Gloria distanced herself from Dodo. Sidney was Jewish, and Dodo had made anti-Semitic comments to Gloria.

By 1973, Gloria and the woman she had thought of as her real mother hadn't spoken in more than a decade. One day, a letter arrived for Gloria from Catholic Charities. When she opened it and saw Dodo's name, she flushed with shame and tore the letter up without reading it, tossing the pieces into a fireplace. A week later, another letter arrived, from a doctor announcing that Dodo had died in her sleep at Catholic Charities, alone. That she was not with Dodo when she died remained one of Gloria's bitterest regrets until the end of her own life. Writing in her nineties to her son, she described the regret as a "silent scream of pain."

Everyone in this story wants something.

Money. Attention. Safety. Security.

But most of all, love. The one thing of which, no matter how privileged the surroundings, how polished the chauffeur-driven cars or delicate the crystal sherry glasses, there still never seems to be enough.

Gloria at La Côte Basque

November 28, 1966

Part of our public life is, of course, concerned with what others see when we venture forth from the social security of our homes. Can we pay a call with grace and terminate it within the accepted time without being brusque? Can we go into restaurants, theaters, and other public places so that we fit in in a well-mannered, unobtrusive way? If the circumstances of our lives are such that we are more or less public figures, can we treat the press and the public courteously, without arrogance—and also have a real sense of noblesse oblige?

—*Amy Vanderbilt's Complete Book of Etiquette,*
Part VII, "Your Public Life"

On November 28, 1966, the crowds of gawking onlookers started gathering on Fifth Avenue in the afternoon, shuffling their feet against the biting chill of the Monday after Thanksgiving. "It was not a day like any other day," reported the *New York Times.* "The rain came down and the women poured out—from penthouses, town houses, duplexes and hotels." Word had been circulating in the city for weeks about the party. Everyone knew about it, even the cab drivers picking up passengers at John F. Kennedy Airport. After attending a series of small and intimate dinners in

well-appointed homes all over the city, the most prominent people in the worlds of media, politics, literature, and society would
be gathering in the Grand Ballroom of the Plaza Hotel beginning
at ten that evening.

The guest list consisted of only five hundred people so carefully hand-selected that single people were not even permitted to
bring a plus-one. The host had been seen conspicuously carrying
around a notebook for weeks leading up to the event, to which he
was constantly adding and scratching out names. Guards were
stationed at the various stairwells snaking through the hotel, to
make sure that no well-attired gatecrashers sneaked inside. The
only way to gain access to the Grand Ballroom was by presenting
a nontransferable crimson admission card and then riding up in
one of two closely protected elevators. The most intriguing part
of the whole soiree was that everyone would be arriving wearing
a mask, which wasn't to come off until midnight.

The dress designer Halston was exhausted. "I've never seen
women putting so much serious effort into what they're going to
wear," he said. He had been charged with crafting many of the
masks, some of which were towering confections involving jewels
and feathers.

The dress code for the ball was also unique: everyone was to
wear only black and white. The host professed to be inspired by
the Ascot scene designed by Cecil Beaton for the Audrey Hepburn film *My Fair Lady*, and had even considered making note
on the invitations that ladies were to wear no jewels other than
diamonds. The chairs at Kenneth's salon were packed that afternoon as women rushed to have their hair teased into the right
shape to accommodate their selected masks. In some quarters
of the city, social also-rans were spotted hanging out casually
in black-and-white outfits, to give the impression that they had
been invited. No one could stand the idea of being left out, not

from what some newspapers were already calling the greatest party of the twentieth century: Truman Capote's Black and White Ball.

Truman and his guest of honor, *Washington Post* and *Newsweek* owner Katharine Graham, received the stream of guests who started trickling in under the bright Plaza overhang around a quarter past ten, stepping out of taxicabs and limousines and black cars and onto the plush red entryway carpeting, finally giving the hordes of reporters and photographers and security men something to make note of and photograph and secure. Crowds of onlookers pressed close, hoping for a glimpse of international royalty; of Frank Sinatra and his new young wife, Mia Farrow; of the Maharaja of Jaipur; of Marlene Dietrich; of the reigning queens of New York society. The host and mastermind of this breathtaking event, which as it turned out bore a striking resemblance to a black-and-white-themed black-tie party thrown by Dominick Dunne and his wife, Lenny, in 1964, a party which Truman Capote attended, wore a black Halloween mask that he had picked up at a five-and-dime for thirty-nine cents.

The 1880s had Ward McAllister, the courtly gentleman who'd burst onto the New York scene from Savannah, Georgia, and invented "the Four Hundred" out of thin air. The 1910s had Harry "King" Lehr, the court jester from Baltimore who'd picked up McAllister's mantle after it was stripped from him in disgrace. But the 1960s had Truman Capote, the "Tiny Terror" from New Orleans with the poison pen.

In 2012, longtime gossip columnist Liz Smith reflected on Capote's unique status and role in the mid-twentieth-century New York social pantheon to *Vanity Fair*: "New York doesn't seem to have epic characters like Truman Capote anymore. There are no major writers today that matter in the way that he mattered." Of course, the nature of fame has changed radically since then, and

the nature of "society" has as well. *Vogue* editor and Manhattan social fixture Louise Grunwald, quoted in the same article, agreed:
"There's no one like him anymore, not that there ever was anyone
like him. Just as there are no places like La Côte Basque."

La Côte Basque was a Manhattan restaurant—expensive, tra-
ditional, formal, and French. It opened on Fifty-Fifth Street in
the 1950s and quickly became one of those restaurants where the
map of tables in the dining room could function as a simulacrum
for the map of social hierarchies among the diners seated at them.
The treasured tables were the chilliest ones, by the door, where
everyone could be seen. The dining room in the back was more
comfortable, but it was social Siberia. For a certain slice of New
York society in the 1960s and '70s, La Côte Basque was one of a
tiny handful of places that mattered.

"It's all changed," Louise Grunwald continued to *Vanity Fair*.
"Truman wouldn't recognize New York anymore. It's ghostly."
But before the city was ghostly, it glittered, and in the center of
the glitter—knowing everyone, invited everywhere, petted by
elegant society women whom he would come to refer to as his
"swans"—was a small-statured Southerner who had wanted to
be a writer since he was eight and who yearned, deeply, to belong.

After spending his early childhood with relatives in Monroe-
ville, Alabama, where he lived next door to Harper Lee, Truman
Streckfus Persons arrived in New York City in 1932. He settled
in with his mother and her second husband, a Cuban bookkeeper
who adopted him, giving him the name "Truman Garcia Capote."
Near the end of high school, Truman stepped into the sophisti-
cated waters of New York literary life when he started working
as a copy boy at *The New Yorker* magazine. Robert Frost got him
fired after Truman walked out of a poetry reading he was giving,
but the young Truman began writing in earnest around this time
and quickly established himself in the New York literary scene of

the 1940s, a pretty young man with a swoop of blond bangs who was as adept at flattery as he was at fiction. He spent his twenties penning short stories that were widely published and increasingly celebrated, with his byline appearing in *The New Yorker*, *The Atlantic Monthly*, and *Harper's*, among many others. The success of one of his stories attracted the attention of an editor at Random House, and his first novel, a semiautobiographical volume called *Other Voices, Other Rooms*, was published to some acclaim in 1948.

One of the tall, thin, beautiful women whom Capote christened "swans" as he began to carve his path into literary and social New York was Gloria Vanderbilt. Gloria had spent much of her twenties in New York City pursuing artistic dreams of her own, first in painting and then, later, in theater. She was at a crossroads in her second marriage, to Leopold Stokowski, forty-two years her senior, and beginning to feel like her most secret heart was withering in the face of his control and disapproval. She yearned to break free, but was young and unsure of herself and didn't know how. Years later, she recalled that "waiting on the other side of the glass wall I could see a tiny pied piper. His name was Truman Capote, and he had just appeared on the scene with a book of short stories, *Other Voices, Other Rooms*, told with a literary skill that had captured everyone's imagination." Gloria was in a unique position to know what "everyone" thought. Her fame lay waiting for her before she was even born. She knew everyone whom Truman wanted to know. To him, she represented an opportunity.

One afternoon, Gloria invited Truman to hang out with her at the painting studio she had rented. Her childhood friend Russell Hurd was staying on the couch there, as his trust fund was running on fumes. Russell was gay, but they had, as she put it, "been in love with each other ever since the day when we tea-danced at the Plaza." For months, he camped out in her studio, a sounding board for her romantic anxieties, sharing an intimacy with her of which Truman might have been mildly envious.

"Where did you find him, honey?" asked the writer when he set eyes on delectable Russell.

From then on, every time Gloria and Truman met for lunch, he would ask her probing questions about Russell. Gloria could tell that Truman thirsted for confidences. She could comfortably call Truman a close friend while never entirely trusting him. "He really wanted to be the only one to hear the ins and outs of love affairs, especially mine," Gloria wrote later. But despite Truman's seductively listening ear, she never discussed her failing marriage with anyone besides Russell.

"But what I didn't know yet," Gloria went on, "was that Truman had started weaving Russell into a story set in a brownstone very much like mine, and that the heroine was a girl whose confidant was a man very like Russell. The girl in some ways was like me, in other ways like Carol Marcus." Carol Marcus was another of Gloria's closest friends, who was just then fleeing her own marriage, to writer William Saroyan, and about to displace Russell on Gloria's studio couch. Carol would later marry actor Walter Matthau.

"With Truman I kept up a front," Gloria wrote years later, "never giving the Tiny Terror a toehold into my oh-so-secret heart." Her friend Carol had no such compunction, unloading all her divorce frustrations on Truman's eagerly listening ears. Gloria professed shock at Carol's lack of caution, but then, divorce will sometimes make people do shocking things. "And Truman, sly puss that he was, lapped it up and wove it into *Breakfast at Tiffany's*," Gloria wrote with some satisfaction.

Released in 1958, the novella *Breakfast at Tiffany's* was Truman's first really major success. The story catalogues heroine Holly Golightly and her taste for the famous Fifth Avenue jewelry store and her nameless cat. It would be made into a 1961 film that provided a star-making turn for Audrey Hepburn. Following the story's publication, a new game bubbled up within New York society, of which we've just seen an example: Truman called it "the Holly Golightly Sweepstakes." Every society woman wanted to have been the model for Holly Golightly and claimed with authority that she was the inspiration: Carol Marcus, Doris Lilly, Phoebe Pierce, Oona Chaplin, Gloria Vanderbilt. This keen competition is perhaps a bit surprising, given that Holly is, for all intents and purposes, a prostitute and was based, in many respects, on Truman himself—the beautiful outsider arriving in New York City and trying to break his way in. But Holly's beauty and independence and glamour so dazzled some of the society girls that they looked past the rest, and each of them wanted to be seen as more beautiful and independent and glamorous than the others. (In truth, each swan probably wanted to be Audrey Hepburn more than she wanted to be Holly Golightly.)

With the smash hit of *Breakfast at Tiffany's*, Truman's literary triumph could begin to be tracked alongside his social one, and for the rest of his career, the two would be closely intertwined.

If, as critic Ralph F. Voss has suggested, Truman Capote's career can be mapped along a "year-to-year, double-line graph," one line of which represents artistic achievements, and the other of which represents celebrity, both would trend steadily upward from the mid-1940s to 1958 and would then "turn radically upward and peak at new heights" in 1966, which saw the publication of *In Cold Blood* on the one hand and the Black and White Ball on the other. *In Cold Blood* was Truman's pinnacle literary achievement, the true crime account of the brutal murder of a family in Kansas and the ensuing trial and execution of the killers. Truman grew emotionally close to the killers, and close to many people in Garden City, Kansas, over the six years he spent working on the book, which he called his "nonfiction novel." It was also a run-away success, a bestseller. Truman went on television talk shows, was invited everywhere, and fine liquor began to flow like blood through his veins.

In 1966, Truman was forty-two years old and had achieved a kind of success that his awkward boyhood self could never possibly have imagined. "I've gotten rid of the boy with the bangs," he said of himself. It was also the first time he had tasted real money—even the film sale of *Breakfast at Tiffany's* hadn't brought him this kind of financial gain. He bought a two-bedroom apartment in "the most important new address," 870 United Nations Plaza, where Gloria Vanderbilt would also move a few years later. The apartment was on the twenty-second floor, with a panoramic southern view of Lower Manhattan. His friend and biographer Gerald Clarke described Truman at this moment: "Alexander after the Battle of Issus, Napoleon after Austerlitz could not have been cockier than Truman was after *In Cold Blood*. He had the golden touch, and he was already looking forward to his next triumph, a party that would end the year as it had begun—with all eyes focused on him."

A party wouldn't only guarantee that the bright klieg light of public acclaim stayed focused warmly on him. It would also be an opportunity to repay the kindnesses of his society hosts and hostesses—all those yacht trips in the Mediterranean, those glamorous dinners, those weekends at plush country estates. And really, there is nothing Southerners love more than a theme party. One of his swans, Slim Keith, knew this. "He wanted to give the biggest and best goddamned party that anybody had ever heard of," she said. "He wanted to see every notable in the world, people of importance from every walk of life, absolutely dying to attend a party given by a funny-looking, strange little man—himself."

Truman's great insight in planning the Black and White Ball

was to understand that the guest list made the party, even more than the music, the liquor, the theme, or the food. In fact, the food would be something of an afterthought—spaghetti Bolognese and chicken hash at midnight. The décor would be simple as well: red tablecloths, white taper candles, translucent balloons, and "miles of smilax," an affordable greenery. "Unlike fabled gatherings from New York's past," wrote Gerald Clarke, with visions of the Gilded Age dancing in his head, "in which champagne spurted from fountains, live swans floated on artificial lakes, or gilded trees were hung with golden fruit, his would be a model of good taste and simplicity." But the guests were a different thing altogether. The *Times* called them "as spectacular a group as has ever been assembled for a private party in New York." Mrs. Nicholas Longworth, the elegant eighty-something daughter of Teddy Roosevelt, was overheard saying that the party was "the most exquisite of spectator sports." Writer and editor Leo Lerman smirked that "the guest book reads like an international list for the guillotine."

The real appeal, of course, was that making a loud show of strictly limiting the number of guests to five hundred gave Truman complete power and control over a group of otherwise very powerful and controlling people. Being on the list not only meant attendance at what promised to be a memorable party; it also telegraphed one's importance, through association with the other people on the list. Truman had learned Ward McAllister's lesson well in this regard—power devolved to the man who held the list. Competition over invitations was so fierce that Truman joked he might as well have called the party *In Bad Blood*. Those privileged ones who were included were so excited to have made the cut that they often forgot that they actually disliked Truman. Katherine Anne Porter, for example, was delighted to receive an invitation and conveniently forgot that she had hated Truman on sight when they were together at Yaddo and had publicly called him "the pimple on the face of American literature."

The Black and White Ball was a success. Everyone knew that the event was something special even as it was happening, though no one could quite put their finger on why. The *Washington Post* reported that "this city's normally blasé social set is flapping like a gaggle of geese over a not-so-private party being thrown by author Truman Capote for 500 guests here Monday night. The New York newspapers are calling it variously the party of the year, the decade or the century." The verdict was in even before the first limousine rolled up to the revolving doors of the Plaza that night.

"We used to do this sort of thing in Newport in the old days," said Mrs. William Woodward, described by the *Times* as "the grande dame who has been giving and going to elegant parties since before World War I." "Why, I remember we all dressed up in lavish costumes and the Ziegfeld Follies came up from New York to perform." And like those lavish fêtes of Alva's day, the guest list—which would be published the following day in the *Times*, just as the list of the famed Four Hundred had eventually been leaked to the press by Ward McAllister—included names that had held sway in New York society for generations. Vanderbilts were there, and Astors, too, scattered among the media and Hollywood and jet set elites. Alfred Gwynne Vanderbilt II complained that his black velvet mask itched, so he took it off and put it in his dinner jacket pocket shortly after he arrived. His cousin Gloria Vanderbilt was there, too, with her fourth husband, Wyatt Cooper, whom she had married in 1963. She was nearly three months pregnant with her fourth child, who would be me—though, at the time, she was sure I would be a girl, whom she planned to name Morgan. She wore a simple, chic maternity dress—black velvet, with a high and wide starched white Puritan collar. But unlike the grand amusements of the Gilded Age, the

Black and White Ball was a relative bargain. All told, throwing it cost Truman between $13,000 (per the *New York Times*) and $16,000 (per his biography)—a fraction of what Alva would have shelled out just for flowers in the "old days." It's quite probable several attendees spent more on their outfits for that one night than Truman spent on their amusement. The Museum of the City of New York even made a point of collecting people's masks as the evening wound down.

Truman Capote rode high on the twin successes of *In Cold Blood* and the Black and White Ball as the 1960s drew to a close. He surfed his fame from one nighttime talk show couch to another, and started talking up the book that was going to leave the towering achievement of *In Cold Blood* in its dust. The new novel was to be a Proustian magnum opus about social life in New York City, and it was to be called *Answered Prayers*. The title derived from a truism that weighed heavily on Truman's mind from his discovery of it in 1958 until his death thirty-odd years later: that more trouble comes from answered prayers than unanswered ones. But as the 1970s dawned, the book did not appear. He missed one deadline, then the next. His social life roared on unchecked, and his drinking grew worse. But there was no novel.

Finally, in 1975, a short story appeared in *Esquire* that was meant to be a chapter from the long-simmering, long-awaited book. Entitled "Mojave," it was warmly received, generating a frisson of buzz and publicity and attention and, of course, a small pot of money. Quickly, Truman let slip that another chapter would be forthcoming in the magazine in November, and it would be even greater than the first. Fires of anticipation stoked, New York social and literary circles were on high alert for the promised next chapter.

"La Côte Basque, 1965" crash-landed in *Esquire* magazine in November 1975, and its publication sent an earthquake through

Manhattan society. But it was not the earthquake of love and acclaim that Truman had anticipated. Instead, in thirteen thousand
carefully chosen, venomous words, "La Côte Basque" brought
both his social and literary careers to a flaming, cataclysmic end.
It's hard to imagine today something as simple as the publication
of a short story in a magazine causing that kind of radioactive
fallout for a writer. But no short story before or since has been
quite as poisonous as "La Côte Basque." One critic memorably
called it "shit served up on a gold dish."

Biographer Gerald Clarke recalled that he first read a draft of
it "one summer day in Gloria Vanderbilt's swimming pool in the
Hamptons when Gloria and her husband, Wyatt Cooper, were
away. I was reading it while Truman was floating in the pool on a
raft. I said, 'People aren't going to be happy with this, Truman.'
He said, 'Nah, they're too dumb. They won't know who they are.'
He could not have been more wrong."

Nominally the account of a society fixture, Lady Ina Coolbirth, who has been stood up for lunch by the Duchess of Wind-
sor and takes along a Trumanesque cipher named Jonesy instead,
"La Côte Basque" is told as a series of stories within stories like
The One Thousand and One Nights or, more accurately, *The 120
Days of Sodom*. Lady Coolbirth is desperate for someone to talk
to—or, rather, at. As the lunch unfolds, she dishes some of the
most sordid, and true, tidbits of gossip from New York society
over the past couple of decades. They touch upon every manner
of moral outrage: murder, adultery, rape, even bestiality. Every
detail of gruesome human frailty that Truman had absorbed in
his years as the petted toy at society dinners and holidays came
vomiting up in "La Côte Basque," at times, veiled in only the
lightest gossamer of anonymizing details, and at other times, actually accompanied by names. From the moment the issue of *Esquire* hit the newsstands, New York's elites spoke about little else.

What do the tasteful rich talk about with one another when no one else is listening? If the story is to be believed, they discuss their sordid lives and those of everyone they know, in coarse language and with zero emotional affect. "Taste" is usually defined as a marker for the recognition of, and turning away from, that which is vulgar. But the stories being served for lunch at La Côte Basque are the very definition of vulgar. Not cocktail party chit-chat, not even standard-issue lunchtime gossip, but rank immorality. In Truman's telling, the elite are revealed to be not just as vulgar as the next person—which would be a humanizing position, bringing his exclusive list of five hundred down to an earthly plane—but *the most* vulgar. The world as represented in the story is soul-deadening, unredeemable, unredeeming. To wit: at one point, Jonesy is too distracted wondering about the structural details of a diamond brooch worn by one of the other diners to listen to his dining partner's account of her own sexual assault.

Ina Coolbirth, an impossible-to-mistake version of Truman's swan Slim Keith, says while examining a leaf of Bibb lettuce on the end of her fork, "There is at least one respect in which the rich, the really very rich, *are* different from . . . other people. They understand *vegetables*." (There's that Fitzgerald quote again.) And that is essentially Truman's point: apart from their weird appreciation for tiny peas and corn so minute as to be practically "unborn," the really very rich are awful, just as awful as anyone in, say, Garden City, Kansas. Characters in the story feast on gossip as they dine on rich and expensive French food, consuming one another's lives as a perverse kind of nourishment. The anecdotes are meant not just to entertain, but to obscure the emptiness of the lives doing the telling—like heavy French sauces smothering otherwise bland and simple food.

The story is actually a masterful experiment in the forced denial of empathy. None of the characters expresses any concern for another, even when recounting, or eavesdropping on, some of the most gut-wrenching episodes of another's life. But any writer faces a challenge if he seeks to force his reader not to identify with anyone. The reader *wants* to identify with a character, even if that character is an antihero. But through quick pacing, shifting narrative perspectives, and a flatness of tone that treats a story about a woman blowing her husband away with a shotgun with the same level of seriousness as the characterization of a governor's wife as the kind of woman who wears "tweed brassieres," Truman refuses to allow so much as a hairline crack that would let empathy bubble to the surface. Moreover, he seems to suggest that the people mentioned in the story—all of them real people, living people, people whose ears were burning crimson as they paged through the magazine—wouldn't want our concern even if we were inclined to offer it. They don't want it from each other, and they certainly don't want it from the likes of us. That would suggest that we have something in common with them—in which case, they would no longer be the superterrestrial elite. Instead, reading "La Côte Basque, 1965" is an exercise in pure disgust.

It was the most important piece of new fiction Truman Capote had published since the watershed moment of *In Cold Blood* ten years before. But the literary adulation he had come to expect was not only withheld, but also turned on its head, curdled into disdain and, ultimately, expulsion. The story is typically read now from the standpoint of psychobiography, grist for the mill of Truman's personal viciousness, insecurity, and self-doubt. Disgust for the subjects of his writing morphed quickly and totally into disgust for the writer himself.

The response by the elites portrayed in the story was not shame for their own behavior, but round condemnation of Truman for his lack of discretion, and for his audacity in using their stories and their names. This redeployment of disgust worked. It even clings to him in death. The social hierarchy he had attempted to critique was instead shored up.

The swift and total expulsion of Truman Capote from New York society quickly became a story of its own. He hotfooted it out of town, to Los Angeles, where he was due to play a version of himself in the spoof film *Murder by Death*. *New York* magazine sent gossip columnist Liz Smith chasing after him for an interview about the fallout. "It's one thing to tell the nastiest story in the world to all your 50 best friends," Smith wrote in the resulting article. "It's another to see it set down in cold Century Expanded type."

"Truman was thrilled I was going to do it," Smith told *Vanity Fair* years later. "I'll never forget how distraught he was because the pressure was building. In the Padrino bar, in the Beverly Wilshire, he said 'I'm going to call [*Vogue* editor Diana] Mrs. Vreeland, and you'll see that she's really on my side.' So he caused a big ruckus and they brought a phone. He called her. He said, 'I'm sitting here with Liz Smith, and she tells me that everyone is against me, but I know you're not.' He went on and on, holding the phone out for me to hear." Vreeland said some things "meaning everything and nothing—but Truman didn't get the vote of confidence he was hoping for." *New York* magazine put Smith's story on the cover, with an illustration of Truman literally biting the hand of a society hostess who had not just fed him, but fêted him as well.

Though he struck a defensive posture in public, in private, Truman hid out with his friend Joanne Carson, who was married to Johnny Carson. She was one of many whose marital problems had been presented for delectation in "La Côte Basque," but also one of the few who, upon reading it, didn't immediately call for Truman's banishment. "But they know I'm a writer," he complained to her plaintively. "I don't understand it."

And who were some of the other real people mentioned in this poison pen letter masquerading as a short story? Other than Lady Coolbirth and Jonesy, the closest thing the story has to protagonists are none other than not-even-tokenly-anonymized Carol Matthau (née Marcus) and her very good friend Gloria Vanderbilt—or, as Truman characterizes her, Gloria Vanderbilt DiCicco Stokowski Lumet Cooper, "women in their late thirties, but looking not much removed from those deb days when they were grabbing Lucky Balloons at the Stork Club."

Jonesy and Ina sink their forks into a soufflé Furstenberg—surely named for designer Diane—a "froth of cheese and spinach" with poached eggs that make "rivers of egg yolk" when pierced with a fork. While eating this foodstuff so rich and decadent that reading about it is almost enough to make one reach for an Alka-Seltzer, the ostensible main characters eavesdrop on Gloria and Carol.

"Incidentally, did you go to the Logans' party?" says Carol. (Josh and Nedda Logan were also real people, who were similarly incensed at being included in the story by name.)

"For an hour," Truman has Gloria answer.

"How was it?"

"Marvelous. If you've never been to a party before."

The story continues: "The two women laughed together, their laughter like a naughty but delightfully sung duet. Though they were not physically similar . . . one sensed they were two of a kind: charmingly incompetent adventuresses."

Truman then has his fictional Gloria tell a story about a friend of J. D. Salinger's drinking himself to death in the snow in New Hampshire. And then . . .

An exiting customer, a florid-at-the-edges swarthy balding Charlie sort of fellow, stopped at their table. He fixed on Mrs. Cooper a gaze that was intrigued, amused and . . . a trifle grim. He said: "Hello, Gloria"; and she smiled: "Hello, darling": but her eyelids twitched as she attempted to identify him; and then he said: "Hello, Carol. How are ya, doll?" and she knew who he was all right: "Hello, darling. Still living in Spain?" He nodded; his glance returned to Mrs. Cooper: "Gloria, you're as beautiful as ever. More beautiful. See ya . . ." He waved and walked away.

Mrs. Cooper stared after him, scowling.

Eventually Mrs. Matthau said: "You didn't recognize him, did you?"

"N-n-no."

"Life. Life. Really, it's too sad. There was nothing familiar about him at all?"

"Long ago. Something. A dream."

"It wasn't a dream."

"Carol. Stop that. Who is he?"

"Once upon a time you thought very highly of him. You cooked his meals and washed his socks"—Mrs. Cooper's eyes enlarged, shifted—"and when he was in the army you followed him from camp to camp, living in dreary furnished rooms—"

"No!"

"Yes!"

"No."

"Yes, Gloria. Your first husband."

They drop the subject when they are distracted by Jackie Kennedy coming in with her sister, Lee Radziwill.

It's a pitiless representation, by any stretch. How could anyone be so self-absorbed, so vapid, that she doesn't recognize her own first husband when he stops by her table at lunch? The exchange paints a brutal picture, made even worse by the possibility that it was, in some respect, true. Much else he wrote was.

When Liz Smith approached the real-life Gloria to get her take on the story, and presumably her starring role in it, Gloria's response was elegant and brief. "I have never seen it and have heard enough about it to know I don't want to," she was quoted as saying in *New York*. But that's not the whole truth.

Gloria's husband Wyatt Cooper was more forthcoming. "I hate talking when my feelings are negative," he told Liz. "It isn't constructive. I'm very fond of Truman." The two had been good friends. They were both from the South, both had spent their young years in New Orleans, both were writerly and observant and had, through force of personality, propelled themselves into the same glittering circles in New York and Hollywood. Three years earlier, in 1972, the two men had even cowritten a screenplay for *The Glass House*, a well-received TV movie starring Alan Alda. "We used to have lunch, gossip, and it was fun," Wyatt continued. "But lately it wasn't. His viciousness ceased to make it fun. I even talked to him about it two years ago and he thanked me later for caring. I think this destroys all the things he has built up. He can't really pretend to sneer at these people in the Jet Set. He worked too hard to be 'in' himself.

"But, you know," Wyatt reflected, "he has always had a love-hate for all these beautiful women he has been close to . . . Truman would like to be glamorous and beautiful. He has often acted out fantasies of his own by telling his women friends how to act, who to have love affairs with, by manipulating them. Now he has his ultimate revenge, by making them ridiculous in print."

Wyatt knew whereof he spoke. In her 2004 memoir, Gloria elaborates on this theory, that Truman urged his swans toward misbehavior as stand-ins for himself. "Truman and I had been friends since our twenties and remained so until he [published a chapter from] *Answered Prayers*, a book about his friends," she recalls in her memoir. "I, along with a lot of others, felt betrayed, as well we might. Truman manipulated people, and because he was so intuitive, sensitive, and extraordinary, people trusted him. Many times he tried (sometimes successfully, sometimes not) to manipulate me."

Gloria confides in the reader that one day over lunch, Truman tried to persuade her to have an affair with Bill Paley, the powerful president of CBS and the husband of socialite and "swan" Babe Paley, Truman's dearest friend. "Now wait, honey, just listen to me," Gloria remembered Truman saying. "Now, Babe knows that he has other girlfriends and she handles it beautifully, but sometimes it gets out of hand and it gets complicated and messy; it's upsetting to her, naturally. She likes you, you know, respects you; if he was involved with you it would be fun for you, ease things up for her; it would even in a way be doing everyone a favor—so to speak."

Gloria demurred.

Though there was one afternoon meeting, which Gloria would go on to characterize as a "French farce," complete with a chase around the sofa, the affair between her and Bill Paley as brokered by Truman Capote didn't get very far off the ground. But this didn't stop Truman from putting a nasty little anecdote about Bill Paley's notorious infidelity in "La Côte Basque, 1965." At the time of the story's publication, Babe was dying of cancer. Despite Truman's entreaties and yearning to apologize, she never spoke to him again.

The doors to New York society slammed shut, and the deadbolt shot behind them. Notably, Truman didn't just lose the friendships of women. He lost the friendships of their husbands. The gay society gadfly's success depends on the support of husbands—he is not a sexual threat, but he must make himself amusing, like Harry Lehr did, in order to be accepted.

Ostracism followed. As society once was closed to divorced women in the nineteenth century, so it closed to Truman Capote in the late twentieth. "In the long run, the rich run together, no matter what," he told *Playboy* in 1980. "They will cling, until they feel it's safe to be disloyal, then no one can be more so." Truman sought solace among the demimonde of Studio 54, and with Andy Warhol and the Factory scene, none of whom gave a damn about Babe Paley's approval, or even knew who she was. He drank heavily and used a lot of cocaine. He gained weight, and his drinking spiraled out of control. He published a few more pieces, here and there, journalism and short stories, and still appeared on television, often rambling and incoherent. One of his favorite swans, Lee Radziwill, reflected sadly, "I mean, I never forgot about him, but we didn't see each other, because he wasn't making any sense whatsoever. It was pitiful."

Truman Capote would die in Joanne Carson's guest room in California in 1984. *Answered Prayers* remained unfinished. And his reputation, both literary and social, in some respect, has never recovered.

One question hangs over every evaluation of "La Côte Basque, 1965," and that is this: Why? Why would Truman Capote deploy his singular literary talents against a group of people who had not only taken him into their confidence, and their homes, and onto their yachts and private planes, but who also had the distinct ability to end his access to the privileged life he yearned to enjoy? And if he was going to do it, why would he release the most vicious and incendiary chapter before finishing and publishing the book?

Novelist William Styron described Truman's decision to give

the story to *Esquire* magazine when he did, the way he did, in this way: "It was disastrous. And to me, inexplicable."

One of Truman's boyfriends at the time, John O'Shea, agreed: "There's something there that defies analysis."

"All literature is gossip," Truman told *Playboy* after the brouhaha—but this is hardly an explanation.

A "psychobiographer" of Truman Capote has suggested that one reason *Answered Prayers* remained perpetually unfinished was that it was less the Proustian magnificence that he claimed than an insurance policy in case Gloria Vanderbilt, Babe Paley, Diana Vreeland, and the other swans should happen to turn on him, a sword of Damocles that he could dangle over their exquisite Kenneth coiffures. But then, he published "La Côte Basque" in 1975, while he was still in the inner circle. Perhaps the move could be explained as preventive abandonment—he left them so that they could never leave him. He guarded against his own victimization—always an unspoken risk for an outsider both small, strange, and queer—by going on the attack and making his domination unmistakable.

Maybe he was just sick of being a plaything, closing in on middle age. After all, not even Harry Lehr was Harry Lehr forever. But maybe the logic behind his decision was as simple as Truman's craving the literary attention he had grown accustomed to at a time when his own private demons, drinking and drugs, were making it impossible for him to produce work of the caliber that he used to. He has been called "largely incoherent" from the late 1960s until his death. It's hard to produce good writing without being able to produce clear thoughts.

Or, maybe, at root, the glamorous Five Hundred spinning under the Plaza chandeliers at the Black and White Ball never understood Truman Capote at all. They saw in him what they wanted to see, and not what he was.

"I'm a writer," Truman Capote said, "and I use everything. Did all those people think I was there just to entertain them?"

Let's look at Truman's relationship with Gloria from a different perspective. Gerald Clarke wrote that their friendship had been tenuous from the beginning, when they were both in their twenties. It seems that Gloria's uneasy distrust of Truman was wise. Of her, Truman wrote rather bitterly, "she was a nasty little girl," which is a tough thing to say about a child. "She lied about her mother during her custody trial, and she was terrible to her until shortly before she died. She had a father complex. . . . I introduced her to Sidney Lumet, and she only married him because she thought he would make her a movie star. . . . When she found out he wasn't going to make her a star, she dumped him quick."

Harsh.

And consider the forcible denial of empathy for Gloria that Truman imposes on his readers, with the story of her failing to recognize her first husband. Truman makes her out to be indifferent, imperious, self-absorbed. But there is another way to understand that exchange, if it indeed took place as described. In a late-in-life memoir, Gloria notes that upon seeing her mother for the first time in seventeen years, she didn't recognize her and wouldn't have known her if they'd passed one another in the street. Her mother, of course, was at the center of every trauma of Gloria's considerably traumatic childhood except one: Gloria's teenage marriage to Pat DiCicco, an ostensible Hollywood agent, inveterate gambler, and possible mobster and murderer. (His first wife, actress Thelma Todd, had died under mysterious circumstances, and there were rumors DiCicco was involved—rumors that a seventeen-year-old Gloria, eager to get out of her aunt Gertrude's house, chose to ignore.) In their four short years together, DiCicco was controlling and abusive, and he siphoned off a chunk of Gloria's money. He mocked her body, wrecking her already fragile self-esteem, and used to throw her against the wall, leaving her bruised and with blackened eyes.

A more empathetic viewer of Gloria's failure to recognize him at lunch twenty years later might have pointed out that over half her lifetime had passed since she had seen Pat DiCicco, and while he had been an attractive man in his early thirties, decades of hard living and alcohol had taken a toll by 1965. It is also worth considering that the marriage was so traumatic for Gloria that she could deal with it only by stuffing it in a box inside her mind, closing the lid, and throwing away the key. But Truman Capote wasn't interested in humanizing Gloria Vanderbilt, even while he floated in her majestic swimming pool. Instead, he wanted to resent her.

Truman closed Gloria's appearance in "La Côte Basque, 1965" with an exchange with Carol Matthau that would be funny if it weren't so bitter:

> Mrs. Cooper said: "D-darling, there's the most m-m-marvelous auction at Parke Bernet this afternoon—Gothic tapestries."
>
> "What the fuck," asked Mrs. Matthau, "would I do with a Gothic tapestry?"
>
> Mrs. Cooper replied: "I thought they might be amusing for picnics at the beach. You know, spread them on the sands."

He even mocks Gloria's occasional soft stutter, which she developed as a child after the custody battle. As Gerald Clarke concluded in his biography of Truman Capote:

> Those who believed themselves betrayed by "La Côte Basque" had not been wrong. He was a fifth columnist. "They assumed

that I was living by their values. Which I never was. It's as though, by writing that, I was saying to them: 'Everything you lived for, everything you did, is a lot of shit!' Which is true! I was saying that!"

Shit on a gilded plate.

"That was Truman," Gloria wrote many years later, about the former friend she once called True Heart. "He drew you into a web, intimating he knew things about you, things you didn't know yourself. How could he betray me when he didn't really know me at all?"

12

The Last Vanderbilt

October 28, 1978, and June 17, 2019

*Celebrities and notorious characters, scandal and helpful pub-
licity, all go into the potpourri of the gossip column. Next to
the doings of one of society's most conservative older hostesses is
the latest witticism of an underworld character, with the writer,
or so one assumes by his easy reference, on intimate terms with
both.*

—Amy Vanderbilt's *Complete Book of Etiquette,*
Part VII, "Your Public Life"

On October 28, 1978, a boy of eleven sat in the back of a limousine, buttoned into dress-up clothes, watching the lights of Midtown streak past the windows of the car. He had just attended
a premiere of a movie that was directed by one of his mother's
ex-husbands, whom she was involved with once again. It was a
musical based on the story of *The Wizard of Oz*, but modernized,
with an all-Black cast. *The Wiz*, it was called, and it starred Diana Ross and Richard Pryor. The musical had been a huge hit
on Broadway, and now it was going to be a huge hit movie, too.
Maybe. The boy, like most critics and all audiences, had found
the film sort of bizarre. (The movie, unfortunately, became a notorious flop, infamous for stopping Diana Ross's film career in its

tracks. Consensus was that it was too strange for adults but too frightening for children.) Now they were slowly driving a few blocks to an afterparty at a place called Studio 54, which was a kind of Oz of its own.

In one of the cars in front of his was another boy—or, young man, really—accompanied by his mother and father. He had just turned twenty and was playing the Scarecrow in the movie. He was already famous as a singer, but the movie was only going to make him more so. He had grown up in a family that was used to commanding lots of attention. Earlier, the younger boy had watched as several women who had been waiting outside the theater, hoping to catch a glimpse of the just-past teenager, ran after his departing limousine screaming his name: Michael.

The younger boy didn't know much about Michael Jackson. He had met him briefly at the premiere and thought he seemed shy. He'd heard he had been performing almost since he was born, and that his relationship with his father was troubled, but the boy thought Michael was lucky to have a father, and talent. He could sing, he could dance, people were interested in him and wanted to know him . . .

It meant that he would always be safe. He would always be able to look out for himself.

That was something the younger boy worried about a lot—looking out for himself and the people he loved.

The younger boy had a mop of brown, adolescent hair that fell sweetly over his forehead, and though he had the slightly upward-tilting eyes of a Vanderbilt, they were the arresting pale blue of a Cooper. At thirteen, those eyes would help net him occasional modeling jobs, which he liked because they provided him with his own money, which he squirreled away in a savings account his father had helped him open at the Bowery Savings Bank when he was eight.

At the end of each school day, he would use a pay phone to call a booker at the Ford modeling agency and ask if there were any "go-sees" for him. If there were, he would take the bus to the address he'd been given, usually somewhere in Midtown, and hand his portfolio to the person in charge of casting, and maybe pose for a Polaroid. The other kids vying for the job were usually accompanied by their moms, but the boy came alone. He liked that. He, too, was shy, sometimes painfully so, but it was like a test for him, something he had to push himself to do. No one knew it, but the boy was worried. He felt he was on a slowly sinking ship with no captain at the helm.

Women all over New York City in 1978 wore tight-fitting, high-waisted jeans with his mother's name embroidered on the back pocket, as well as her signature swan on the front. She was suddenly flush, earning millions promoting the brand. But the boy knew it would not be enough. It never was. Money ran away from his mother like water. And his father wasn't there anymore to try to stanch the flow.

"I had lunch with him just before he died," Truman Capote once wrote about the boy's father. "He seemed fine, but he kept talking about those boys. 'If only I can live another ten years,' he said, 'everything will be all right. But Gloria just isn't responsible enough to raise them.'"

The boy's father had died during open heart surgery earlier that year, in January, after suffering a heart attack in December. When he died, the boy felt like his own heart had broken, too, a wound that might scar over but would never properly heal.

His older brother and mother were riding in the car with him. The boy could not really remember spending a great deal of time with his mother before his father died. She was always going somewhere, it seemed, working in other cities, or painting in her studio. She worked hard, but she sometimes drank wine, and when she did, her voice changed and she became someone else. It scared the boy, but he loved her fiercely. He knew something had happened to her as a child that still made her sad, and he wanted to protect her. Around his mother, everything was exciting, but little was certain, and as he gazed out the window of the car, he felt somewhere deep inside his wounded heart that none of it was real—the musical, the limousine, the way people looked at him and his brother and his mom.

The Vanderbilt era was long past by 1978, and the eleven-year-old boy knew it, even if he didn't know he knew it. People looked at him and his brother as heirs to an American dynasty, but the boy knew that such a thing didn't exist and that no good could come from imagining that it did. He'd heard the stress in his father's voice while he was talking over the phone to friends about Gloria's spending, and his father had explained it to the boy as best he could. The boy wanted to be ready when the ship finally sank.

History tends to look only at exceptional moments. Studio 54, for instance, and the boy on his way to it, at all of eleven years old, in a line of cars with Michael Jackson. That is an exceptional moment. Like Alva's ball one hundred years before, or the Black and White Ball at the Plaza in 1966, Studio 54 in 1978 was the party everyone wanted to be invited to, but few were. It lives on in our fantasy lives, colors our perception of its historical epoch. We have all seen the pictures: Bianca Jagger in a tequila-sunset-red, off-the-shoulder dress riding onto the dance floor on the back of a snow-white horse—a hearkening back, wittingly or not, to a sumptuous dinner on horseback at Sherry's in 1903, each saddle outfitted with a tray and a champagne bucket. Liza Minnelli and Andy Warhol lounged on banquettes. Even Truman Capote himself, after he was expelled from café society, giggled when the giant man in the moon over the dance floor brought the spoonful of white powder up to its nose. The Hustle was like a late twentieth-century quadrille, a dance of prescribed steps done in unison, forms joining under the lights and breaking apart in patterns, with admission granted only to the most beautiful, to those dressed in the right clothes, knowing the right people. "Le Freak (C'est Chic)" blasted through the speakers. Unchic need not apply.

But exceptional moments are not often what matter most to us, when we reflect on the lives we have lived. Alva Vanderbilt Belmont, for instance, recalled in the notes for her memoir lazy summer afternoons with her children digging in the garden at their summer house on Long Island. They planted flowers and vegetables and kept a little rowboat on the pond nearby, to which was added a small mast and sail when the children were big enough. Harold, her baby son, the great America's Cup defender, had his first sail with his mother and sister, Consuelo, as a tiny boy on a calm summer pond in a rejiggered rowboat. That's what Alva remembered. Her memoir doesn't include her costume ball at all, not even a passing mention of it.

The story of one life, or a constellation of lives tossed into the firmament to make a dynasty, will never entirely be what history thinks it is. Gloria Vanderbilt kept a journal, too. She described July 12, 1971, as "a day of clear crystal. The sound of the children calling to each other across the lawn. Anderson in a raspberry shirt. Berry brown and freckled, blue blue of eyes. Playing in the pool—he, a fat minnow caught for Old Brown. Carter brings me Queen Anne's Lace—big like fireworks."

A few days later, she wrote, "Carter and Anderson—such perfect beings it sometimes frightens me. 'Oh, you make me so happy, Mummy,' Carter says. His face as he rus[hes] towards me holding Queen Anne's lace behind his back to surprise me. A flower—sunlit, flooded with a beauty that blinds me. I wish the summer and living here would never end." In between these flashes of sunlight through lacy flower petals sound echoes of Alva's children's laughter on a different drowsy summer afternoon ninety years before.

That blue-eyed boy—Andy Cooper, as his mom sometimes called him—can remember some exceptional moments trailing along in his Vanderbilt mother's substantial wake. But they are not what matter. What matters to him—to me, who even now, in middle age, still remembers what it felt like to be that young boy—are the unexceptional moments, lived far from the watching and judging eye of history or the scribbled notes of the gossip columns. Moments as simple as going out to the movies with your mother when your dad and your brother are both dead, and it's the holidays, and you've long since given up trying to cook or decorate or celebrate. When you are grieving, sometimes all you want to do is escape, and the movies can take you both away, together, for a little while. Not a movie premiere, with fancy clothes and photographers and limos and parties—just going to the movies: Buying tickets. Sharing popcorn. Walking the winter streets of Manhattan on the way home after the credits roll, on one of those days when it's warmer outside than it looks, but you still wish you'd remembered your gloves. Just the two of us, walking together, nursing our private hurts on Christmas Day.

I think of my mother as the last Vanderbilt. There are others, of course, who still carry the name and are keepers of family history, and some who seem closely related but aren't—like Amy Vanderbilt, the etiquette author, who was a far distant cousin laterally descended from the Commodore, but who built a brand for herself on her famous last name. And there are many more descendants who may seem unrelated but are actually deeply entwined with the Vanderbilt story, like me. We stalk around, unnoticed, riding next to you on the subway. But my mother was the last to live what we might think of as a Vanderbilt life. The dynasty ended with Gloria. She was the last living Vanderbilt who'd slept at The Breakers when it was still a private home, owned by her grandmother Alice, who'd built it with her grandfather Cornelius Vanderbilt II before the advent of air-conditioning, to escape the stifling heat that made even their sprawling mansion in Manhattan feel oppressive. She was the last child to ride in cars driven by liveried chauffeurs, guarded by private detectives in overcoats and fedoras. She was the last to be born before the Depression, when the Vanderbilt riches seemed as limitless and eternal as the stars in the sky. She knew that vanished world, with all its opulence and uncertainty and coldness. She had lived her entire life in the public eye, and she was the last Vanderbilt whose birth and obituary would make the front page of newspapers around the world. She was a symbol of an era, of a set of values or experiences—the way that money can bend and warp relationships, the way that one family's ambition can either uplift or infect the members of that family, sometimes for good, but more often than we might think, for ill. The way that American inequality in the Gilded Age could echo and reverberate all the way into the late twentieth century.

That's what she would be to history, anyway.

But not to me. To me, she was my mom.

"No matter what our age, death is not in the distant future," my mother wrote to me in 2015, when she was in her early nineties. "It is here in this present moment, right now, alive and waiting."

Gloria, the last Vanderbilt, died on June 17, 2019, in a jewel box of a room in her apartment on Beekman Place, a quiet cul-de-sac in Manhattan named after descendants of Wilhelmus Beekman, treasurer of the Dutch West India Company, who'd arrived in New Amsterdam in the years before Jan Aertsen van der Bilt, my mother's seventh great-grandfather. She had lived in the two-bedroom apartment for twenty-three years, far longer than she'd ever lived anywhere in her life. She'd decorated and redecorated its rooms dozens of times, her eye never quite satisfied with the story she wanted them to tell. "Everything we do is autobiographical," she would say, and the rooms in that apartment certainly were. The way she had them painted, the fabrics she chose, how she placed objects on a table—all told a story about her life, or how she wanted her life to be.

"Those born to the storm, find the calm very boring," her friend Dorothy Parker once said, and my mother's restlessness was testament to that. She would move into a house or an apartment convinced that it was all she would ever want, but quickly, doubts would begin to set in. As a child, she'd been shuttled among gilded mansions and hotel suites, rented châteaus and country estates. She dreamt of having a family and a home with a white picket fence and love that would make her feel safe and complete, that would quiet the pounding hurt and sadness visible sometimes behind her eyes. But when she had all that, it was never quite enough, because underneath all those desires, she had a drive to make something of herself, to create, to contribute, to be "seen, heard, and felt," as she once wrote to me, and to be loved. It was a drive as relentless as her heartbeat.

There was the penthouse apartment at 10 Gracie Square, where she lived with her second husband, Leopold Stokowski, and then with Sidney Lumet. Then there was the grand old town house on Sixty-Seventh Street that she loved and then hated for its lack of light. It was there that she and Wyatt Cooper, my father, gave dinners and parties for Charlie Chaplin, Dorothy Parker, Truman Capote, and so many others. There was the apartment at 870 United Nations Plaza, a few floors above where Truman lived, which was fun until it wasn't. Then the apartment on Fifty-Seventh Street that we moved into after my father died, but that didn't last long. And then it was back to another penthouse, at

10 Gracie Square, which seemed to be the solution, but after my brother's death there by suicide, she couldn't remain. Then it was another town house; then 30 Beekman, where she steeled herself to stay.

She remembered every inch of every room she had ever lived in, and with the gnawing sense that something didn't feel quite right and needed to be changed, she would be seized by an idea and would ask Nora, her beloved friend and housekeeper for nearly sixty years, to track down the solution. "I need that small oval table," she might say. "You remember, the one with pearl inlay that was in the patchwork bedroom in the house on Sixty-Seventh Street?"

Nora would indeed remember; she remembered everything, never mind that the table hadn't been used in twenty years and was packed away in an enormous storage unit my mother had rented for decades somewhere in Queens—a secret archive for physical memories as vast and necessary and inaccessible as her own subconscious. The next day, Nora would disappear deep into the recesses of the storage space, a place my mother never actually visited, embarking on a spelunking excursion into Gloria's past. A few days later, the table would appear and be welcomed like a long-lost friend my mother had loved and then grown disenchanted with, but now was ready to embrace once again. The love affair never lasted for long.

"It's no longer right," she would say ruefully after several weeks or months, and back to storage the table would go. "I don't know; it worked for a little while," she would say, "but it didn't get to the root of the problem."

Nothing ever would.

On my mother's ninety-first birthday, she sent me an email recalling a birthday message her aunt Gertrude had sent upon her turning seventeen. My mother said she still felt like that teenage girl. I decided to start a conversation with her that I'd always wanted to have, about all the things we had never discussed. It took the form of letters exchanged over email and evolved into a book called *The Rainbow Comes and Goes*, and an HBO documentary, *Nothing Left Unsaid*. We were both moved to discover how many people responded to these conversations. After all, take away the Vanderbilt trappings, and we were just a mother and her adult son, finally coming to know one another as human beings. We did a lot of interviews and speaking engagements and publicity around the project, which my mom was very accustomed to, and secretly loved.

"I am a big ham," she would say, and laugh with delight. But by the time the book publicity tour was over, my indefatigable mother was tired. Her energy was flagging. Then, one afternoon, she tripped on a carpet in her apartment and fell on the floor outside her bedroom. There was no one else there that day. She hadn't had a live-in housekeeper for twenty years. She lay on the floor for some time before reaching her cell phone and calling for help. She had sprained her back and would recover, but I knew then I had to get involved in the day-to-day aspects of my mom's life I had always tried to avoid. I suppose all adult children delay for as long as possible the moment when they must step in, take charge, and become the parent. It's scary to be the one in charge, no matter how responsible and authoritative we are accustomed to being in our regular adult lives.

I found a company with wonderful nurses, who were sent to be with my mother as she recovered. It was supposed to be a temporary situation. When she felt better, she would let me know, and we would switch from registered nurses to home care attendants. But the weeks turned into months, and then the months turned into years. Her back recovered, but she grew accustomed to the nurses. They were kind and attentive, and as my mom would say,

"Who doesn't love that?" The few times I suggested that perhaps it was time to replace them, since she didn't really need registered nurses, she would look at me as though I were speaking gibberish. After a while, I just gave up.

I began working more to cover the additional expenses, allowing myself just one weekend off a month, the adult version of my thirteen-year-old self, finishing the school day and then calling up his agent to see if there was any modeling work to be had. I also found myself lying in bed at night obsessively worrying about her, something I'd routinely done in the years after my father died. I'd make endless calculations in my head about her expenditures and tax problems—only, now it was about the hourly rate for her nurses or her late-night online shopping expeditions.

"You know, Mom, saving money is making money," I would occasionally say to her, but we both knew she would never change her ways.

She started getting depressed at the turn her health had taken, and the lack of energy she felt. For a time, she wasn't getting out of bed. Hoping to revive her spirits, I suggested we set up an Instagram account. "I'm not sure anyone would really be interested in following me," she said, but agreed. We spent several hours discussing what photos she should initially post, and when I mentioned she'd joined Instagram on my own Instagram account, she suddenly saw her number of followers rise. When she hit one hundred thousand followers, she called me, breathless. "Wow, I can't believe it," she said, sounding like a teenager who has just discovered her crush likes her back.

To motivate her to start painting again, I set up another account for her artwork. She'd had many exhibits over the decades, but with Instagram, she wouldn't have to wait for a gallery to show and sell her paintings. The first drawing she posted sold within a few minutes. She was thrilled. She felt productive again and connected to an audience of people who sent her lovely messages about her work. She no longer wanted to risk going down the stairs to her studio one floor beneath her apartment, so her nurses set up a makeshift workspace by her dining room, and every day, she spent hours painting and drawing. It gave her new life.

She didn't have anyone to handle the logistics of sales, so I told my mom I would do it. When someone would message her on Instagram that they wanted to buy a drawing, I would then reach out to them to complete the sale, but I didn't want them to know it was me. My mom suggested we invent a studio assistant for her named "Monica." She loved the idea of this imaginary character and, after much discussion, decided that Monica should be a "lady of a certain age, fiercely loyal, who had been with Ms. Vanderbilt for years." I would be on assignment in some far-flung place, and in my spare time, as "Monica," I'd be conversing about frame sizes and shipping information with my mom's customers. Her friend and housekeeper, Leonor, who took over after Nora died, would then bring the drawing to the framers and have it shipped.

My mom turned ninety-five on February 20, 2019. Over the next few months, she began to feel more tired and found it harder to move around. She stopped wanting to go to her doctor's office. I found another doctor to make house calls, but by June, she took a serious turn. She was admitted to a hospital for tests, and that is how we learned she had cancer in her stomach that had spread. Her remarkable doctor, Thomas Nash, called me with the results, and we both sat with my mom to tell her.

"How long do you think I have?"

"It's hard to say," he said, explaining that if she wanted to go through treatments, that was an option, but they would require frequent hospitalizations and were unlikely to be effective.

"I see," she said. I held her hand tight, and she was quiet for a few seconds. "Well, it's like that old song, 'Show me the way to get out of this world, 'cause that's where everything is.'"

She was discharged a few hours later, and we brought her home.

"At the very least," she'd written to me once, "when we die we will be as if asleep, in the same place we were before birth, so why fear death? Scattered on the wind, unaware as we were before we came into this world, with no memory of any of it."

My mom did not return to the mirrored, soft-pink bedroom she had painstakingly designed over many years. The white four-poster bed was too large and too difficult for her nurses to attend to her in. She had always resisted having a hospital bed in the apartment, but to the surprise of everyone, she agreed we could rent one to make it easier on the nurses. Before my mother saw it, Leonor covered the bed in Porthault sheets and concealed the metal handles on either side in antique quilts and shawls.

For as long as I can remember, my mom always insisted that she would end her life by taking pills. "You can always find someone to get you a hundred Seconal," she'd say as though this were a known fact. "I won't stick around to be a burden on you," she told me countless times over the years. But dying in theory is one thing; the reality is far different. "I would like to see how it all turns out," she said, settling into her new bed. I reminded her that she had once said she wouldn't want to live after she "lost her beauty."

"What a stupid thing to say. I don't know what I was thinking; I must have been drunk." She laughed.

It was the first time she had ever made a joking reference to drinking. Her father drank himself to death, and while her own drinking was not nearly so frequent or severe, it had been a big issue for me during my childhood. It wasn't until after my brother, Carter, killed himself in 1988 that I spoke to her about it, and as far as I know, she never drank alcohol again.

We spent the next two weeks together, and they were among the best times we ever had together. My mom's sons from her marriage to Leopold Stokowski, Chris and Stan, were there, and Stan's family as well. Most days and nights we would talk and laugh, or we would just sit in silence holding hands. Her skin looked almost translucent, and it was remarkably soft, almost like silk—the result, I suppose, of her lifelong aversion to the sun and, perhaps, of the bottles of Erno Lazlo lotion she applied to her face and hands every night of her adult life.

One night shortly before she died, we had just finished watching a video on YouTube of Peggy Lee singing "Is That All There Is?" We both loved the song and the grainy black-and-white video of Lee's nightclub performance of it. While it played, I held her hands and we sang the chorus, pretending we were dancing.

"It's so marvelous," she said, giggling with a sound of delight and mischief, knowing that she was on the cusp of discovering if that was all there was.

"I suppose people will think you are inheriting the Vanderbilt millions," she said. "Boy, won't they be surprised."

She was right. Just as they had when the Commodore died, and when Billy the Blatherskite died, and when everyone else on the Vanderbilt tree right on down to her father, Reggie, died, reporters speculated about the fortune they imagined my mom left behind. A website that somehow claims to know the net worth of celebrities had estimated that my mother had $200 million—a combination, they confidently stated, made up of interest on the millions she had inherited from a Vanderbilt trust when she turned twenty-one and the money she had made in her foray into fashion. The *New York Post* ran with that figure as well, though decades before, they had gleefully published a front-page story claiming my mom was broke. As with many things surrounding the Vanderbilts, the truth, the reality of her life, was much different from the fantasy created by reporters and gossip columnists and strangers.

She had inherited fortunes and lost them and made them again and lost them again. She had been taken advantage of by Pat DiCicco, her first husband; and was later robbed by her psychiatrist Christ Zois, who had his medical license taken away, and by her lawyer Thomas Andrews, who was disbarred. She had made bad deals that wrecked her business and snarled her taxes, but she had persevered. She lived her life on her own terms.

My mom never understood wealthy people who talked about money and regaled others with stories about their winning stock selections. "They know the cost of everything and the value of nothing," she used to say, meaning to reveal where her priorities lay, but also revealing the kind of life she had been able to live. She knew the value of friends and work and love, but she did not know the actual cost of anything. The numbers were of no interest to her and, therefore, no impediment to her spending. Since her death, I've found boxes of files with letters from accountants over the decades warning her to stop spending so much. My dad had agonized over the waste, to little effect. His powerlessness before her spending ate away at him, just as it ate away at me, always.

Helen Gurley Brown, the founder of *Cosmopolitan* magazine, was always trying to set Gloria up with someone rich, but rarely did any of these men hold my mother's attention. It would have been convenient if she had been able to force herself to love any of them. But she couldn't. Love was the only thing she cared about and believed in. In our correspondence, she once wrote, "Love Is All," capitalizing each word to underscore its importance. From her perspective, there had always been money somewhere, and when suddenly it wasn't there, she was able to make it, or find it, or borrow it, or sell her apartment for a profit. Money bought beautiful things, and those beautiful things made her feel safe, secure, clear . . . until they didn't and were relegated to the storage vault.

Once, when I got a significant raise at a job and signed a new contract, I told my mother how much it was for. She was thrilled for me, of course, but I instantly knew that I should not have said anything. The next day, she called to tell me she "had to" redecorate several of the rooms in her apartment. Browsing online, she had found two screens made from antique, hand-painted Chinese wallpaper that once hung in the dining room of the house we lived in on Sixty-Seventh Street when I was born. My mother had sold the valuable wallpaper when we moved, and now here it was again. She had to have the screens. They cost fifty thousand dollars.

"Honey, we have to get them," she said to me breathlessly on the phone. It was not a request, not a discussion. In that moment, she *needed* them; they were the answer to something, something she had been searching for—a reminder of my father, my brother, the life we had had on Sixty-Seventh Street: the party for Charlie Chaplin, that night Judy Garland and Liza Minnelli came by the house, the silver pheasants used as table settings in that dining room all those years ago.

I swallowed hard, pained with the extravagance, but was powerless before her insistence. Once I had bought the screens and they arrived, she then explained, as though there could be no doubt, that the whole room had to be changed because of them. It wouldn't be right any other way. Eventually, she asked me to come over and see the transformation.

"It's really beautiful," I told her, happy that it made her so happy. "It's perfect," I said, and it was.

Six months later, she emailed asking me if I had room for the screens somewhere in my basement. "It's just not working," she explained. "I found a lovely chandelier, and the screens just don't work there anymore." No one can make money evaporate into thin air like a Vanderbilt.

In 1945, when Gloria turned twenty-one, she received an inheritance that had grown to about $4 million, over which her mother and her aunt had sparred when she was a child. That is the equivalent today of nearly $60 million, a staggering sum.

"Remember," Gloria wrote to me during our year of focused correspondence. "Whenever money is involved it brings out horrific things in people."

By the late 1960s, only about a million dollars remained. Like her globe-trotting mother, Gloria Morgan, and like Reggie, with his taste for horses and cars, she spent lavishly, almost heedlessly, on anything that might bring pleasure: on houses and furnishings, gifts for friends, charities, and fine clothes.

She worked hard, however, she always had, painting and designing fabrics and home furnishings, and by the late 1970s she began to make millions on her own in fashion, with the licensing of those famous jeans—a whole generation of Gen X women still thinks of blue jeans before railroads when they hear the name "Vanderbilt"—but she never thought to put any of it aside. She invested in her houses and in making them beautiful. Like so many Vanderbilts before her, she thought there would always be more she could make. And there was—until there wasn't. She accepted her financial situation with grace and humor, though she never fully understood it. She would still spend money she didn't have, acting on a belief that she might make millions once again, and even if she didn't, she knew I was earning a good income and would always be there to help.

There was no subject about her that she had not mulled over, no scene from her past she had not played and replayed in her mind: the trauma of the custody battle she was the center of as a child;

the horror of witnessing and trying to prevent my brother Carter's death; conversations she had with my father in the hospital in the days before he died. So much of her life had been shaped by loss, and yet she never allowed it to harden her. That was her greatest strength. She remained open and vulnerable even when it would have been easier not to. At ninety-five she was still the most optimistic, youthful, and modern person I ever met.

In the last ten years or so of her life, she would send me handwritten notes or emails out of the blue: "When I'm dead, make sure Biko does my makeup" and "I want to be buried in the yellow Fortuny. I've hung it in the closet in the studio, and Leonor knows where it is."

She had also taken to writing on the back of all the framed photographs hanging on her walls. Ostensibly, this habit was to help me catalogue them after she was gone. But I couldn't help thinking back to a motel we stayed in once in Mississippi, on a rare trip down south to visit my father's large extended family. My mom always felt like an alien on such trips, out of the circle, a stranger. She hadn't had a family of her own in any even remotely conventional sense, and she didn't always know how to behave when she was confronted with one. In the motel room, Carter and I were rummaging around, as children are wont to do in new places. We pulled open the drawer of the nightstand and found that some previous guest had written "I WAS HERE" inside. A stranger's voice shouting into the darkness, *I exist. I was here. This all really happened.* It's nice, now, stumbling upon her handwriting on the back of those framed photos. Her words feel like surprise messages from her, as if the conversation between us has continued, even now that she is gone.

She was here. This all really happened.

She wrote me a letter a few years ago, instructing me to "keep it somewhere in a box," so that I could refer to it whenever I needed to after she died. It talked about my father and how proud he would have been of me and how proud she was of me, too. She also wrote, "I fervently hope that you will become a father," perhaps because she saw how fully himself my father, Wyatt Cooper, became when they had Carter and me.

As I complete this manuscript right now, my son, Wyatt Morgan—named for my father and for my mother's mother—is nearing the end of his babyhood. He has just started walking, no longer using his arms to drag himself around like a tiny soldier trying to sneak under barbed-wire fortifications. He'll be a little boy himself soon—sooner than I can believe—buttoned into his own dress-up clothes, inevitably, at some point, and staring out the window of a car at the passing lights of Midtown. My dream is for him to feel safe and loved and unafraid. My mother didn't get to meet him, but she knew that I was planning and hoping for him to happen. Fortune smiled, and he is here, and he amazes me.

Some friends who knew I was going to have a child inquired if I was going to give him the middle name "Vanderbilt." I never even considered it. I don't want my son to be thought of, or to think of himself, as a Vanderbilt. He is not a scion or an heir. He is, and will be, his own person. He will make his own way. Forge his own path. And perhaps, one day, he will read this book and understand.

As Gloria wrote in her journal in 1971, reflecting on the deaths of people she knew and loved, "So many, and then there's no one left but oneself. Then one knows it's only the long walk of the blood—one's children—that endure."

EPILOGUE

Christmas Eve

1930

Most cemeteries provide perpetual care of graves as part of the purchase price, but families usually visit and tend their plots from time to time, especially among Christians on Memorial Day, Easter, and Christmas, and arrange for special care of plantings.

—Amy Vanderbilt's Complete Book of Etiquette,
Part I, "The Ceremonies of Life"

Whoever they were, they didn't bring the sledgehammer with them.

On Christmas Day 1930, the *New York Times* reported that vandals had attempted to break down the stone doors of the Vanderbilt mausoleum in the Moravian Cemetery in what the paper called "a lonely section of Staten Island." Detective Thomas Lynch reported that the outer doors were cracked and that the bronze reliefs had been defaced, battered by what seemed to be a sledgehammer. The night was frigid, with a blanket of glistening snow coating the streets and lining the naked branches of New York City's trees. Snow frosted the imposing gates of the Vanderbilt crypt, a pale sheen of transitory beauty hiding the corruption within, and it deadened the sound of the intruders' footfalls and grunts and conversation. The clanging of the hammer and chisels against bronze panels would have echoed dully through the otherwise silent and sleeping night. Who knows how long they tried to bust the doors wide open, but their project was a failure: the heavy doors stayed locked up tight.

The *Daily News* was, typically, more colorful in its account of the break-in the following day: "From a maze of footprints about the impressive tomb," the *Daily News* wrote, "detectives picked up a trail that led to the wall of the cemetery and for two miles across fields, finally disappearing in a region of brush and undergrowth." The *Times* guessed there were two or three vandals, but the *Daily News* estimated five or six, and suggested that they might have used metal-cutting saws and heavy levers in their efforts to break open the door. The culprits had planned ahead, to some extent, but had helped themselves to the sledgehammer from an obliging tool shed at the cemetery gates.

In response to the thwarted raid, the Vanderbilt family hired private watchmen to guard the mausoleum around the clock. Imagine that job: standing alone in the cold and snow at a mausoleum, making sure no one got in . . . or out. Pacing there, all day, and then all night, at Christmas. A more joyless endeavor would be hard to conceive.

"Midst the eerie surrounds of the bleak, deserted Moravian cemetery, at New Dorp, Staten Island," the *Daily News* reported the next day, "two uniformed private watchmen last night kept a chilly, grisly Christmas vigil before the sombre but majestic mausoleum which houses the bones of the long line of departed Vanderbilts. Only the glow from their cigarettes and the echoes from their oft-clapped hands told the outside world that the peaceful sleep of old Commodore Vanderbilt and his sons had recently been disturbed." And only the sons. Perhaps because the Commodore had only really cared about male heirs who would carry the Vanderbilt name, only those with the name "Vanderbilt" can be interred inside. Everyone else is buried in the ground in the surrounding acres.

What did the robbers want? Why would they go to such herculean efforts, in the frosty winter night, hours before a holiday, to bust into a mausoleum? There was nothing of value inside: No Vanderbilt wealth. No secret treasure. Inside, the mausoleum held only people, just like all other tombs at the Moravian Cemetery. The Vanderbilt tomb contained no special brilliance, no royalty, no deference, no skill, no slander—just twenty-odd human remains journeying their slow way back to dust.

On the twenty-sixth, a notice appeared in the paper saying that if no leads developed in the case, the family was prepared to offer a lucrative reward and hire private detectives to solve the mystery themselves. The notice was buried near the back of the paper, easy to overlook. Did the Vanderbilts follow through on their promise? The newspapers don't say, so probably not. Workmen set to repairing the doors, and soon enough, the foiled robbery would be forgotten.

Where were the living Vanderbilts at Christmastime in 1930 while that watchman oversaw the family crypt?

Little Gloria was six years old and still in Europe with Dodo while Gloria Morgan provided elegant cover for her sister Thelma's torrid affair with Edward, the Prince of Wales.

Consuelo was long divorced from the Duke of Marlborough and had remarried dashing French aviator Jacques Balsan.

Alva was living in France, where she'd moved to be closer to Consuelo, leaving Marble House shuttered and its contents swathed in dust covers.

Alice of The Breakers was chafing under the realization that she was no longer the reigning Mrs. Vanderbilt, as her attempt to disinherit her son Neily for marrying Grace Wilson had actually done nothing to stop Grace's social ascendancy.

Harold had just appeared that September on the cover of *Time*, posing at the helm of his America's Cup defender yacht, *Enterprise*.

And in October, Gertrude's husband, Harry Payne Whitney, had died suddenly of pneumonia, and she had called for a craftsman to come help her make a death cast of his face.

What about the rest of the world? The same issue of the *New York Times* that carried the family's offer of a reward features the front-page headline "Cheer Reigns in City for Christmas but Breadlines Are Long." The paper also reported on the rise of Stalin in Russia and on the visit of Santa Claus to the Hoover White House, to the awe of the Hoover grandchildren, all of whom were apparently more interested in the mechanics of how he had managed to emerge from the chimney than they were in the presents he had brought them. New York City logged five Christmas Day deaths from "poison alcohol," along with fifty-nine cases of alcoholism in city hospitals, down from eighty-three in the prior year. "Dr. Charles Norris said that while the alcoholic death rate was much lighter than on Christmases in the previous two years," the paper remarked, "it was considerably higher than the city's average of about one death per day." This was during the height of Prohibition—death from diseases of despair, we would call them today. Poverty was stalking the streets of New York, as the Depression sank its teeth into lives much more modest than those of the Vanderbilts.

The well-guarded, imposing mausoleum edifice had been designed by Richard Morris Hunt, Alva's dear friend and favorite architect, and built between 1885 and 1886. From its steps, there is a large courtyard and a gently sloping hill. To one side, through a screen of trees, a visitor can spy the neighborhood that once held the farm where the Commodore grew up. Then, farther beyond, the hilltop spot offers a vista out over lower New York Bay, where the Commodore made his first fortune. The view is splendid and commanding, as befits an American dynasty. In 1930, it might have seemed like the only place where the Vanderbilts were vulnerable, where they were close enough to touch.

The tomb cost an estimated two hundred and thirty-five thousand dollars when it was built forty-five years before the vandals tried to break it down, and they did around three thousand dollars' worth of damage. It's possible they were after the copper tomb lining, much as brownstone shells in struggling neighborhoods are sometimes stripped of copper pipes today, to be sold for cash at scrap yards. A Long Island cemetery had recently been robbed of a bronze sculpture, the *Daily News* pointed out, presumably to be sold as scrap. When the fortress proved impregnable, the robbers reportedly made off with a bronze door valued at around two thousand dollars, more than a year's salary in 1930 for a lot of people. There's something poetic to be said about robbing the tomb of the richest family in America for metal decorations to be sold as junk, but men wielding stolen sledgehammers on Christmas Eve probably don't have a lot of spare time for poetry. So, maybe that's all they were after: scraps.

William Schutzendorf, the real estate agent in charge of the Vanderbilt property on Staten Island, had a different idea about what the robbers might have been looking for. He theorized that the vandals had been attempting to steal some bodies—maybe even that of the Commodore himself—and hold them for ransom.

This idea wasn't as outlandish as it probably sounds. Fifty-three years earlier, in 1877, a year of class unrest all over the country following another depression, marked by the first national railroad strike and the construction of armories in cities to put down urban riots, the body of department store magnate A. T. Stewart, who had attended the same operas and the same lavish balls, nodding to Vanderbilts and Goelets and Astors on Fifth Avenue at the crowded hour, was stolen from its crypt in St. Mark's-in-the-Bowery. The body was ransomed for twenty-five thousand dollars, and though the ransom was paid, it's possible the remains were never actually recovered. That's a lot more than one is liable to get for copper scrap.

A strong mausoleum—all the more important then, and the perfect Gilded Age example of American eclecticism for the dead—was the brainchild of Billy the Blatherskite. William Henry Vanderbilt clearly had death on his mind as the nineteenth century drew to a close.

In the six years before his death in 1885, he redrafted his will nine times.

In December 1884, he drove to the old Dutch cemetery in New Dorp, on Staten Island, where the Commodore was already buried, and told his sons Cornelius II and Willie that he wanted to build a family crypt there. He went back and forth with the cemetery, but he couldn't settle on a price for the acreage he wanted, and so, instead, he bought fourteen acres on top of the hill next door for the mausoleum. Billy told Richard Morris Hunt that he wanted it to be "roomy and solid and rich" without being ostentatious—whatever that might mean, given that we are talking about Vanderbilts.

The final design, though called "Moorish" in the newspapers, was that of a Romanesque chapel modeled after one in the South of France, built of heavy gray granite. Construction commenced in 1885. From the steps swept away a view of all of Staten Island, all the way down to the Narrows and the paths of every steamship coming into or out of New York Harbor. The landscaping would be the purview of Frederick Law Olmsted, who had also designed

Central Park. The nineteenth century was a moment for garden cemeteries, like Mount Auburn in Massachusetts or Green-Wood in Brooklyn. Before cities discovered the necessity of designating public space as parkland for the health and well-being of city residents, cemeteries were often the only green space available for urban dwellers seeking relief from the overcrowding of narrow streets and tenements. At the time the mausoleum was built, it was common, even pleasant, to picnic among the dead.

Billy died of a stroke on December 8, 1885, and was buried in the vault next to the Commodore, to await completion of the grand mausoleum he had planned. Mindful of what had happened to the Stewarts, the family hired Pinkerton guards to defend against body snatchers, and the watchmen stayed there around the clock for the next several decades. After lifetimes spent courting public attention, the Vanderbilt clan wanted to be free from the grasping hands of the public after death. But the public, once courted and seduced, will not be spurned so easily.

Maybe the robbers went there looking for ghosts.

But the Vanderbilt ghosts aren't to be found on Staten Island. (Well, the Commodore's mother, Phebe, might be there, and maybe the Commodore, too, out of sentiment.) To step through the specters of long-departed Vanderbilts, you'd do better to visit Manhattan.

Sneak upstairs to the grand ballroom at the Plaza Hotel and listen for the sounds of the Peter Duchin Orchestra. If you can hear it, faintly, then look around for Gloria Vanderbilt and Wyatt Cooper, Gloria, newly pregnant, beaming her dazzling smile in her Puritan-inspired floor-length black maternity gown with wide white collar and cuffs; Wyatt dapper in a three-piece tuxedo lined in satin piping; he in a black mask, she in white, laughing near red-clothed tables decked in long white taper candles while, overhead, nestled in among the glittering crystal chandeliers and grandiose arches were bunches of translucent white balloons, waiting to fall.

Trip down the steps of the Plaza Hotel, past the Pulitzer Fountain in Grand Army Plaza, across from where FAO Schwarz used to be, and you will be treading on the site of what was once Alice Vanderbilt's private, circular driveway, opposite Central Park. Slip through the revolving doors and browse the perfume counters of Bergdorf Goodman. On that spot from 1883 to 1926, filling an entire city block, stood the Cornelius Vanderbilt II house, which still holds the record for the largest private residence ever built in New York City. Stop at the Guerlain counter—the company made perfume in the Gilded Age—and try to imagine a five-story Caen stone entrance hall soaring overhead, opening in turn to a book-lined library, a grand salon, a two-story ballroom, a "Moorish"-style smoking room, and a dining room that also served as the art gallery. Next door, right on Fifth Avenue, the house enjoyed its own stable and a private garden.

Alice and Cornelius II's house was a palace designed by— who else?—Richard Morris Hunt, together with George B. Post. Built to last a thousand years, it stood for only forty-three before skyscrapers began their steady march northward. After Cornelius II's death in 1899, Alice lived in the house alone, with only the thirty-seven servants needed to keep it running. The grand ballroom was silent except for the occasional brushing of dust mops and the skitter of tiptoeing mice. Finally, in 1926, no longer able to afford the upkeep on the house (or on The Breakers) with the trusts left for that purpose, Alice was forced to sell to developers, who paid for the land but not the house sitting on top of it. A week before the wrecking ball swung, she opened the house for tours at fifty cents a pop, with proceeds to be given to charity. Not all was lost—Alice Vanderbilt's Augustus Saint-Gaudens mantelpiece now stands in the American Wing at the Metropolitan

Museum of Art, and the gate to her driveway guards the Conservatory Garden in Central Park.

Stroll a few blocks down to 666 Fifth Avenue, between Fifty-First and Fifty-Second Streets—at the time of this writing, a somewhat vacant corporate albatross hanging around the neck of Jared Kushner and his family. This is where Willie and Alva Vanderbilt's Petit Chateau once stood, designed with painstaking attention to detail by Alva herself, working with Hunt between 1878 and 1882. In a style charitably called "Chateau-esque," the sprawling mansion featured pointed turrets out of a fairy-tale castle. The echoing grand hall—sixty feet long—was done all in Caen stone, deeply carved and ornate, with a grand stone staircase winding upward at one end and a massive stone fireplace at the other. The interior design was all pseudo-eighteenth-century French, a style trend from which elite New York has never entirely recovered. A developer bought this house, too, also in 1926. By 1927, it was dust.

Next door to the Petit Chateau stood the famed "Triple Palace" of William Henry Vanderbilt, the Blatherskite himself, the three grand and sprawling connected houses built for his children between 1879 and 1882. Billy hired famed local furniture makers Gustave and Christian Herter to design an interior so lavish that it took between six and seven hundred workmen to complete. When Neily, Alice's black sheep son, took over the Triple Palace in 1915, its lush and costly Gilded Age interior furnishings were thought to be wildly out of date. He and his wife, Grace, undertook a complete redecoration, and the furniture was scattered far and wide, the last of it disappearing into the ether when the mansion was, inevitably, demolished in 1945.

But not entirely into the ether—some of the costliest and most beautifully made furniture of the American nineteenth century was picked up at auction for cheap in 1942 by Warner Bros. Stu-

dios to use as set decorations for period films. Eagle-eyed view-
ers can spot Vanderbilt castoffs in film after film in the 1940s and
later, as the stuff of an American dynastic fantasy was marshaled
to embroider the fantasy lives of Americans all over the country.
(The studio, in deep financial straits, auctioned them off again in
the 2000s.) Some Herter furniture possibly chucked out of Billy
Vanderbilt's mansion even appears, fleetingly, in Hitchcock's
Psycho (1960).

Tool over to Madison Avenue and Fifty-First Street to call
upon Alva in the second stage of her life, for this is where she
built the Mrs. O. H. P. Belmont House in 1909, another of her col-
laborations with Hunt. The three-story neoclassical town house
was covered in limestone, as Alva couldn't abide brownstone.
She built an eighty-five-foot-long gallery expressly to house Oliver Belmont's vast collection of arms and armor. Later, the hall
served nicely for suffragist meetings, before Alva sold it off in
1923. The mansion became a home for Catholic Charities until
the archdiocese unloaded it in 1951, at which point it was razed in
favor of a parking lot.

Moving farther downtown, we can duck into the Duane Reade
pharmacy at the corner of Park Avenue and Thirty-Fourth Street
to buy a Vitamin Water and try to imagine when this was the
lobby and bar of Alfred's tony Vanderbilt Hotel, designed for
wealthy young playboys like him to live sumptuously and well
without all the fuss of keeping a house. Alfred took the top two
stories for his own aerie when the hotel opened in 1912, but he
barely had any time to enjoy it before he went down on the R.M.S.
Lusitania in 1915.

Another ghost haunts Thirty-Fourth Street, two blocks west
of the former Vanderbilt Hotel. Though Caroline Astor was not a
Vanderbilt, she was an important part of the Vanderbilt dynasty,
in her way. On Fifth Avenue and Thirty-Fourth, she built her

fashionable four-bay brownstone in 1862 next door to the home
of her husband's brother, John Jacob Astor III, when Murray Hill
was the very vanguard of New York society and Caroline Astor
its reigning monarch. When her nephew William Waldorf Astor
tore down the family house next door and erected a new and fashionable hotel, the Waldorf, bringing crowds and noise and public
life to Mrs. Astor's exclusive doorstep, she considered exacting her
revenge by tearing down her own house and building a stable so
that the beautiful people would be harassed by the odor of manure.
Instead, she erected a hotel of her own—the Astoria. Eventually,
the two hotels would merge, creating the first Waldorf-Astoria
Hotel, a center of increasingly public fashionable life in Manhattan beginning in 1893. Mrs. Astor decamped to the Upper East
Side, building her own Richard Morris Hunt palace on Fifth Avenue and Sixty-Fifth. The original Waldorf-Astoria was razed
in 1929 and replaced with the building that stands at that address
today—the Empire State Building.

The view from the top of the Empire State Building is breathtaking. Beneath your feet unrolls all of Manhattan Island, yellow
taxicabs crawling slowly along the veins and arteries of the naked
city. If you're facing south, the Hudson shimmers off to the right,
plowed by ferries and the Circle Line and the occasional party
boat strung with lanterns. To the left, the narrower East River
wraps around the hip of Manhattan, the two slender suspen-
sion bridges, Brooklyn and Williamsburg, shimmering with the
movement of vehicles and people into the neighboring boroughs.
The foot of the island is studded with towering glass mono-
liths that would have been unimaginable in the Commodore's
day, so tall that they block the view of the Staten Island Ferry
landing by the Battery, though we can sense where it is. But on a
clear day, tracing through the haze formed where cool Atlantic
air meets the warm, living breath of the city, we can just spot

the Verrazzano-Narrows Bridge, which spans from Brooklyn to Staten Island, over the swirls and eddies of the water flowing into and out of New York Harbor. The Narrows are where, from the Flatlands, the van der Bilts crossed over into Staten Island. The eddies and tides would still be familiar to an eleven-year-old Cornelius Vanderbilt if he were again to pilot his periauger, laden with black-market passengers and vegetables, bound for Manhattan and profit. We can see where the Vanderbilt story begins. And on the shores of Staten Island, behind impregnable doors, we can just glimpse where it ends.

While his fortune has all but disappeared, we can still call upon the Commodore today, as I did with my father as a child. Elevated above the traffic, casting a proprietary gaze down Park Avenue to the south, the statue of the patriarch still stands. Cast in 1869, at the height of Cornelius Vanderbilt's influence, the statue originally graced his train depot in St. James Square, before that site was turned into an on-ramp. In 1929, the statue was moved to Grand Central, where it would have enjoyed an unsurpassed view of his heirs' buildings going up and coming down, wave upon wave of money heaping up and, ultimately, dissolving away. All that remains is the original engine of Cornelius Vanderbilt's wealth and of his own ambition—the keen desire of strangers to come quickly across the waters to arrive in Manhattan, where someday, in some generation yet to come, their fortunes will be made.

Acknowledgments

Writing a book with someone else is a daunting task but it is made easier when you do it with a writer as talented and smart as Katherine Howe. I learned a tremendous amount from her and am so grateful she was willing to take this project on. Thanks also go to Luke Janklow, my literary agent and friend since middle school, and his assistant Claire Dippel. Also to Carole Cooper, Jay Sures, Charlie Moore, and Jeff Zucker for their amazing support, friendship, and advice over the years. Thanks to Jonathan Burnham, Emily Griffin, Doug Jones, Tina Andreadis, Leslie Cohen, Katie O'Callaghan, Rebecca Holland, and everyone at HarperCollins. I was so happy that Chip Kidd agreed to lend his tremendous talent to create the book's cover and endpapers. He did the cover for my first book, and for many of my mom's books, and I appreciate his amazing creativity and friendship. I'm grateful to Gladys and Paul Szápáry for their dedication to preserving the history of The Breakers, and to their mother, Countess Anthony Szápáry (Syvie), who welcomed my brother and me into her beloved home and began to tell us about the Vanderbilts. I would also be remiss if I didn't thank Theresa Roodal Achaiba for caring for my son, Wyatt, so lovingly while I was working, and most of all, thanks to Benjamin Maisani for being such a great Papa to our little boy.

Katherine Howe's Acknowledgments:
I would like to thank first the many people without whom this book would not exist: my agent Suzanne Gluck, at William Morris Endeavor, together with her right hand Andrea Blatt, for their wise guidance and unflagging support; Luke Janklow of

292 & of this book infinitely more complicated

Janklow & Nesbit; Jonathan Burnham at Harper; the fabulous and brilliant Emily Griffin at Harper; and above all, Anderson Cooper, who has been a dream to work with. His wit, intelligence, good humor, and curiosity have made working on this book a joy, and I am so honored to have been a part of it.

Writing an archives-intensive book during a pandemic was challenging to say the least. I am indebted to Melanie Locay and all the librarians and staff at the New York Public Library's Center for Research in the Humanities, where I was fortunate enough to be a resident of the Allen Room. Thank you also to the staff of the Patricia D. Klingenstein Library at the New-York Historical Society for facilitating my whirlwind two-day Vanderbilt paper digitization extravaganza, to the Huntington Library for digitizing images of Alva's unpublished memoir, and to the Cornell University Law Library.

The week I found out I would be working on this book was the same week I found out that I would be having a baby. I would like to thank Charles Gage Hyman Howe for making the writing of this book infinitely more complicated than it otherwise would have been, and for making my life infinitely better at the same time. I dedicate this book in part to him. I am indebted to my mother-in-law, Patty Kuzbida, to my friend Callie Naughton, and to the incredible teachers and staff of the Infant and Toddler House at Harborlight Montessori in Beverly, Massachusetts, especially Hiro Sudachi, Paula Chapman, Donna Hingston, Kerrie Spinney, and Helen Johnson, for their care of Charles while I was writing and my husband was teaching. I am fortunate to have a partner, Louis Hyman, who is the ablest of dads, chefs, cheerleaders, beta readers, and research assistants (being a history professor at Cornell helps in that last regard). We always "joke" about the historians of the 1950s thanking their wives in their book acknowledgments for typing their notes. Loulou, thank you. You typed some great notes this year.

On August 21, 1994, the summer before my senior year in high school, the exhibition "Herter Brothers: Furniture and Interiors for a Gilded Age" opened at the Museum of Fine Arts, Houston, before traveling on to the High Museum in Atlanta and then the Metropolitan Museum of Art in New York. The Herter brothers, as mentioned briefly in this book, were the visionaries behind all the most opulent Vanderbilt interiors. The exhibition was curated by my mother, Katherine S. Howe, then Curator of Decorative Arts at the MFAH, together with her counterparts at the Met. She taught me that "Vanderbilt" meant something other than designer jeans, and more importantly, she peopled my intellectual landscape with an understanding of how objects can inform our narratives of history, of class, and of cultural change. If I have an eye for the telling detail or the revealing primary source, it's because she taught me to see. I would like to dedicate my work on this project to her. Together with my father, George, she gave me the love, education, and courage to dream and succeed.

Bibliography

Secondary Sources

Amory, Cleveland. *The Last Resorts*. New York: Harper and Brothers, 1952.

————. *Who Killed Society?* New York: Harper and Brothers, 1960.

Andrews, Wayne. *The Vanderbilt Legend: The Story of the Vanderbilt Family, 1794–1940*. New York: Harcourt, Brace, and Company, 1941.

Auchincloss, Louis. *The Vanderbilt Era: Profiles of a Gilded Age*. New York: Charles Scribner's Sons, 1989.

Bavier, Robert N. *The America's Cup: An Insider's View, 1930 to the Present*. New York: Dodd Mead and Company, 1986.

Beckert, Sven. *The Monied Metropolis: New York City and the Consolidation of the American Bourgeoisie, 1850–1896*. Cambridge, UK: Cambridge University Press, 2001.

Bradford, Ernle. *The America's Cup*. London: Country Life Ltd., 1964.

Brandon, Ruth. *The Dollar Princesses*. New York: Alfred A. Knopf, 1980.

Braudy, Leo. *The Frenzy of Renown: Fame and Its History*. New York: Vintage, 1997.

Brough, James. *Consuelo: Portrait of an American Heiress*. New York: Coward, McCann and Geoghegan, 1979.

Burrows, Edwin G., and Mike Wallace. *Gotham: A History of New York City to 1898*. Oxford: Oxford University Press, 2000.

Bushman, Richard. *The Refinement of America: Persons, Houses, Cities*. New York: Alfred A. Knopf, 1992.

Carter, Susan B. et al., eds. *Historical Statistics of the United States: Millennial Edition*. Vol. 2: *Work and Welfare*. Cambridge, UK: Cambridge University Press, 2006.

Chauncey, George. *Gay New York: Gender, Urban Culture, and the Making of the Gay Male World, 1890–1940*. New York: Basic Books, 1994.

Churchill, Allen. *The Upper Crust: An Informal History of New York's Highest Society*. Englewood Cliffs, NJ: Prentice-Hall, 1970.

Clarke, Gerald. *Capote: A Biography*. New York: Simon and Schuster, 1988.

Crain, Esther. *The Gilded Age in New York, 1870–1910.* New York: Black Dog and Leventhal/Hachette, 2016.

Dowland, Douglas. "How Disgust Works: Truman Capote's 'La Côte Basque.'" *Journal of Modern Literature* 39, No. 4 (Summer 2016): 67–84.

Dudden, Faye E. *Serving Women: Household Service in Nineteenth-Century America.* Middletown, CT: Wesleyan University Press, 1983.

Eliott, Maud Howe. *This Was My Newport.* Cambridge, MA: The Mythology Co., University Press, 1944.

Foreman, John, and Robbe Pierce Stimson; Introduction by Louis Auchincloss. *The Vanderbilts and the Gilded Age: Architectural Aspirations, 1879–1901.* New York: St. Martin's Press, 1991.

Friedman, B. H. *Gertrude Vanderbilt Whitney: A Biography.* Garden City, NY: Doubleday and Company, 1978.

Goldsmith, Barbara. *Little Gloria . . . Happy at Last.* New York: Alfred A. Knopf, 1980.

Hofstadter, Richard. *The Age of Reform.* New York: Vintage Books, 1955.

Homberger, Eric. *The Historical Atlas of New York City: A Visual Celebration of 400 Years of New York City's History.* 3rd ed. New York: St. Martin's Griffin, 2016.

———. *Mrs. Astor's New York: Money and Social Power in a Gilded Age.* New Haven, CT: Yale University Press, 2002.

Howe, Katherine S. et al. *Herter Brothers: Furniture and Interiors for a Gilded Age.* New York: Harry N. Abrams/Museum of Fine Arts, Houston, 1994.

Hoyt, Edwin P. *The Vanderbilts and Their Fortunes.* Garden City, NY: Doubleday, 1962.

King, Greg. *A Season of Splendor: The Court of Mrs. Astor in Gilded Age New York.* Hoboken, NJ: John Wiley and Sons, 2009.

Lane, Wheaton J. *Commodore Vanderbilt: Epic of the Steam Age.* New York: Alfred A. Knopf, 1942.

Merwick, Donna. *Death of a Notary: Conquest and Change in Colonial New York.* Ithaca, NY: Cornell University Press, 1999.

Montgomery, Maureen E. *"Gilded Prostitution": Status, Money and Transatlantic Marriages, 1870–1914.* London and New York: Routledge, 1989.

Patterson, Jerry E. *Fifth Avenue: The Best Address.* New York: Rizzoli, 1998.

———. *The First Four Hundred: Mrs. Astor's New York in the Gilded Age.* New York: Rizzoli, 2000.

———. *The Vanderbilts.* New York: Harry N. Abrams, 1989.

Pugh, Martin. *The March of the Women: A Revisionist Analysis of the Campaign for Women's Suffrage, 1866–1914.* Oxford: Oxford University Press, 2000.

Riggs, Douglas. *Keelhauled: Unsportsmanlike Conduct and the America's Cup*. London: Stanford Maritime, 1986.

Sirkis, Nancy. Introduction by Louis Auchincloss. *Newport: Pleasures and Palaces*. New York: Viking, 1963.

Stasz, Clarice. *The Vanderbilt Women: Dynasty of Wealth, Glamour, and Tragedy*. New York: St. Martin's Press, 1991.

Stiles, T. J. *The First Tycoon: The Epic Life of Cornelius Vanderbilt*. New York: Alfred A. Knopf, 2009.

Still, Bayrd. *Mirror for Gotham: New York as Seen by Contemporaries from Dutch Days to the Present*. New York: New York University Press, 1956.

Stuart, Amanda Mackenzie. *Consuelo and Alva Vanderbilt: The Story of a Mother and Daughter in the Gilded Age*. New York: Harper Perennial, 2007.

Sutherland, Daniel E. *Americans and Their Servants: Domestic Service in the United States from 1800 to 1920*. Baton Rouge: Louisiana State University Press, 1981.

Trachtenberg, Alan. *The Incorporation of America: Culture and Society in the Gilded Age*. New York: Hill and Wang, 1982.

Vanderbilt, Arthur T., II. *Fortune's Children: The Fall of the House of Vanderbilt*. 1989; repr. New York: William Morrow, 2001.

Vanderbilt, Cornelius. *Queen of the Golden Age: The Fabulous Story of Grace Wilson Vanderbilt*. New York: McGraw-Hill, 1956.

Voorsanger, Catherine Hoover, and John K. Howat, eds. *Art and the Empire City: New York, 1825–1861*. New Haven, CT: Yale University Press/Metropolitan Museum of Art, 2000.

Voss, Ralph F. *Truman Capote and the Legacy of "In Cold Blood."* Tuscaloosa: University of Alabama Press, 2011.

Wallace, Mike. *Greater Gotham: A History of New York City from 1898 to 1919*. Oxford: Oxford University Press, 2017.

Primary Sources: Periodicals

American Mercury

American Queen

Baltimore Sun

Chicago Daily Tribune

Cosmopolitan

Esquire

Frank Leslie's Illustrated Newspaper

Harper's Weekly

Hartford Courant

The Nation

New York Daily News

New York Daily Tribune

New York Evening Post

New York Herald

New York Herald Tribune

New York Magazine

New York Post

New York Times

New York Tribune

Playboy

Town and Country

Town Topics

Vanity Fair

Washington Post

(New York) *World*

Primary Sources: Papers

Anderson Cooper private collection and correspondence.

Gloria Vanderbilt private collection and correspondence.

Vanderbilt papers (Frank Vanderbilt's journal), New-York Historical Society.

C. E. S. Wood papers, 1829–1980, Sara Bard Field (Alva Belmont's memoir), Huntington Library.

Primary Sources: Books

Balsan, Consuelo Vanderbilt. *The Glitter and the Gold*. New York: Harper and Brothers, 1952. Reissued London: Hodder and Stoughton, 2011.

Beresford, Elizabeth Wharton Drexel, Baroness Decies. *"King Lehr" and the Gilded Age*. Philadelphia and London: J. B. Lippincott Company, 1935.

Brown, Eve. *Champagne Cholly: The Life and Times of Maury Paul*. New York: E. P. Dutton and Company, 1947.

Capote, Truman. *Breakfast at Tiffany's and Other Voices, Other Rooms: Two Novels*. New York: Modern Library, 2013.

Cooper, Anderson. *Dispatches from the Edge: A Memoir of War, Disasters, and Survival*. New York: Harper Perennial, 2006.

Cooper, Anderson, and Gloria Vanderbilt. *The Rainbow Comes and Goes*. New York: Harper, 2016.

Croffut, William Augustus. *The Vanderbilts and the Story of Their Fortune*. Chicago: Belford, Clarke, 1886.

Foster, George G. Introduction by Stuart M. Blumin. *New York by Gas-Light and Other Urban Sketches*. Berkeley: University of California Press, 1990.

James, Henry. *The American Scene*. New York: Penguin Classics, 1994.

Longstreet, Abby Buchanan. *Social Etiquette of New York*. New York: D. Appleton and Company, 1880.

McAllister, Ward. *Society as I Have Found It*. New York: Cassell Publishing Company, 1890.

Vanderbilt, Amy. *Amy Vanderbilt's Complete Book of Etiquette: A Guide to Gracious Living*. New York: Doubleday and Company, 1952.

Vanderbilt, Gloria. *It Seemed Important at the Time: A Romance Memoir*. New York: Simon and Schuster, 2004.

———. *Once Upon a Time*. New York: Alfred A. Knopf, 1985.

Vanderbilt, Gloria Morgan. *Without Prejudice*. New York: E. P. Dutton and Company, 1936.

Vanderbilt, Gloria Morgan, and Lady Thelma Furness. *Double Exposure*. London: Frederic Muller, 1959.

Vanderbilt, Harold S. *On the Wind's Highway: Ranger, Rainbow, and Racing*. New York: Charles Scribner's Sons, 1939.

Van Dyke, John Charles. *The New New York: A Commentary on the Place and the People*. New York: Macmillan, 1909.

Veblen, Thorstein. *The Theory of the Leisure Class*. New York: Modern Library, 1934.

Wecter, Dixon. *The Saga of American Society: A Record of Social Aspiration, 1607–1937*. New York: Charles Scribner's Sons, 1937.

Wharton, Edith. *The Age of Innocence*. New York: D. Appleton and Company, 1920.

———. *A Backward Glance*. New York: D. Appleton-Century, 1934.

———. Edited and with an introduction by Viola Hopkins Winner. *Fast and Loose, and The Buccaneers*. Charlottesville: University Press of Virginia, 1993.

Archives

Huntington Library

New-York Historical Society

New York Public Library

Index

About the Authors

ANDERSON COOPER joined CNN in 2001 and has anchored his own program, *Anderson Cooper 360°*, since March 2003. Cooper has won eighteen Emmys and numerous other major journalism awards. He lives in New York with his two sons.

KATHERINE HOWE is a novelist and historian of America. She holds a BA in art history and philosophy from Columbia and an MA in American and New England Studies from Boston University, where she also did doctoral work. She is the author of the *New York Times* bestsellers *The Physick Book of Deliverance Dane* and *The House of Velvet and Glass*, as well as the young adult novels *Conversion* and *The Appearance of Annie van Sinderen*. She served as editor of *The Penguin Book of Witches*. She has appeared on NPR, National Geographic, Smithsonian TV, the Travel Channel, and *Good Morning America*. She lives with her family in New England and New York City.